IRON

IRON MAN

"HEART OF STEEL"
WRITER: Fred Van Lente
PENCILER: James Cordeiro
INKER: Scott Koblish
COLORIST: Studio F's Marte Gracia
LETTERER: Blambot's Nate Piekos
COVER ARTIST: Michael Golden
ASSISTANT EDITOR: Nathan Cosby
EDITOR: Mark Paniccia

"THE TITANIUM TRAP"
WRITER: Fred Van Lente
PENCILER: James Cordeiro
INKER: Scott Koblish
COLORIST: Studio F's Marte Gracia
LETTERER: Blambot's Nate Piekos
COVER ARTISTS: David Nakayama, Gary Martin
& Christina Strain
EDITOR: Nathan Cosby
CONSULTING EDITOR: Mark Paniccia

"SEVEN RINGS HATH THE MANDARIN"
WRITERS: Jeff Parker & Paul Tobin
PENCILER: Alvin Lee
INKER: Terry Pallot
COLORIST: Wilfredo Quintana
LETTERER: Blambot's Nate Piekos
COVER ARTISTS: David Nakayama & Christina Strain
EDITORS: Nathan Cosby & Mark Paniccia

"THERE'S AN APE FOR THAT!"
WRITER: Paul Tobin
ARTIST: Craig Rousseau
COLOR ARTIST: Veronica Gandini
LETTERER: Dave Sharpe
COVER ARTISTS: Ed McGuinness & Chris Sotomayor
ASSISTANT EDITOR: Michael Horwitz
EDITOR: Nathan Cosby

"EMPLOYEE OF THE MONTH"
STORY: Fred Van Lente
SCRIPT: Margot Blankier
ARTIST: Juan Santacruz
COLOR ARTIST: Chris Sotomayor
LETTERER: Dave Sharpe
EDITOR: Nathan Cosby
CONSULTING EDITOR: Mark Paniccia

Collection Editor: Cory Levine
Assistant Editors: Alex Starbuck & Nelson Ribeiro
Editors, Special Projects: Jennifer Grünwald & Mark D. Beazley
Senior Editor, Special Projects: Jeff Youngquist
SVP of Print & Digital Publishing Sales: David Gabriel

Editor In Chief: Axel Alonso
Chief Creative Officer: Joe Quesada
Publisher: Dan Buckley
Executive Producer: Alan Fine

MARVEL UNIVERSE IRON MAN. Contains material originally published in magazine form as MARVEL ADVENTURES IRON MAN #1, FREE COMIC BOOK DAY 2007 (MARVEL ADVENTURES), FREE COMIC BOOK DAY 2008 (MARVEL ADVENTURES), FREE COMIC BOOK DAY 2010 (IRON MAN: SUPERNOVA), IRON MAN: GOLDEN AVENGER #1. First printing 2013. ISBN# 978-0-7851-6794-5. Published by MARVEL WORLDWIDE, INC., a subsidiary of MARVEL ENTERTAINMENT, LLC. OFFICE OF PUBLICATION: 135 West 50th Street, New York, NY 10020. Copyright © 2007, 2008, 2010 and 2013 Marvel Characters, Inc. All rights reserved. All characters featured in this issue and the distinctive names and likenesses thereof, and all related indicia are trademarks of Marvel Characters, Inc. No similarity between any of the names, characters, persons, and/or institutions in this magazine with those of any living or dead person or institution is intended, and any such similarity which may exist is purely coincidental. **Printed in the U.S.A.** ALAN FINE, EVP - Office of the President, Marvel Worldwide, Inc. and EVP & CMO Marvel Characters B.V.; DAN BUCKLEY, Publisher & President - Print, Animation & Digital Divisions; JOE QUESADA, Chief Creative Officer; TOM BREVOORT, SVP of Publishing; DAVID BOGART, SVP of Operations & Procurement, Publishing; RUWAN JAYATILLEKE, SVP & Associate Publisher, Publishing; C.B. CEBULSKI, SVP of Creator & Content Development; DAVID GABRIEL, SVP of Print & Digital Publishing Sales; JIM O'KEEFE, VP of Operations & Logistics; DAN CARR, Executive Director of Publishing Technology; SUSAN CRESPI, Editorial Operations Manager; ALEX MORALES, Publishing Operations Manager; STAN LEE, Chairman Emeritus. For information regarding advertising in Marvel Comics or on Marvel.com, please contact Niza Disla, Director of Marvel Partnerships, at ndisla@marvel.com. For Marvel subscription inquiries, please call 800-217-9158. **Manufactured between 2/18/2013 and 3/15/2013 by SHERIDAN BOOKS, INC., CHELSEA, MI, USA.**

10 9 8 7 6 5 4 3 2 1

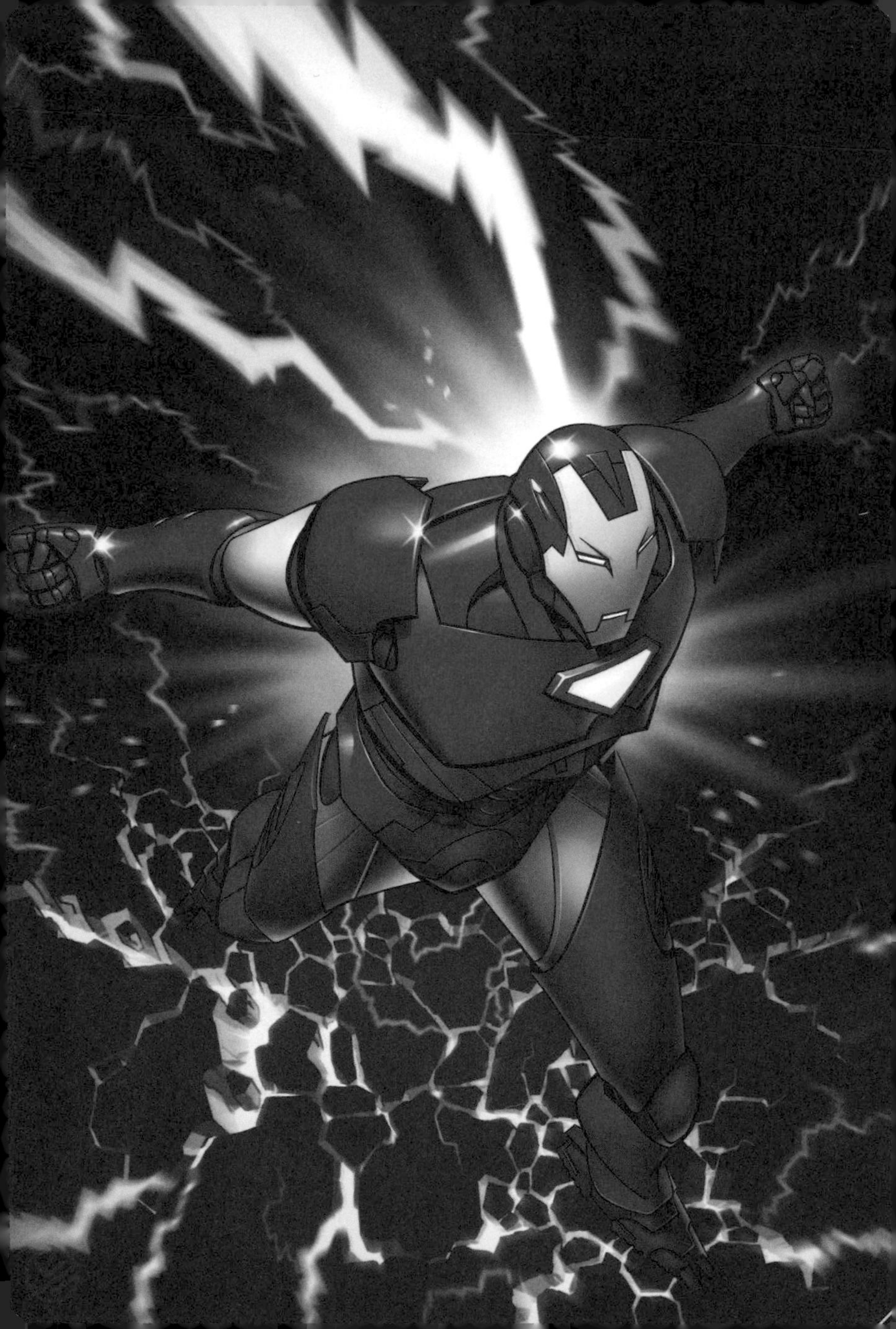

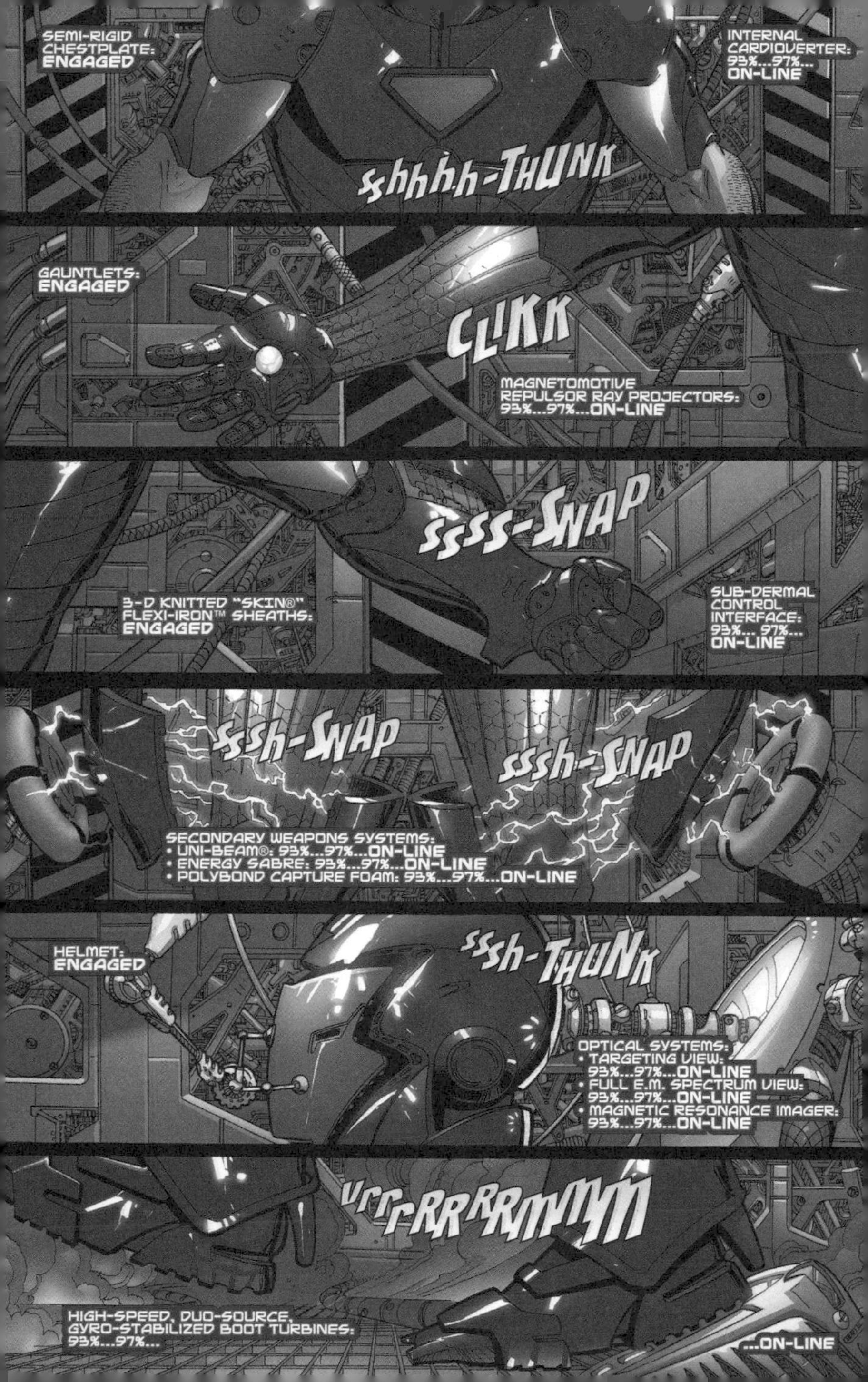
SEMI-RIGID CHESTPLATE: ENGAGED
INTERNAL CARDIOVERTER: 93%...97%... ON-LINE
SSHHHH-THUNK
GAUNTLETS: ENGAGED
CLIKK
MAGNETOMOTIVE REPULSOR RAY PROJECTORS: 93%...97%...ON-LINE
SSSS-SNAP
3-D KNITTED "SKIN®" FLEXI-IRON™ SHEATHS: ENGAGED
SUB-DERMAL CONTROL INTERFACE: 93%... 97%... ON-LINE
SSSH-SNAP
SSSH-SNAP
SECONDARY WEAPONS SYSTEMS:
• UNI-BEAM®: 93%...97%...ON-LINE
• ENERGY SABRE: 93%...97%...ON-LINE
• POLYBOND CAPTURE FOAM: 93%...97%...ON-LINE
HELMET: ENGAGED
SSSH-THUNK
OPTICAL SYSTEMS:
• TARGETING VIEW: 93%...97%...ON-LINE
• FULL E.M. SPECTRUM VIEW: 93%...97%...ON-LINE
• MAGNETIC RESONANCE IMAGER: 93%...97%...ON-LINE
VRRRRRRRRMMM
HIGH-SPEED, DUO-SOURCE, GYRO-STABILIZED BOOT TURBINES: 93%...97%...
...ON-LINE

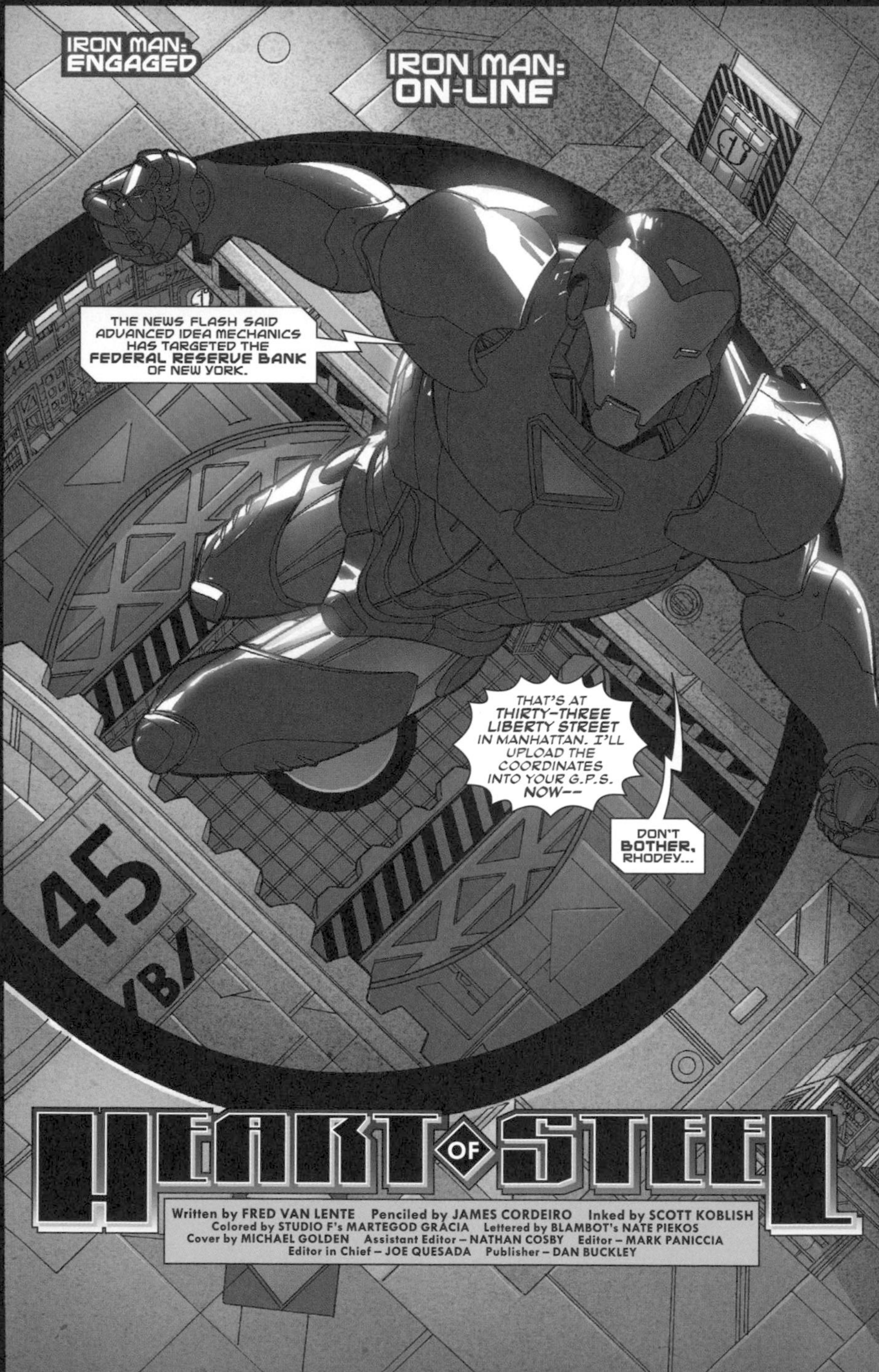

IRON MAN: ENGAGED
IRON MAN: ON-LINE
THE NEWS FLASH SAID ADVANCED IDEA MECHANICS HAS TARGETED THE FEDERAL RESERVE BANK OF NEW YORK.
THAT'S AT THIRTY-THREE LIBERTY STREET IN MANHATTAN. I'LL UPLOAD THE COORDINATES INTO YOUR G.P.S. NOW--
DON'T BOTHER, RHODEY...
45 /B/
HEART OF STEEL
Written by FRED VAN LENTE Penciled by JAMES CORDEIRO Inked by SCOTT KOBLISH
Colored by STUDIO F's MARTEGOD GRACIA Lettered by BLAMBOT's NATE PIEKOS
Cover by MICHAEL GOLDEN Assistant Editor – NATHAN COSBY Editor – MARK PANICCIA
Editor in Chief – JOE QUESADA Publisher – DAN BUCKLEY

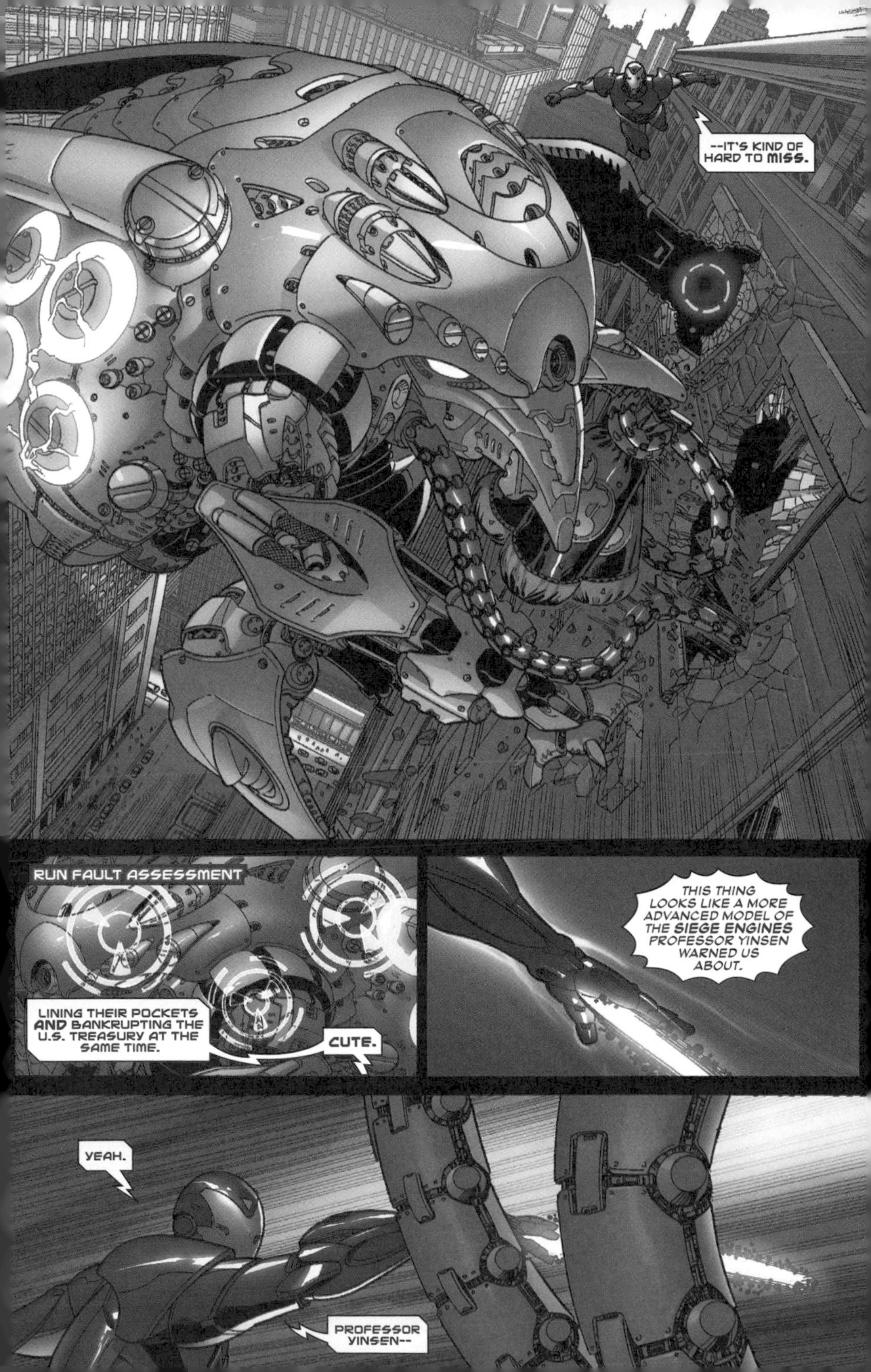
--IT'S KIND OF HARD TO MISS.
RUN FAULT ASSESSMENT
LINING THEIR POCKETS AND BANKRUPTING THE U.S. TREASURY AT THE SAME TIME.
CUTE.
THIS THING LOOKS LIKE A MORE ADVANCED MODEL OF THE SIEGE ENGINES PROFESSOR YINSEN WARNED US ABOUT.
YEAH.
PROFESSOR YINSEN--

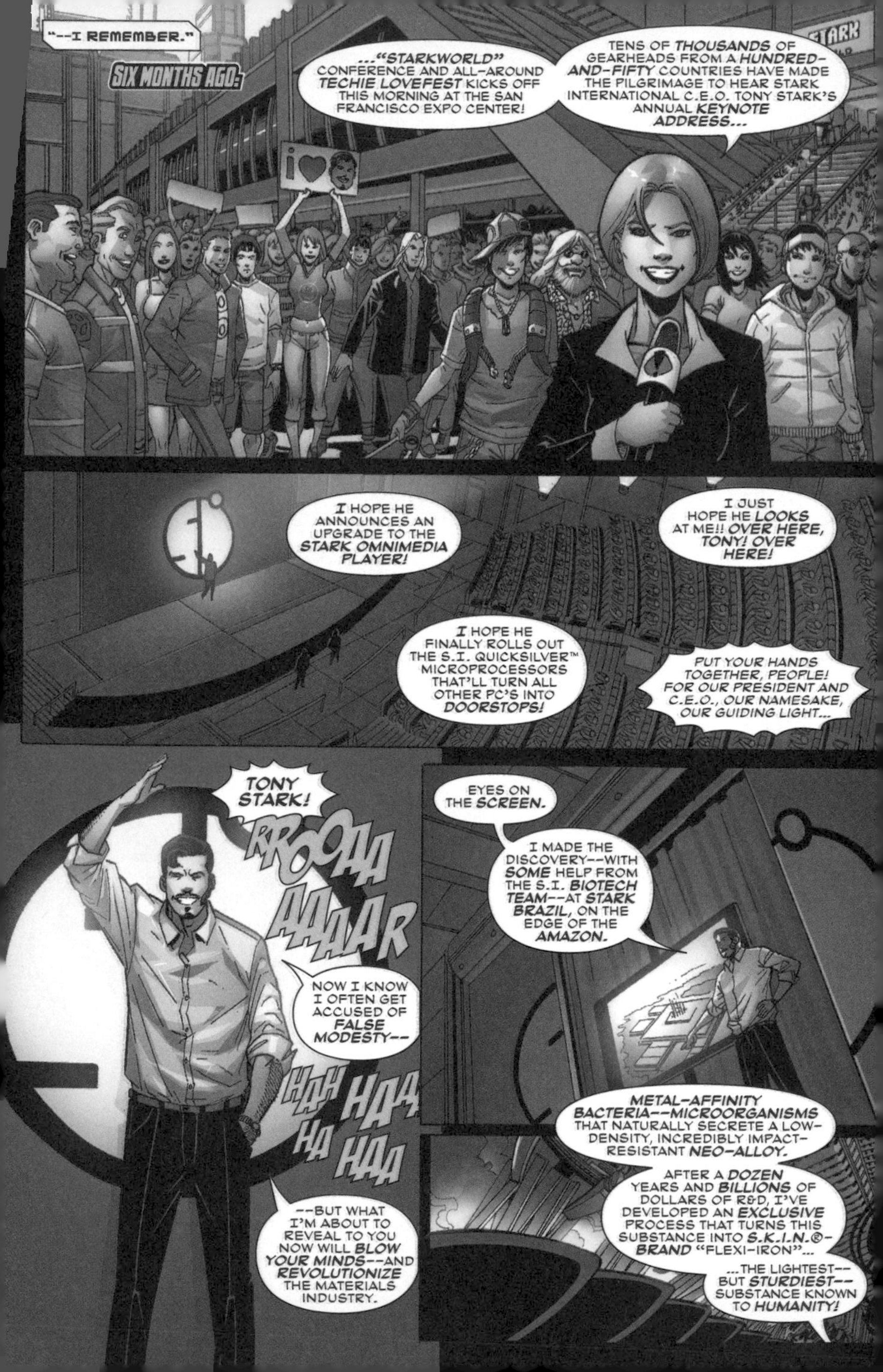

"--I REMEMBER."
SIX MONTHS AGO:
STARK
...“STARKWORLD” CONFERENCE AND ALL-AROUND TECHIE LOVEFEST KICKS OFF THIS MORNING AT THE SAN FRANCISCO EXPO CENTER!
TENS OF THOUSANDS OF GEARHEADS FROM A HUNDRED-AND-FIFTY COUNTRIES HAVE MADE THE PILGRIMAGE TO HEAR STARK INTERNATIONAL C.E.O. TONY STARK’S ANNUAL KEYNOTE ADDRESS...
I HOPE HE ANNOUNCES AN UPGRADE TO THE STARK OMNIMEDIA PLAYER!
I JUST HOPE HE LOOKS AT ME!! OVER HERE, TONY! OVER HERE!
I HOPE HE FINALLY ROLLS OUT THE S.I. QUICKSILVER™ MICROPROCESSORS THAT’LL TURN ALL OTHER PC’S INTO DOORSTOPS!
PUT YOUR HANDS TOGETHER, PEOPLE! FOR OUR PRESIDENT AND C.E.O., OUR NAMESAKE, OUR GUIDING LIGHT...
TONY STARK!
RROOAAAAAAAR
NOW I KNOW I OFTEN GET ACCUSED OF FALSE MODESTY--
HAH HAA HA HAA
--BUT WHAT I’M ABOUT TO REVEAL TO YOU NOW WILL BLOW YOUR MINDS--AND REVOLUTIONIZE THE MATERIALS INDUSTRY.
EYES ON THE SCREEN.
I MADE THE DISCOVERY--WITH SOME HELP FROM THE S.I. BIOTECH TEAM--AT STARK BRAZIL, ON THE EDGE OF THE AMAZON.
METAL-AFFINITY BACTERIA--MICROORGANISMS THAT NATURALLY SECRETE A LOW-DENSITY, INCREDIBLY IMPACT-RESISTANT NEO-ALLOY.
AFTER A DOZEN YEARS AND BILLIONS OF DOLLARS OF R&D, I’VE DEVELOPED AN EXCLUSIVE PROCESS THAT TURNS THIS SUBSTANCE INTO S.K.I.N.®-BRAND “FLEXI-IRON”...
...THE LIGHTEST--BUT STURDIEST--SUBSTANCE KNOWN TO HUMANITY!

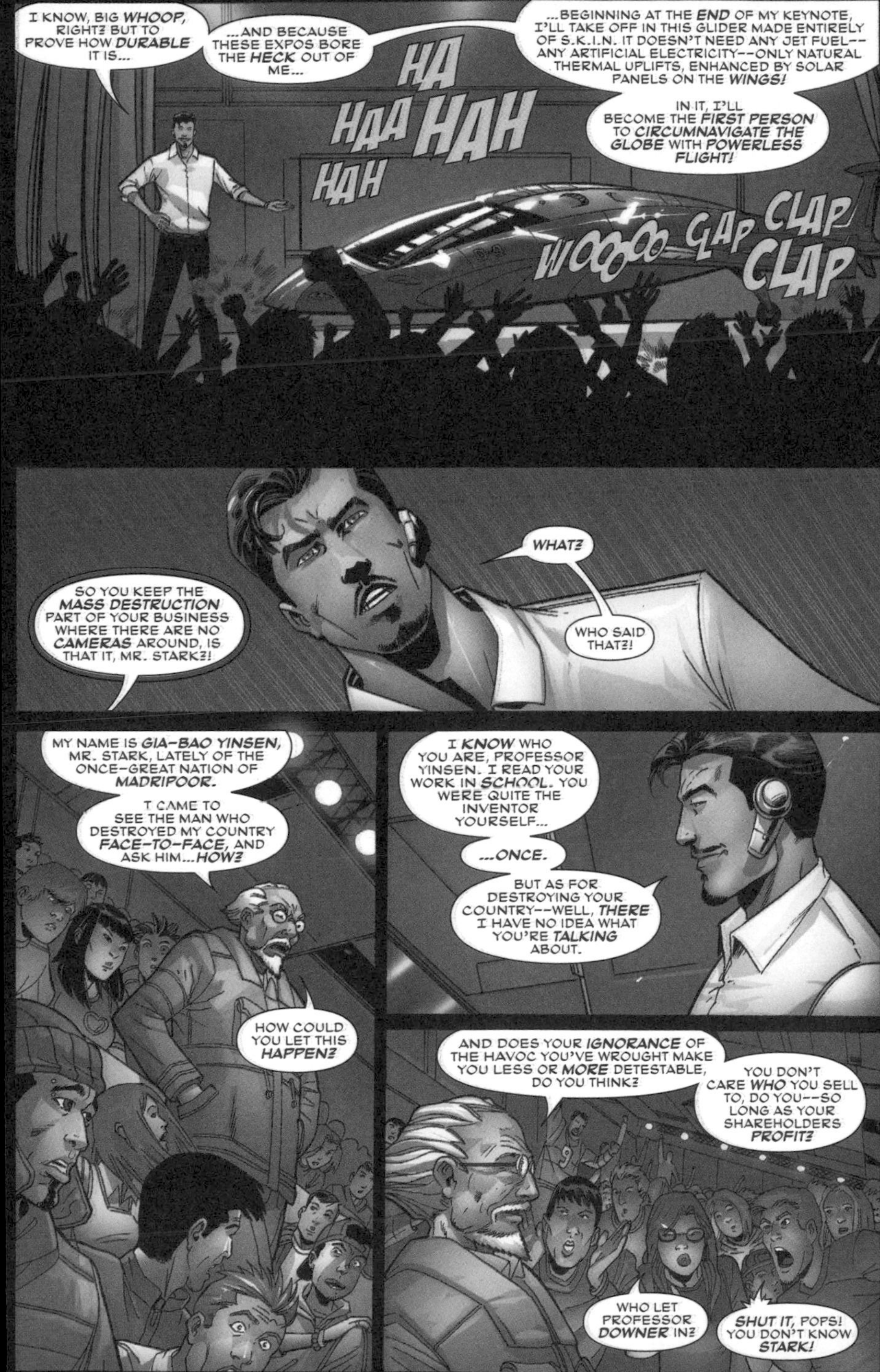
I KNOW, BIG WHOOP, RIGHT? BUT TO PROVE HOW DURABLE IT IS...
...AND BECAUSE THESE EXPOS BORE THE HECK OUT OF ME...
HA HAA HAH HAH
...BEGINNING AT THE END OF MY KEYNOTE, I'LL TAKE OFF IN THIS GLIDER MADE ENTIRELY OF S.K.I.N. IT DOESN'T NEED ANY JET FUEL-- ANY ARTIFICIAL ELECTRICITY--ONLY NATURAL THERMAL UPLIFTS, ENHANCED BY SOLAR PANELS ON THE WINGS!
IN IT, I'LL BECOME THE FIRST PERSON TO CIRCUMNAVIGATE THE GLOBE WITH POWERLESS FLIGHT!
WOOOOO CLAP CLAP CLAP
SO YOU KEEP THE MASS DESTRUCTION PART OF YOUR BUSINESS WHERE THERE ARE NO CAMERAS AROUND, IS THAT IT, MR. STARK?!
WHAT?
WHO SAID THAT?!
MY NAME IS GIA-BAO YINSEN, MR. STARK, LATELY OF THE ONCE-GREAT NATION OF MADRIPOOR.
I CAME TO SEE THE MAN WHO DESTROYED MY COUNTRY FACE-TO-FACE, AND ASK HIM...HOW?
HOW COULD YOU LET THIS HAPPEN?
I KNOW WHO YOU ARE, PROFESSOR YINSEN. I READ YOUR WORK IN SCHOOL. YOU WERE QUITE THE INVENTOR YOURSELF...
...ONCE.
BUT AS FOR DESTROYING YOUR COUNTRY--WELL, THERE I HAVE NO IDEA WHAT YOU'RE TALKING ABOUT.
AND DOES YOUR IGNORANCE OF THE HAVOC YOU'VE WROUGHT MAKE YOU LESS OR MORE DETESTABLE, DO YOU THINK?
YOU DON'T CARE WHO YOU SELL TO, DO YOU--SO LONG AS YOUR SHAREHOLDERS PROFIT?
WHO LET PROFESSOR DOWNER IN?
SHUT IT, POPS! YOU DON'T KNOW STARK!

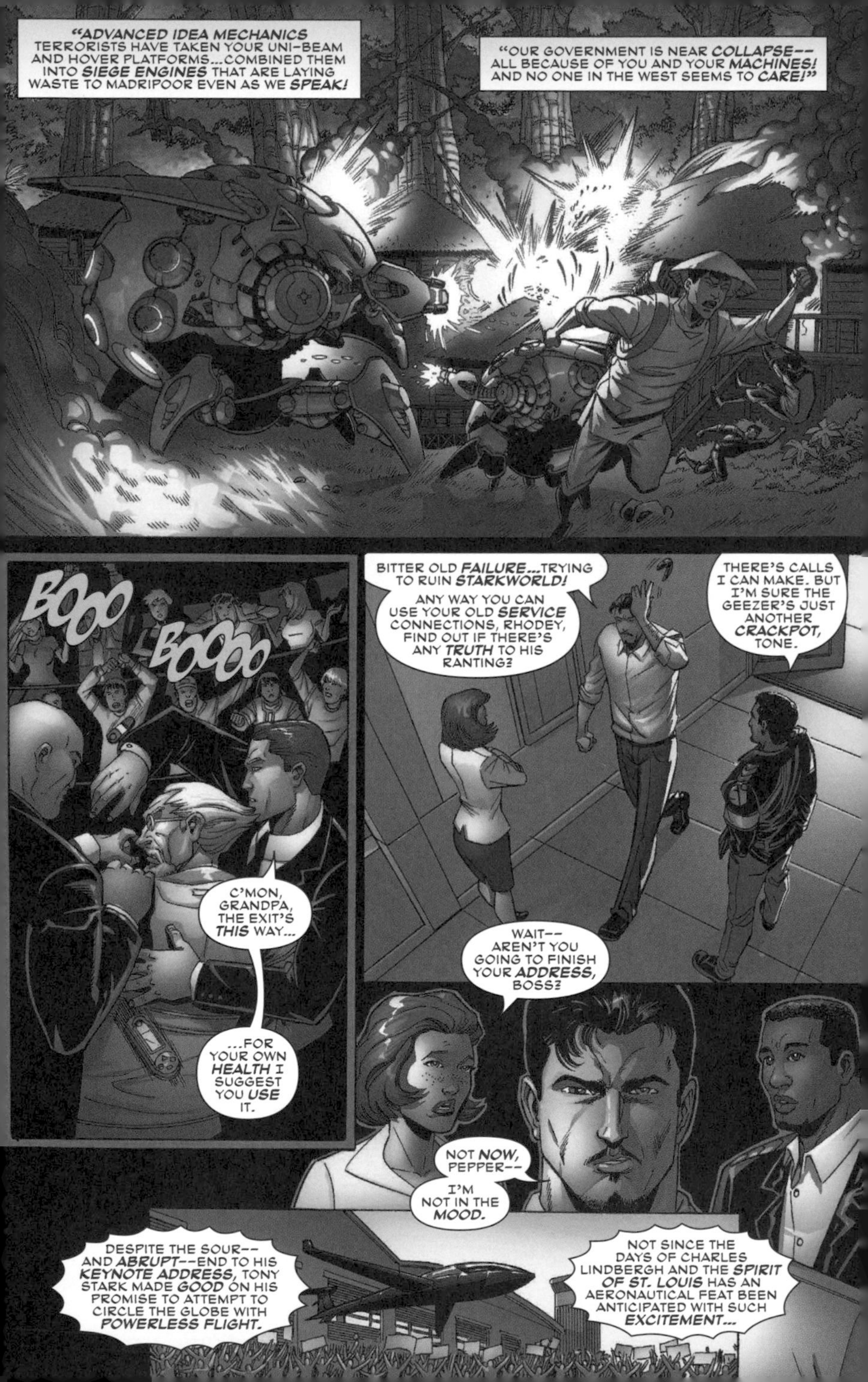
"ADVANCED IDEA MECHANICS TERRORISTS HAVE TAKEN YOUR UNI-BEAM AND HOVER PLATFORMS...COMBINED THEM INTO SIEGE ENGINES THAT ARE LAYING WASTE TO MADRIPOOR EVEN AS WE SPEAK!
"OUR GOVERNMENT IS NEAR COLLAPSE-- ALL BECAUSE OF YOU AND YOUR MACHINES! AND NO ONE IN THE WEST SEEMS TO CARE!"
BOOO
BOOOO
C'MON, GRANDPA, THE EXIT'S THIS WAY...
...FOR YOUR OWN HEALTH I SUGGEST YOU USE IT.
BITTER OLD FAILURE...TRYING TO RUIN STARKWORLD!
ANY WAY YOU CAN USE YOUR OLD SERVICE CONNECTIONS, RHODEY, FIND OUT IF THERE'S ANY TRUTH TO HIS RANTING?
THERE'S CALLS I CAN MAKE. BUT I'M SURE THE GEEZER'S JUST ANOTHER CRACKPOT, TONE.
WAIT-- AREN'T YOU GOING TO FINISH YOUR ADDRESS, BOSS?
NOT NOW, PEPPER--
I'M NOT IN THE MOOD.
DESPITE THE SOUR-- AND ABRUPT--END TO HIS KEYNOTE ADDRESS, TONY STARK MADE GOOD ON HIS PROMISE TO ATTEMPT TO CIRCLE THE GLOBE WITH POWERLESS FLIGHT.
NOT SINCE THE DAYS OF CHARLES LINDBERGH AND THE SPIRIT OF ST. LOUIS HAS AN AERONAUTICAL FEAT BEEN ANTICIPATED WITH SUCH EXCITEMENT...

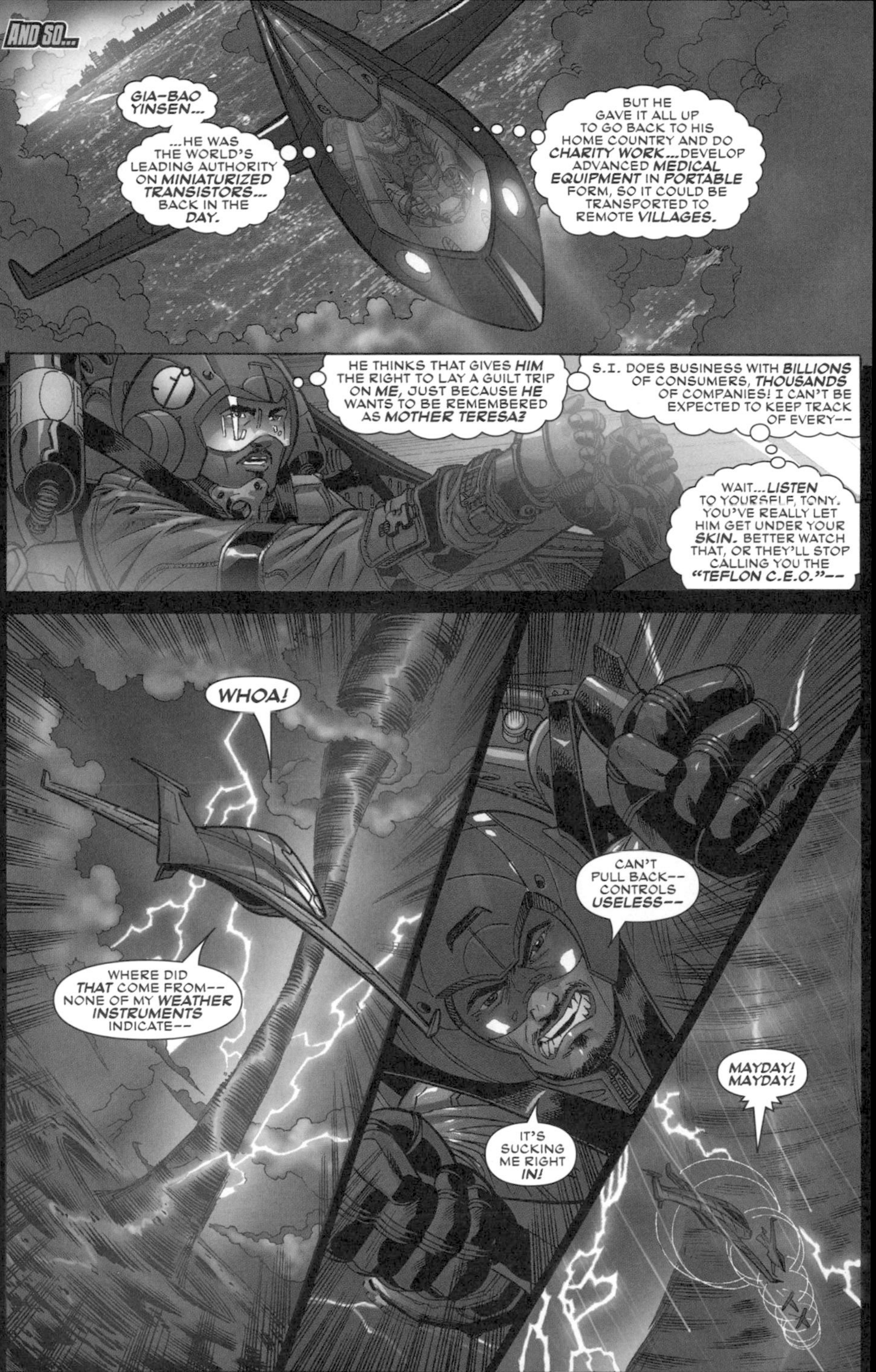
AND SO...
GIA-BAO YINSEN...
...HE WAS THE WORLD'S LEADING AUTHORITY ON MINIATURIZED TRANSISTORS... BACK IN THE DAY.
BUT HE GAVE IT ALL UP TO GO BACK TO HIS HOME COUNTRY AND DO CHARITY WORK... DEVELOP ADVANCED MEDICAL EQUIPMENT IN PORTABLE FORM, SO IT COULD BE TRANSPORTED TO REMOTE VILLAGES.
HE THINKS THAT GIVES HIM THE RIGHT TO LAY A GUILT TRIP ON ME, JUST BECAUSE HE WANTS TO BE REMEMBERED AS MOTHER TERESA?
S.I. DOES BUSINESS WITH BILLIONS OF CONSUMERS, THOUSANDS OF COMPANIES! I CAN'T BE EXPECTED TO KEEP TRACK OF EVERY--
WAIT... LISTEN TO YOURSELF, TONY. YOU'VE REALLY LET HIM GET UNDER YOUR SKIN. BETTER WATCH THAT, OR THEY'LL STOP CALLING YOU THE "TEFLON C.E.O."--
WHOA!
WHERE DID THAT COME FROM-- NONE OF MY WEATHER INSTRUMENTS INDICATE--
CAN'T PULL BACK-- CONTROLS USELESS--
IT'S SUCKING ME RIGHT IN!
MAYDAY! MAYDAY!

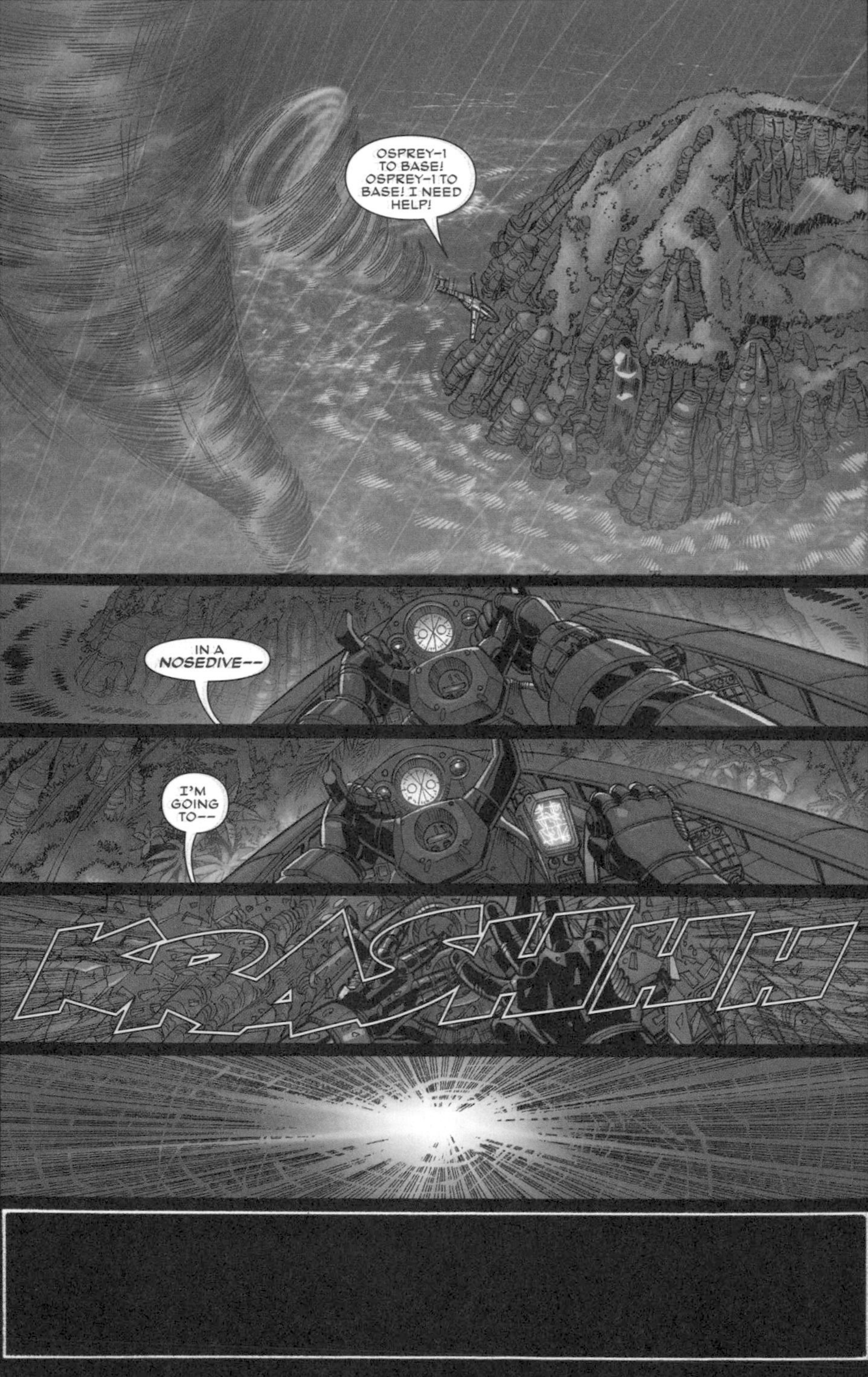
OSPREY-1 TO BASE! OSPREY-1 TO BASE! I NEED HELP!
IN A NOSEDIVE--
I'M GOING TO--
KRASHHH

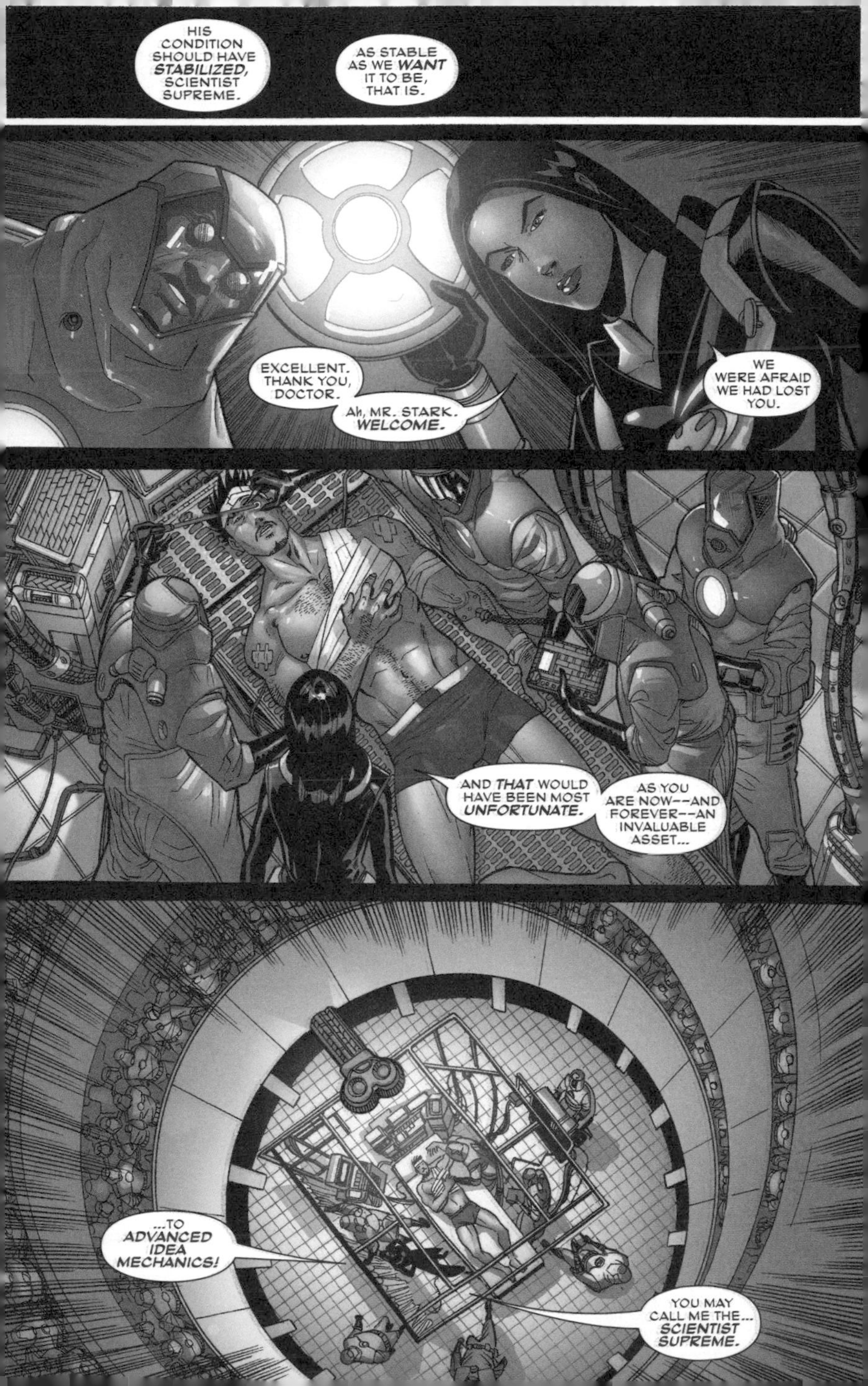
HIS CONDITION SHOULD HAVE STABILIZED, SCIENTIST SUPREME.
AS STABLE AS WE WANT IT TO BE, THAT IS.
EXCELLENT. THANK YOU, DOCTOR.
Ah, MR. STARK. WELCOME.
WE WERE AFRAID WE HAD LOST YOU.
AND THAT WOULD HAVE BEEN MOST UNFORTUNATE.
AS YOU ARE NOW--AND FOREVER--AN INVALUABLE ASSET...
...TO ADVANCED IDEA MECHANICS!
YOU MAY CALL ME THE... SCIENTIST SUPREME.

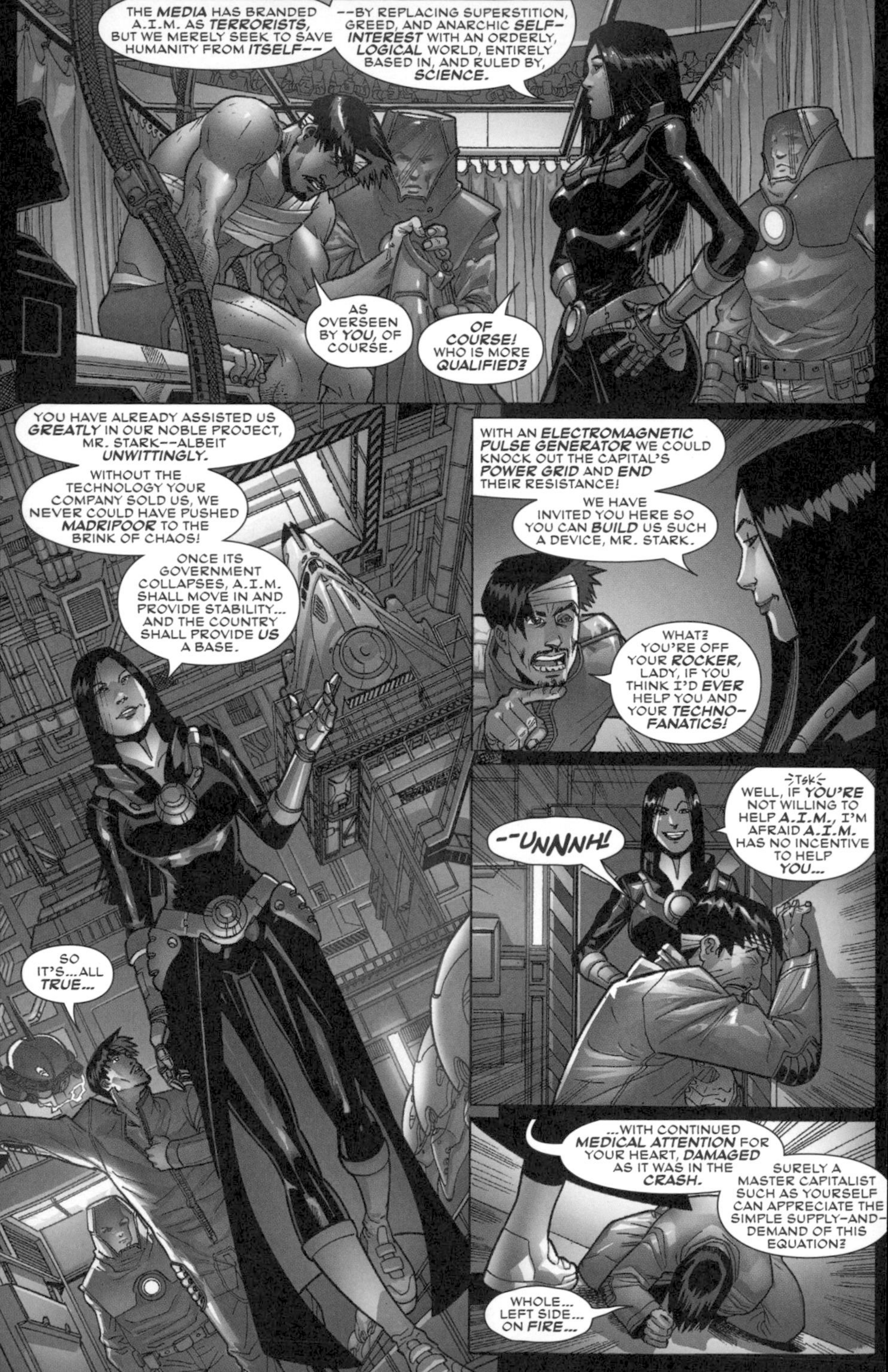
THE MEDIA HAS BRANDED A.I.M. AS TERRORISTS, BUT WE MERELY SEEK TO SAVE HUMANITY FROM ITSELF--
--BY REPLACING SUPERSTITION, GREED, AND ANARCHIC SELF-INTEREST WITH AN ORDERLY, LOGICAL WORLD, ENTIRELY BASED IN, AND RULED BY, SCIENCE.
AS OVERSEEN BY YOU, OF COURSE.
OF COURSE! WHO IS MORE QUALIFIED?
YOU HAVE ALREADY ASSISTED US GREATLY IN OUR NOBLE PROJECT, MR. STARK--ALBEIT UNWITTINGLY.
WITHOUT THE TECHNOLOGY YOUR COMPANY SOLD US, WE NEVER COULD HAVE PUSHED MADRIPOOR TO THE BRINK OF CHAOS!
ONCE ITS GOVERNMENT COLLAPSES, A.I.M. SHALL MOVE IN AND PROVIDE STABILITY... AND THE COUNTRY SHALL PROVIDE US A BASE.
SO IT'S...ALL TRUE...
WITH AN ELECTROMAGNETIC PULSE GENERATOR WE COULD KNOCK OUT THE CAPITAL'S POWER GRID AND END THEIR RESISTANCE!
WE HAVE INVITED YOU HERE SO YOU CAN BUILD US SUCH A DEVICE, MR. STARK.
WHAT? YOU'RE OFF YOUR ROCKER, LADY, IF YOU THINK I'D EVER HELP YOU AND YOUR TECHNO-FANATICS!
-TSK-
WELL, IF YOU'RE NOT WILLING TO HELP A.I.M., I'M AFRAID A.I.M. HAS NO INCENTIVE TO HELP YOU...
--UNNNH!
...WITH CONTINUED MEDICAL ATTENTION FOR YOUR HEART, DAMAGED AS IT WAS IN THE CRASH.
SURELY A MASTER CAPITALIST SUCH AS YOURSELF CAN APPRECIATE THE SIMPLE SUPPLY-AND-DEMAND OF THIS EQUATION?
WHOLE... LEFT SIDE... ON FIRE...

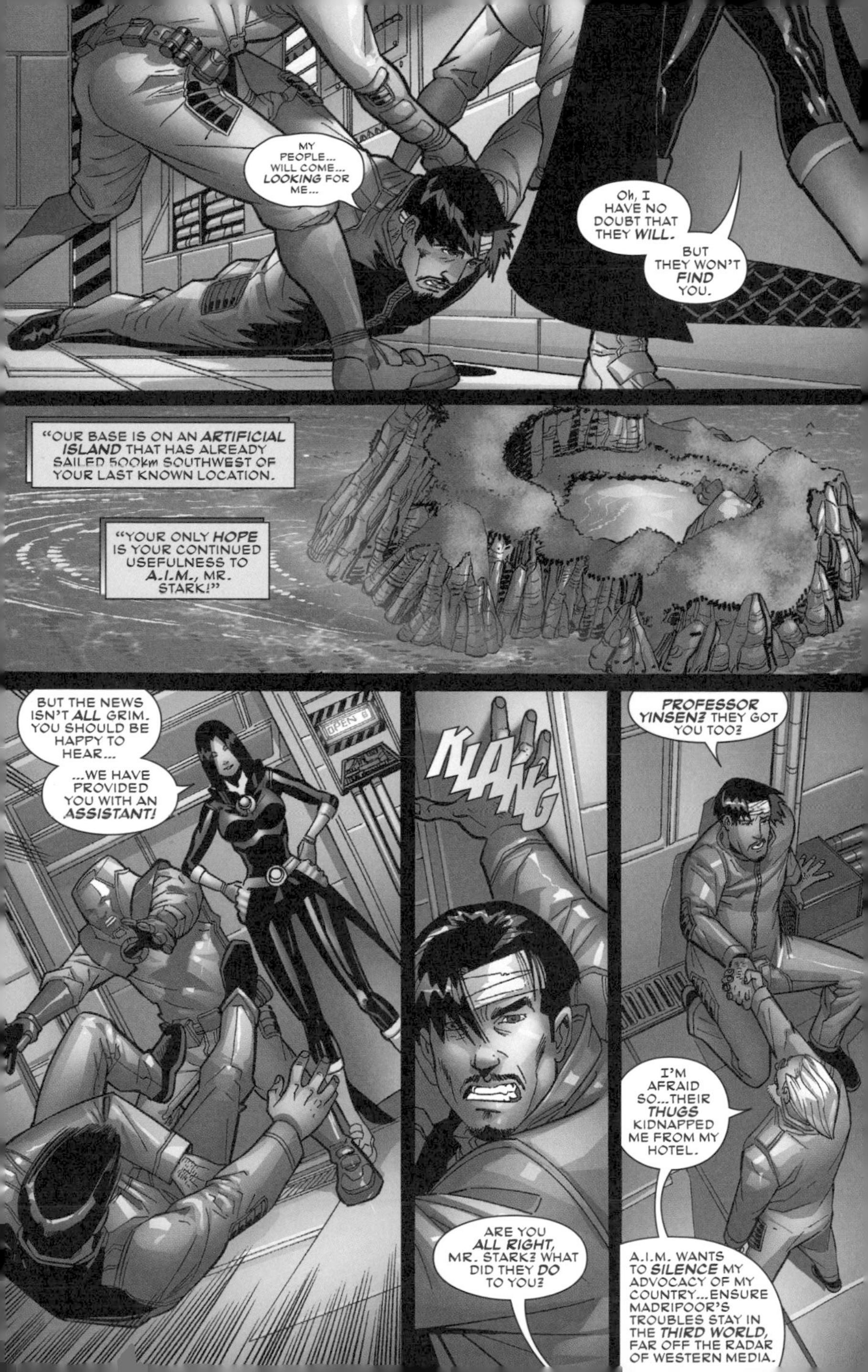
MY PEOPLE... WILL COME... LOOKING FOR ME...
Oh, I HAVE NO DOUBT THAT THEY WILL.
BUT THEY WON'T FIND YOU.
"OUR BASE IS ON AN ARTIFICIAL ISLAND THAT HAS ALREADY SAILED 500km SOUTHWEST OF YOUR LAST KNOWN LOCATION.
"YOUR ONLY HOPE IS YOUR CONTINUED USEFULNESS TO A.I.M., MR. STARK!"
BUT THE NEWS ISN'T ALL GRIM. YOU SHOULD BE HAPPY TO HEAR...
...WE HAVE PROVIDED YOU WITH AN ASSISTANT!
OPEN
KLANG
ARE YOU ALL RIGHT, MR. STARK? WHAT DID THEY DO TO YOU?
PROFESSOR YINSEN? THEY GOT YOU TOO?
I'M AFRAID SO...THEIR THUGS KIDNAPPED ME FROM MY HOTEL.
A.I.M. WANTS TO SILENCE MY ADVOCACY OF MY COUNTRY...ENSURE MADRIPOOR'S TROUBLES STAY IN THE THIRD WORLD, FAR OFF THE RADAR OF WESTERN MEDIA.

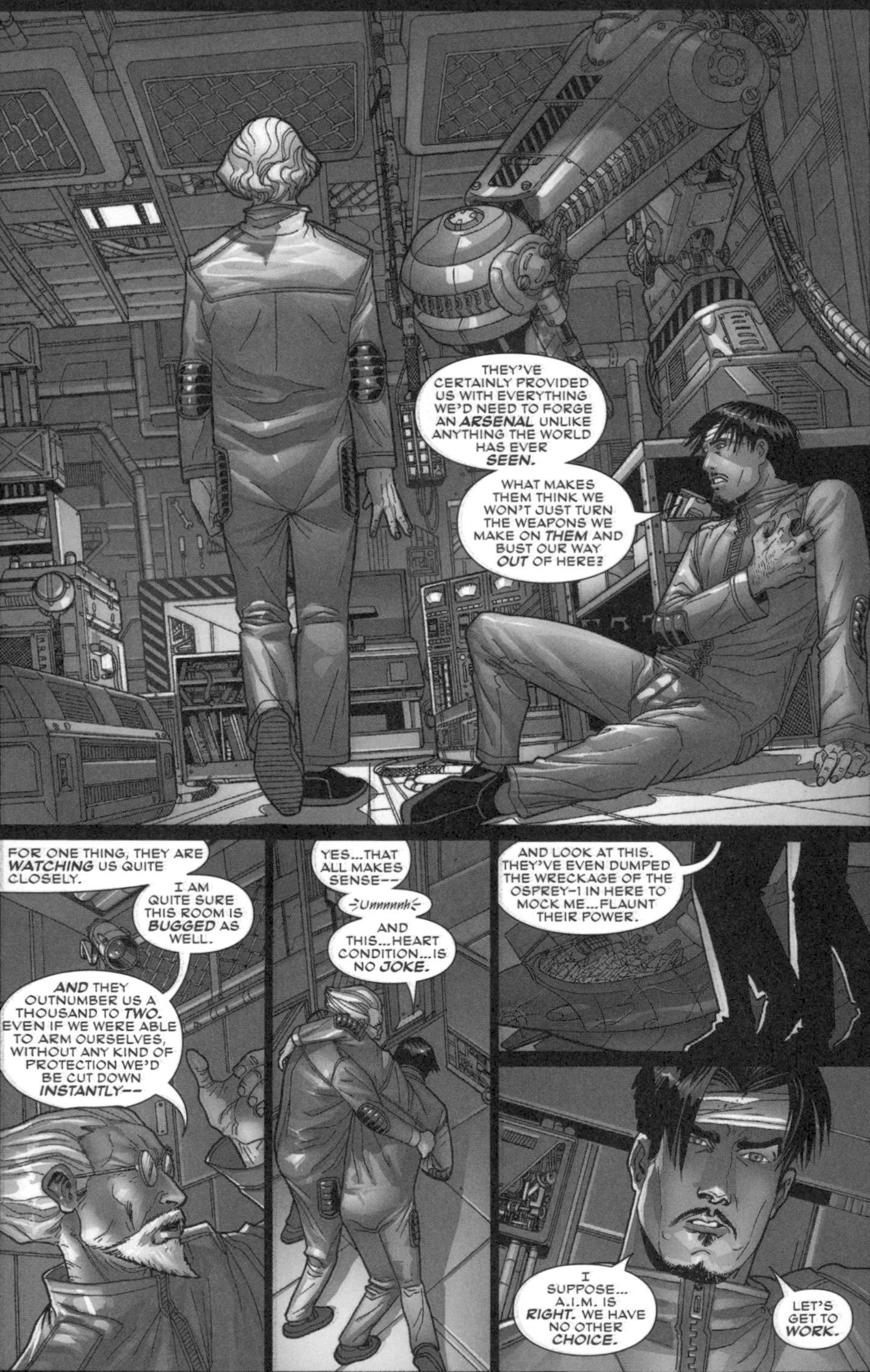
THEY'VE CERTAINLY PROVIDED US WITH EVERYTHING WE'D NEED TO FORGE AN ARSENAL UNLIKE ANYTHING THE WORLD HAS EVER SEEN.
WHAT MAKES THEM THINK WE WON'T JUST TURN THE WEAPONS WE MAKE ON THEM AND BUST OUR WAY OUT OF HERE?
FOR ONE THING, THEY ARE WATCHING US QUITE CLOSELY.
I AM QUITE SURE THIS ROOM IS BUGGED AS WELL.
AND THEY OUTNUMBER US A THOUSAND TO TWO. EVEN IF WE WERE ABLE TO ARM OURSELVES, WITHOUT ANY KIND OF PROTECTION WE'D BE CUT DOWN INSTANTLY--
YES...THAT ALL MAKES SENSE--
Unnnnnh
AND THIS...HEART CONDITION...IS NO JOKE.
AND LOOK AT THIS. THEY'VE EVEN DUMPED THE WRECKAGE OF THE OSPREY-1 IN HERE TO MOCK ME...FLAUNT THEIR POWER.
I SUPPOSE... A.I.M. IS RIGHT. WE HAVE NO OTHER CHOICE.
LET'S GET TO WORK.

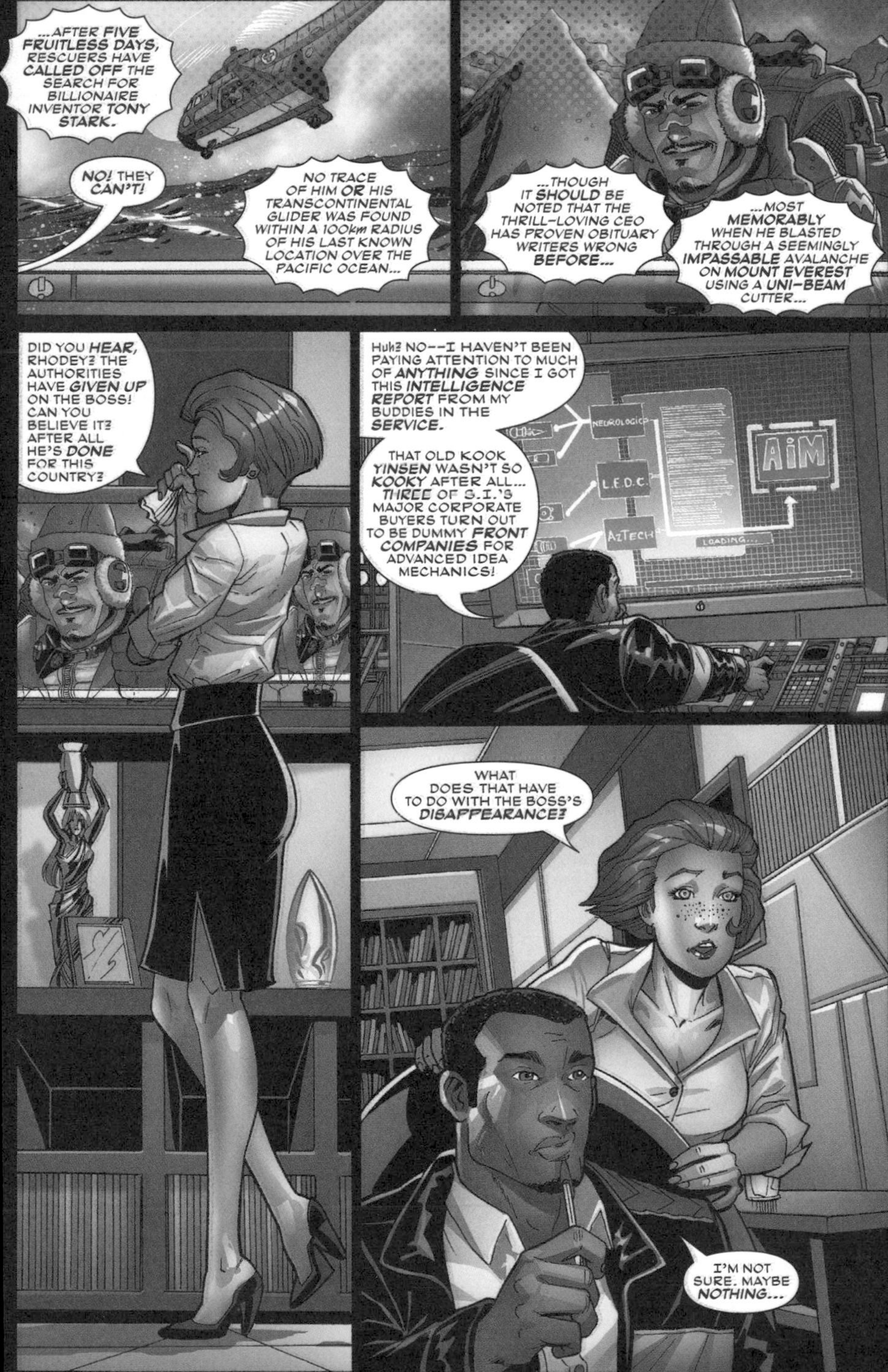

...AFTER FIVE FRUITLESS DAYS, RESCUERS HAVE CALLED OFF THE SEARCH FOR BILLIONAIRE INVENTOR TONY STARK.
NO! THEY CAN'T!
NO TRACE OF HIM OR HIS TRANSCONTINENTAL GLIDER WAS FOUND WITHIN A 100km RADIUS OF HIS LAST KNOWN LOCATION OVER THE PACIFIC OCEAN...
...THOUGH IT SHOULD BE NOTED THAT THE THRILL-LOVING CEO HAS PROVEN OBITUARY WRITERS WRONG BEFORE...
...MOST MEMORABLY WHEN HE BLASTED THROUGH A SEEMINGLY IMPASSABLE AVALANCHE ON MOUNT EVEREST USING A UNI-BEAM CUTTER...
DID YOU HEAR, RHODEY? THE AUTHORITIES HAVE GIVEN UP ON THE BOSS! CAN YOU BELIEVE IT? AFTER ALL HE'S DONE FOR THIS COUNTRY?
Huh? NO--I HAVEN'T BEEN PAYING ATTENTION TO MUCH OF ANYTHING SINCE I GOT THIS INTELLIGENCE REPORT FROM MY BUDDIES IN THE SERVICE.
THAT OLD KOOK YINSEN WASN'T SO KOOKY AFTER ALL... THREE OF S.I.'S MAJOR CORPORATE BUYERS TURN OUT TO BE DUMMY FRONT COMPANIES FOR ADVANCED IDEA MECHANICS!
NEUROLOGIC
L.E.D.C.
AzTECH
AiM
LOADING...
WHAT DOES THAT HAVE TO DO WITH THE BOSS'S DISAPPEARANCE?
I'M NOT SURE. MAYBE NOTHING...

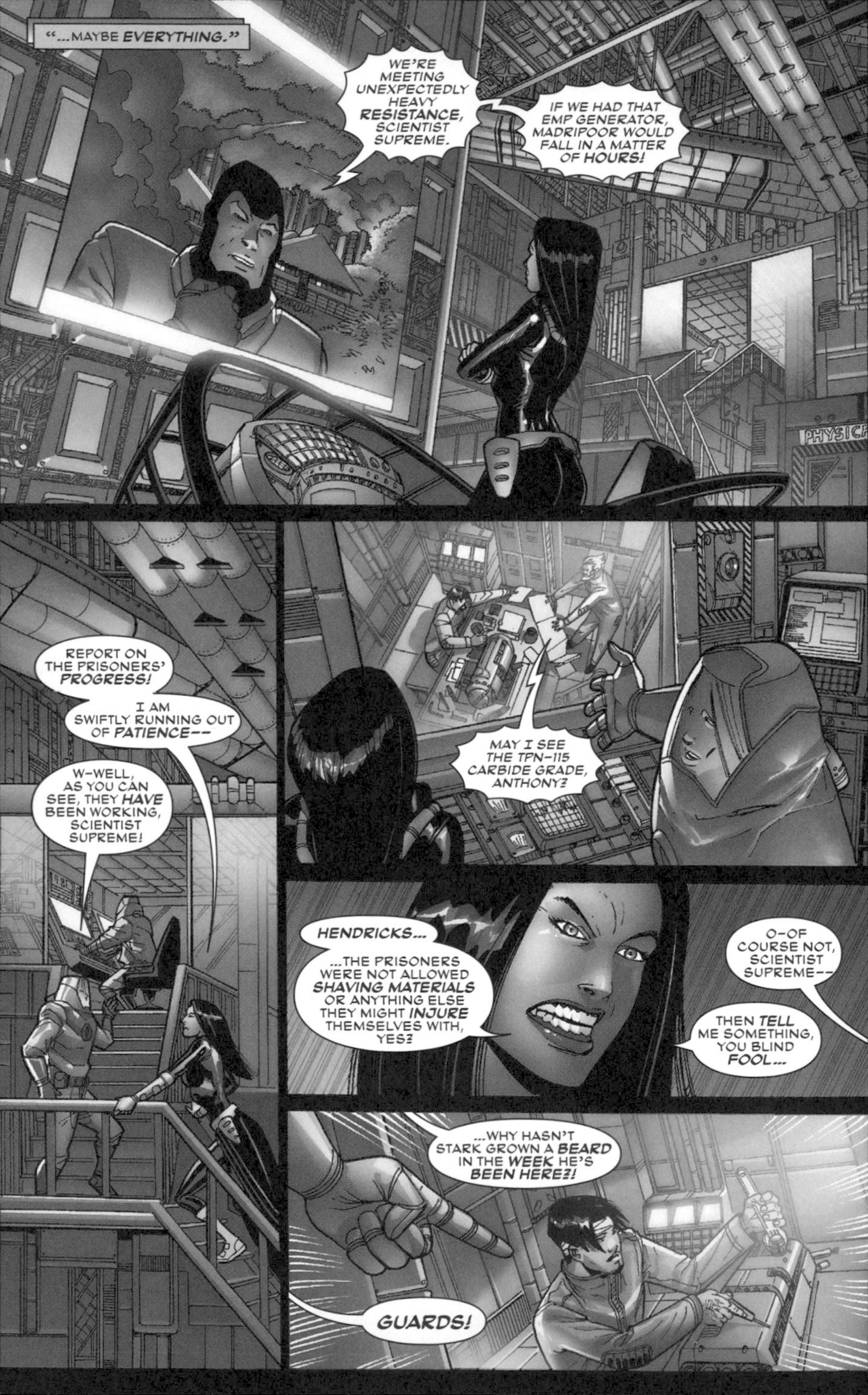
"...MAYBE EVERYTHING."
WE'RE MEETING UNEXPECTEDLY HEAVY RESISTANCE, SCIENTIST SUPREME.
IF WE HAD THAT EMP GENERATOR, MADRIPOOR WOULD FALL IN A MATTER OF HOURS!
PHYSIC
REPORT ON THE PRISONERS' PROGRESS!
I AM SWIFTLY RUNNING OUT OF PATIENCE--
W-WELL, AS YOU CAN SEE, THEY HAVE BEEN WORKING, SCIENTIST SUPREME!
MAY I SEE THE TPN-115 CARBIDE GRADE, ANTHONY?
HENDRICKS...
...THE PRISONERS WERE NOT ALLOWED SHAVING MATERIALS OR ANYTHING ELSE THEY MIGHT INJURE THEMSELVES WITH, YES?
O-OF COURSE NOT, SCIENTIST SUPREME--
THEN TELL ME SOMETHING, YOU BLIND FOOL...
...WHY HASN'T STARK GROWN A BEARD IN THE WEEK HE'S BEEN HERE?!
GUARDS!

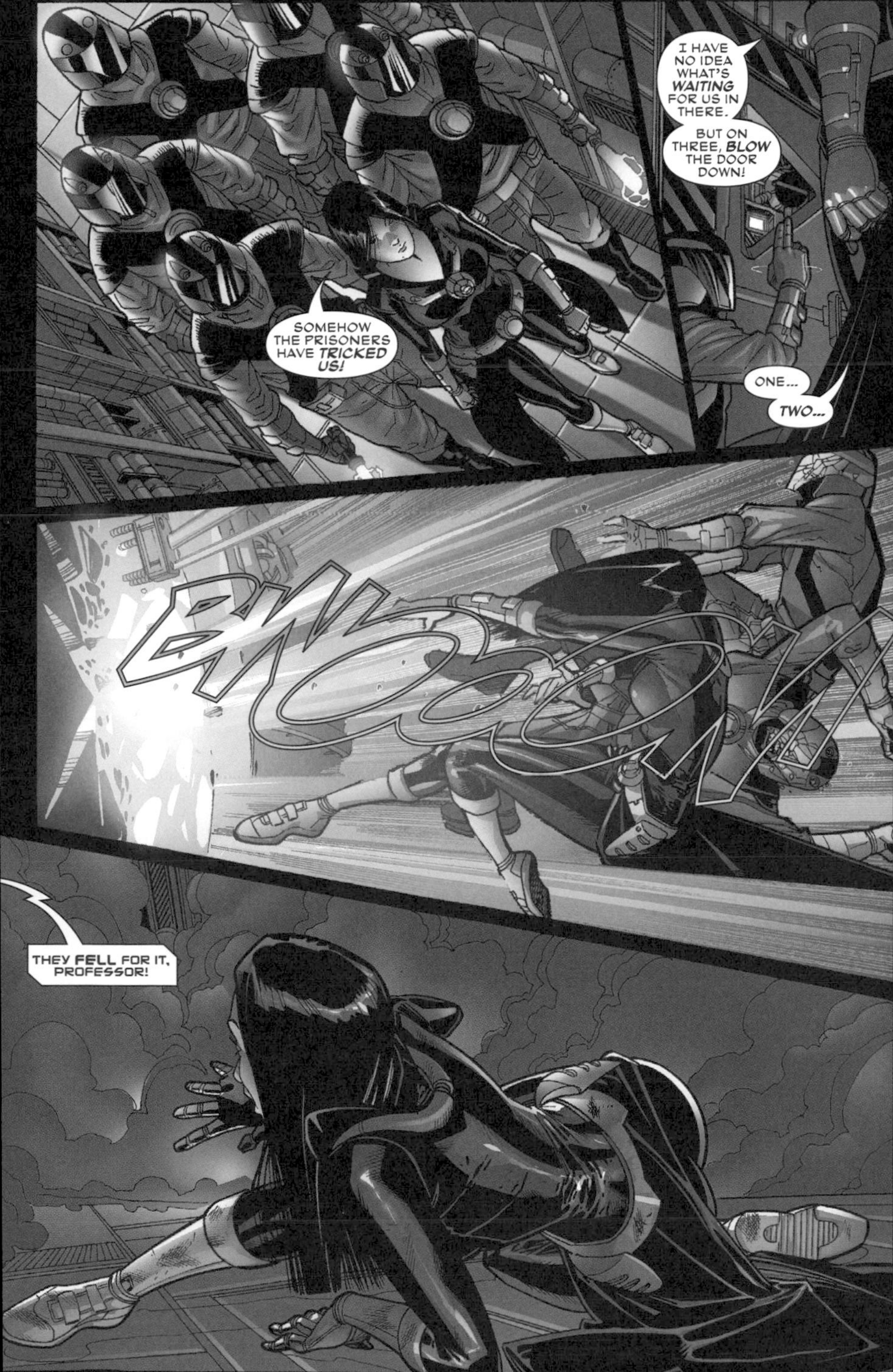
SOMEHOW THE PRISONERS HAVE TRICKED US!
I HAVE NO IDEA WHAT'S WAITING FOR US IN THERE.
BUT ON THREE, BLOW THE DOOR DOWN!
ONE...
TWO...
THEY FELL FOR IT, PROFESSOR!

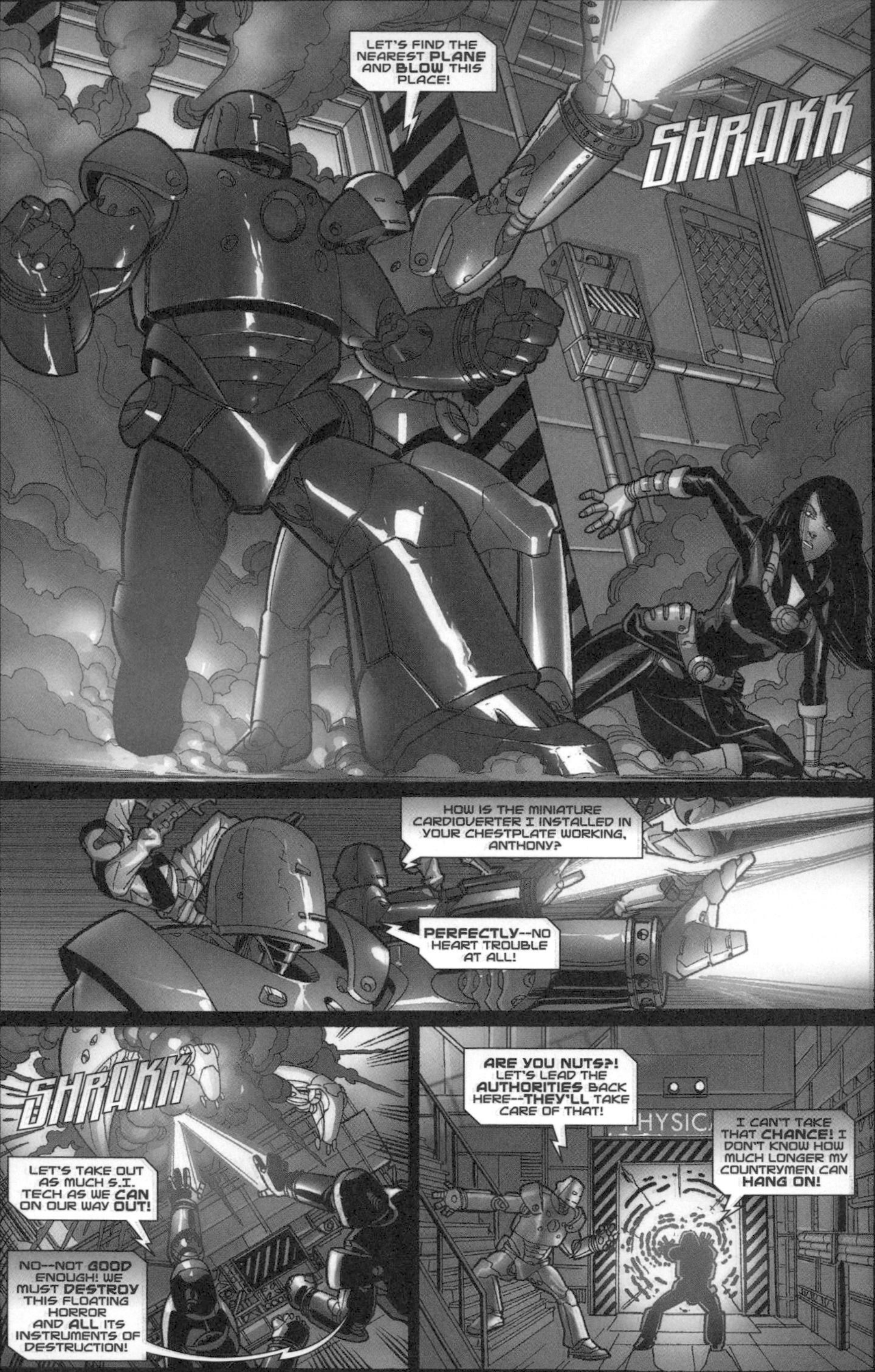
LET'S FIND THE NEAREST PLANE AND BLOW THIS PLACE!
SHRAKK
HOW IS THE MINIATURE CARDIOVERTER I INSTALLED IN YOUR CHESTPLATE WORKING, ANTHONY?
PERFECTLY--NO HEART TROUBLE AT ALL!
SHRAKK
LET'S TAKE OUT AS MUCH S.I. TECH AS WE CAN ON OUR WAY OUT!
NO--NOT GOOD ENOUGH! WE MUST DESTROY THIS FLOATING HORROR AND ALL ITS INSTRUMENTS OF DESTRUCTION!
ARE YOU NUTS?! LET'S LEAD THE AUTHORITIES BACK HERE--THEY'LL TAKE CARE OF THAT!
I CAN'T TAKE THAT CHANCE! I DON'T KNOW HOW MUCH LONGER MY COUNTRYMEN CAN HANG ON!

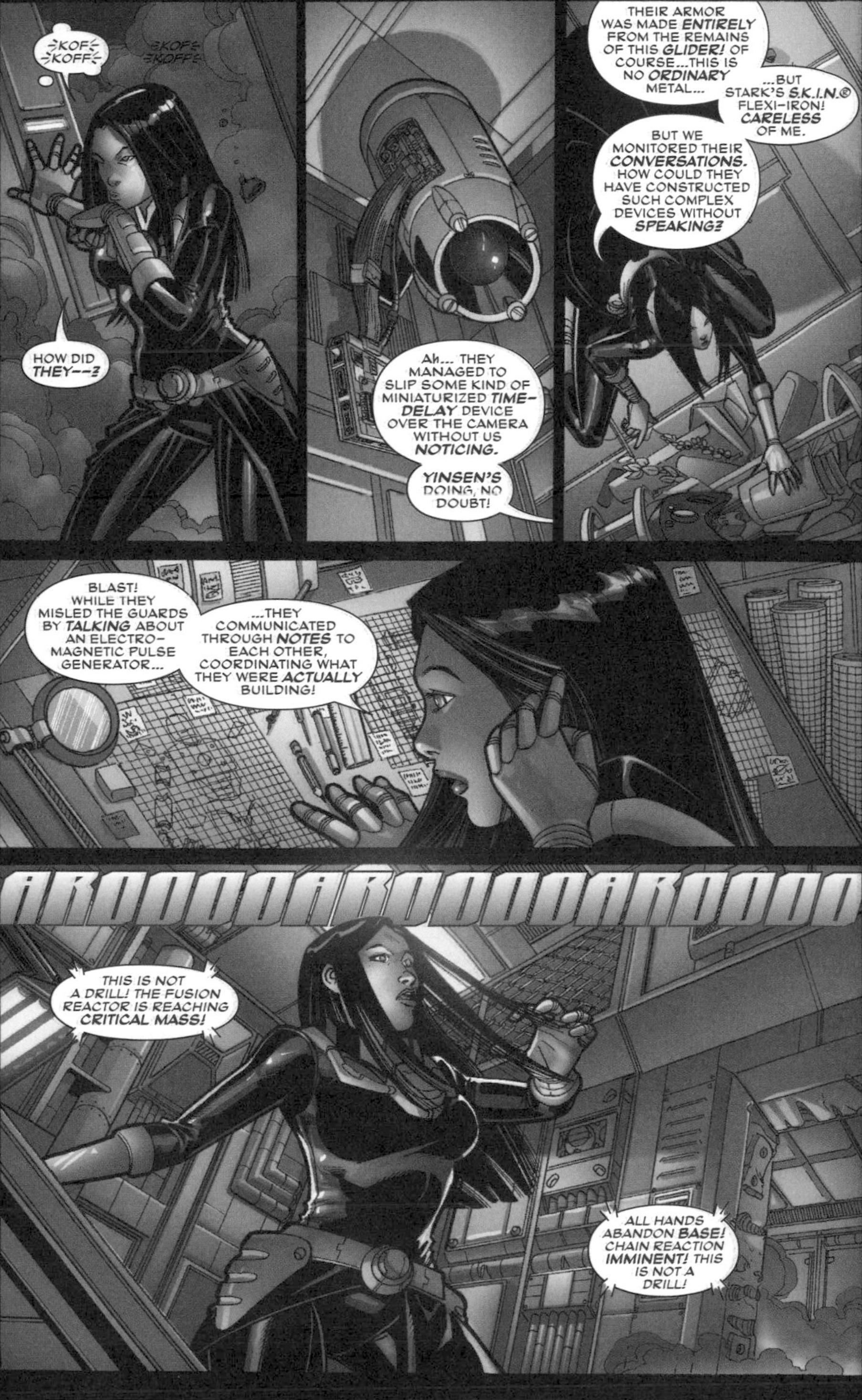
KOF KOFF
KOF KOFF
HOW DID THEY--?
AH... THEY MANAGED TO SLIP SOME KIND OF MINIATURIZED TIME-DELAY DEVICE OVER THE CAMERA WITHOUT US NOTICING.
YINSEN'S DOING, NO DOUBT!
THEIR ARMOR WAS MADE ENTIRELY FROM THE REMAINS OF THIS GLIDER! OF COURSE...THIS IS NO ORDINARY METAL...
...BUT STARK'S S.K.I.N.® FLEXI-IRON! CARELESS OF ME.
BUT WE MONITORED THEIR CONVERSATIONS. HOW COULD THEY HAVE CONSTRUCTED SUCH COMPLEX DEVICES WITHOUT SPEAKING?
BLAST! WHILE THEY MISLED THE GUARDS BY TALKING ABOUT AN ELECTRO-MAGNETIC PULSE GENERATOR...
...THEY COMMUNICATED THROUGH NOTES TO EACH OTHER, COORDINATING WHAT THEY WERE ACTUALLY BUILDING!
AROOOOAROOOOAROOOO
THIS IS NOT A DRILL! THE FUSION REACTOR IS REACHING CRITICAL MASS!
ALL HANDS ABANDON BASE! CHAIN REACTION IMMINENT! THIS IS NOT A DRILL!

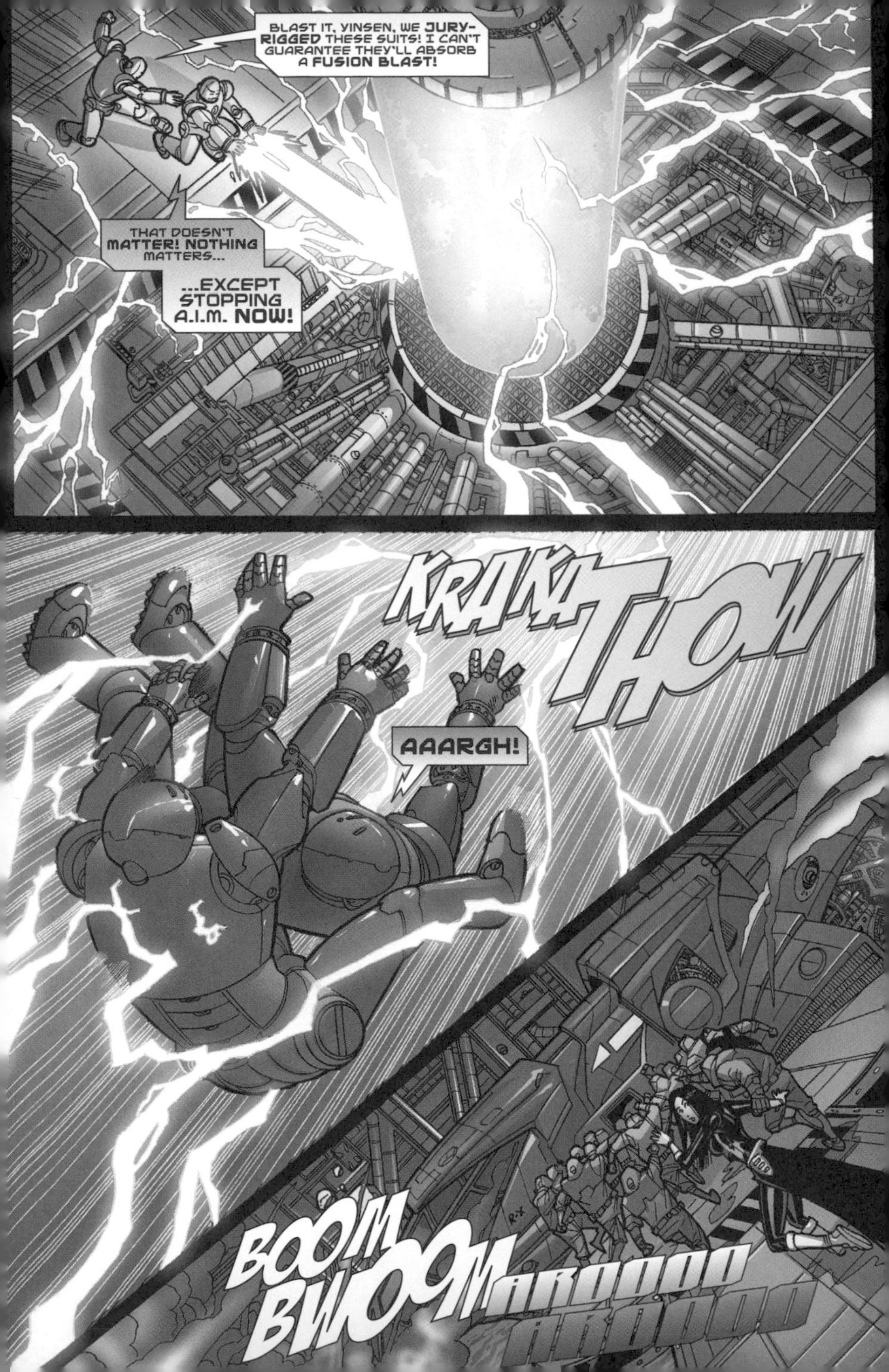

BLAST IT, YINSEN, WE JURY-RIGGED THESE SUITS! I CAN'T GUARANTEE THEY'LL ABSORB A FUSION BLAST!
THAT DOESN'T MATTER! NOTHING MATTERS...
...EXCEPT STOPPING A.I.M. NOW!
KRAKATHOW
AAARGH!
BOOM
BWOOM
AROOOO
AROOOO

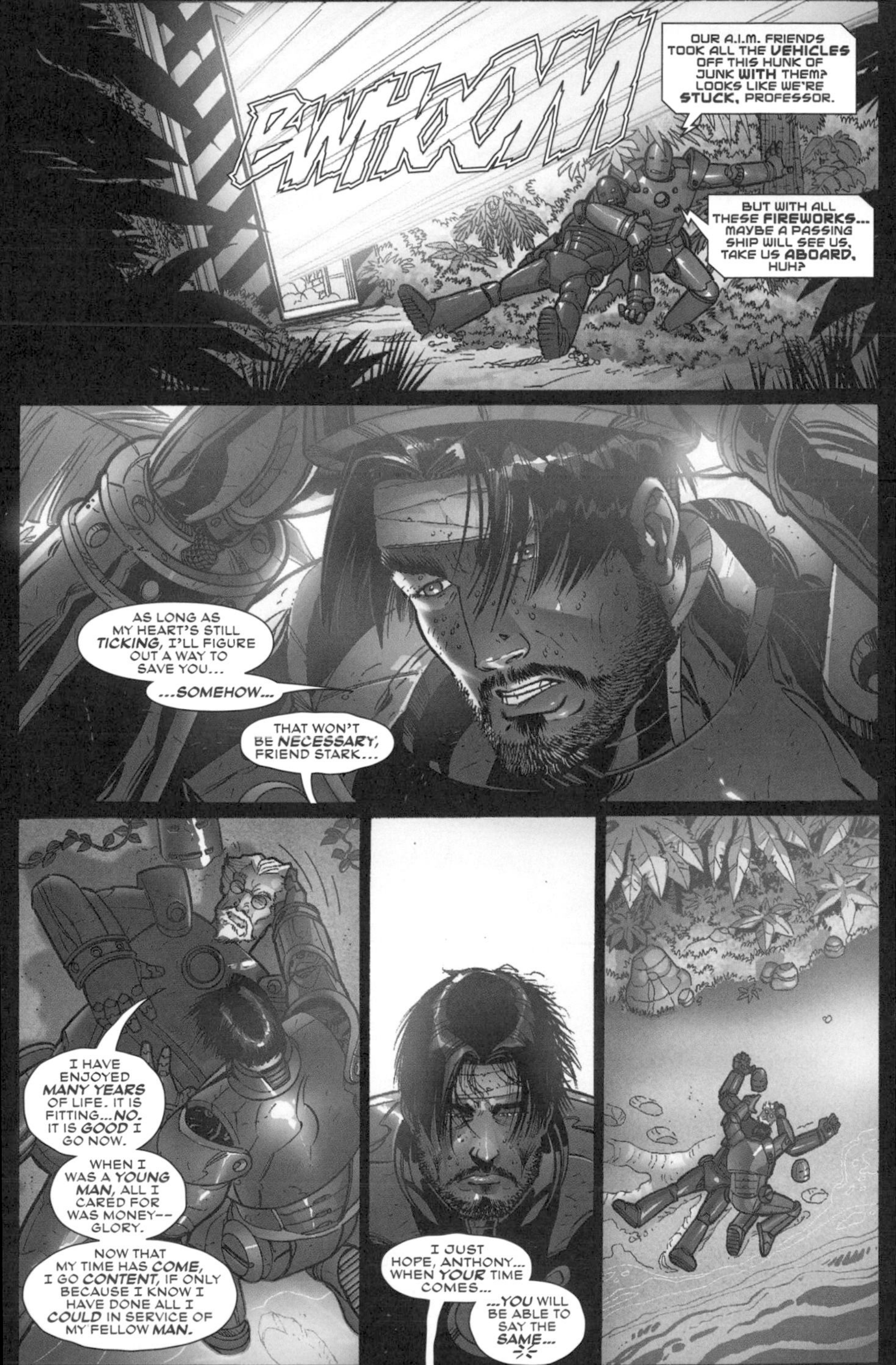
BWHOOM
OUR A.I.M. FRIENDS TOOK ALL THE VEHICLES OFF THIS HUNK OF JUNK WITH THEM? LOOKS LIKE WE'RE STUCK, PROFESSOR.
BUT WITH ALL THESE FIREWORKS... MAYBE A PASSING SHIP WILL SEE US, TAKE US ABOARD, HUH?
AS LONG AS MY HEART'S STILL TICKING, I'LL FIGURE OUT A WAY TO SAVE YOU...
...SOMEHOW...
THAT WON'T BE NECESSARY, FRIEND STARK...
I HAVE ENJOYED MANY YEARS OF LIFE. IT IS FITTING...NO. IT IS GOOD I GO NOW.
WHEN I WAS A YOUNG MAN, ALL I CARED FOR WAS MONEY-- GLORY.
NOW THAT MY TIME HAS COME, I GO CONTENT, IF ONLY BECAUSE I KNOW I HAVE DONE ALL I COULD IN SERVICE OF MY FELLOW MAN.
I JUST HOPE, ANTHONY... WHEN YOUR TIME COMES...
...YOU WILL BE ABLE TO SAY THE SAME...

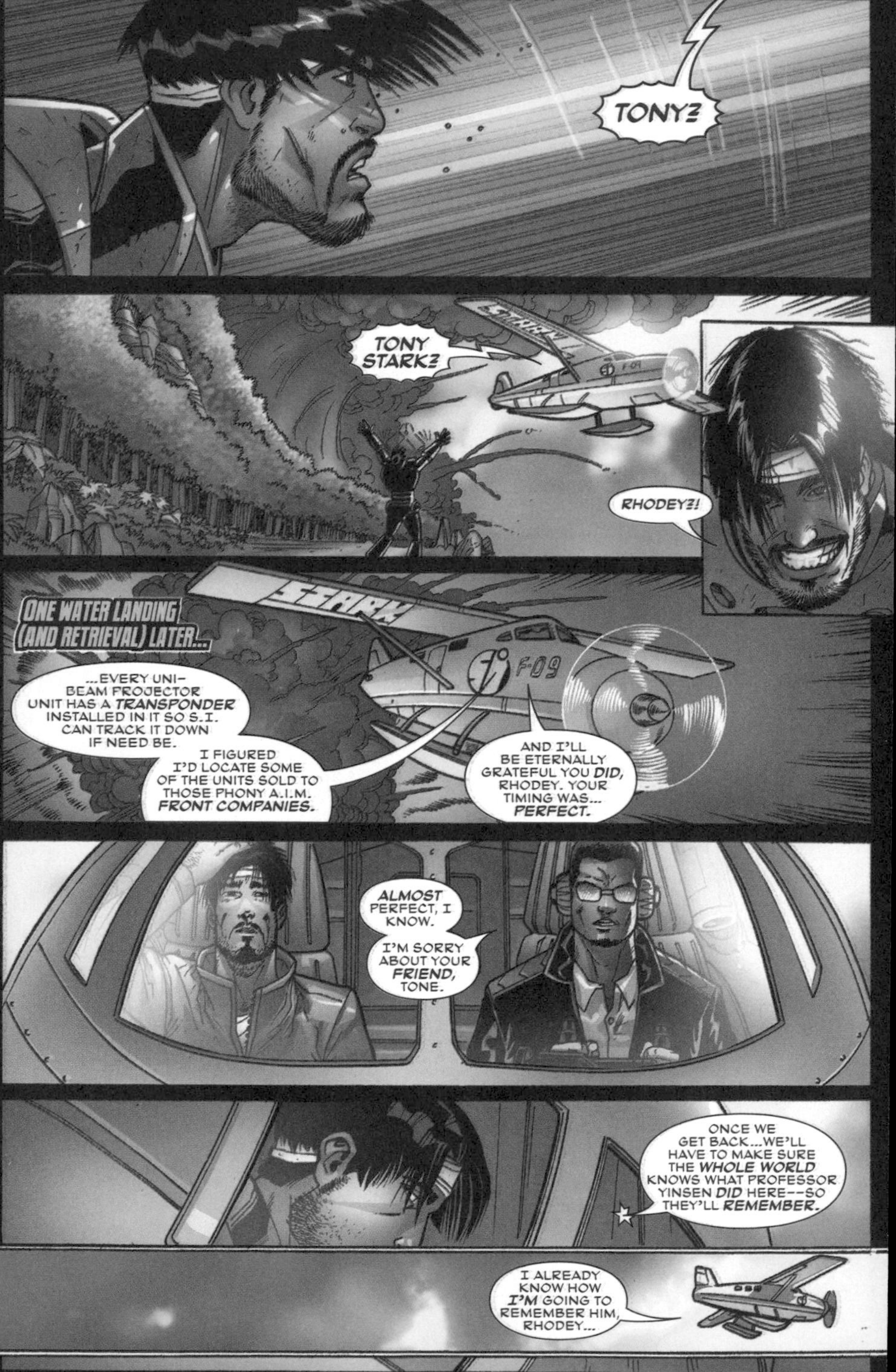
TONY?
TONY STARK?
RHODEY?!
ONE WATER LANDING (AND RETRIEVAL) LATER...
...EVERY UNI-BEAM PROJECTOR UNIT HAS A TRANSPONDER INSTALLED IN IT SO S.I. CAN TRACK IT DOWN IF NEED BE.
I FIGURED I'D LOCATE SOME OF THE UNITS SOLD TO THOSE PHONY A.I.M. FRONT COMPANIES.
AND I'LL BE ETERNALLY GRATEFUL YOU DID, RHODEY. YOUR TIMING WAS... PERFECT.
ALMOST PERFECT, I KNOW.
I'M SORRY ABOUT YOUR FRIEND, TONE.
ONCE WE GET BACK...WE'LL HAVE TO MAKE SURE THE WHOLE WORLD KNOWS WHAT PROFESSOR YINSEN DID HERE--SO THEY'LL REMEMBER.
I ALREADY KNOW HOW I'M GOING TO REMEMBER HIM, RHODEY...

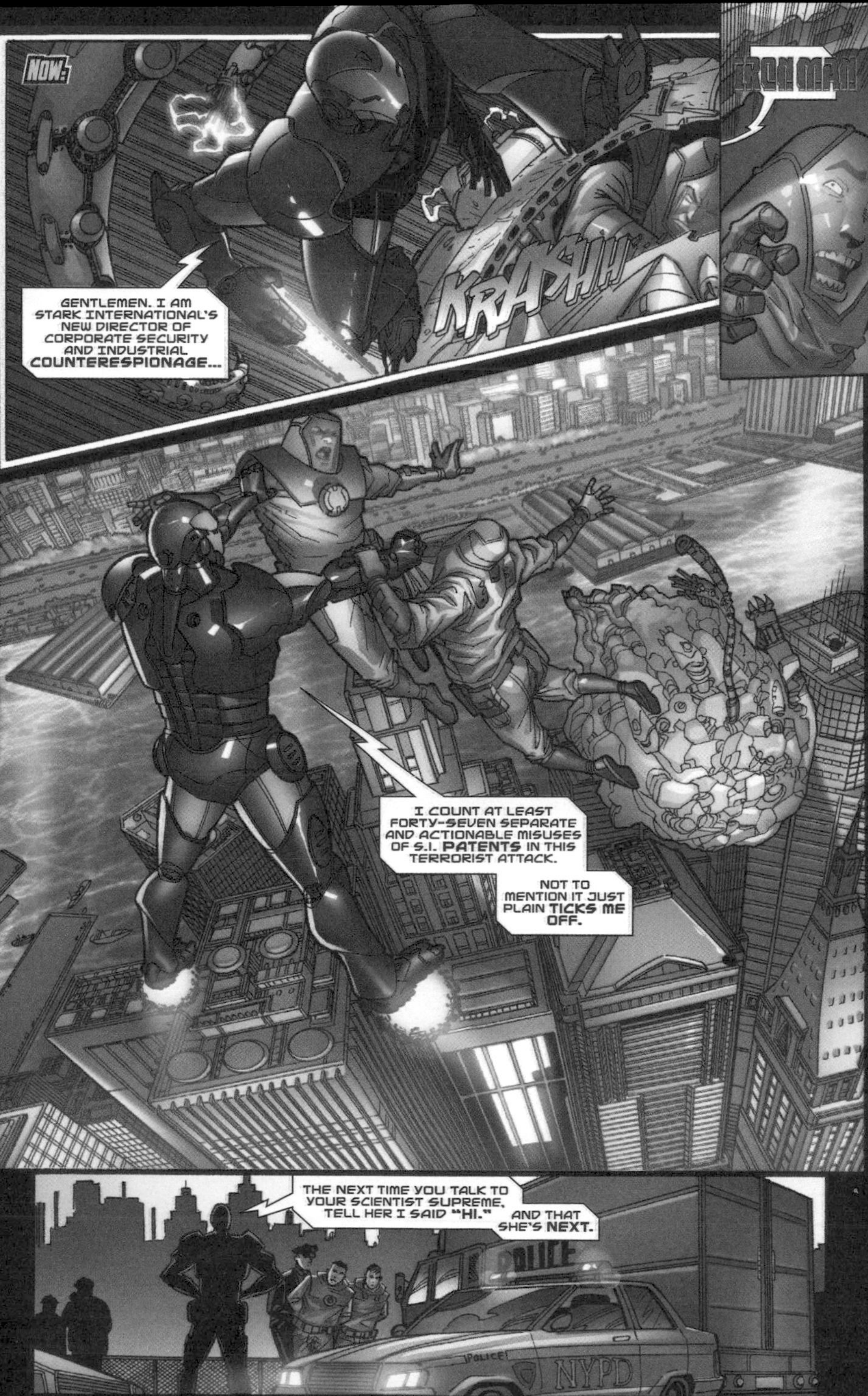

NOW:
IRON MAN
KRASHH
GENTLEMEN. I AM STARK INTERNATIONAL'S NEW DIRECTOR OF CORPORATE SECURITY AND INDUSTRIAL COUNTERESPIONAGE...
I COUNT AT LEAST FORTY-SEVEN SEPARATE AND ACTIONABLE MISUSES OF S.I. PATENTS IN THIS TERRORIST ATTACK.
NOT TO MENTION IT JUST PLAIN TICKS ME OFF.
THE NEXT TIME YOU TALK TO YOUR SCIENTIST SUPREME, TELL HER I SAID "HI."
AND THAT SHE'S NEXT.
POLICE
NYPD

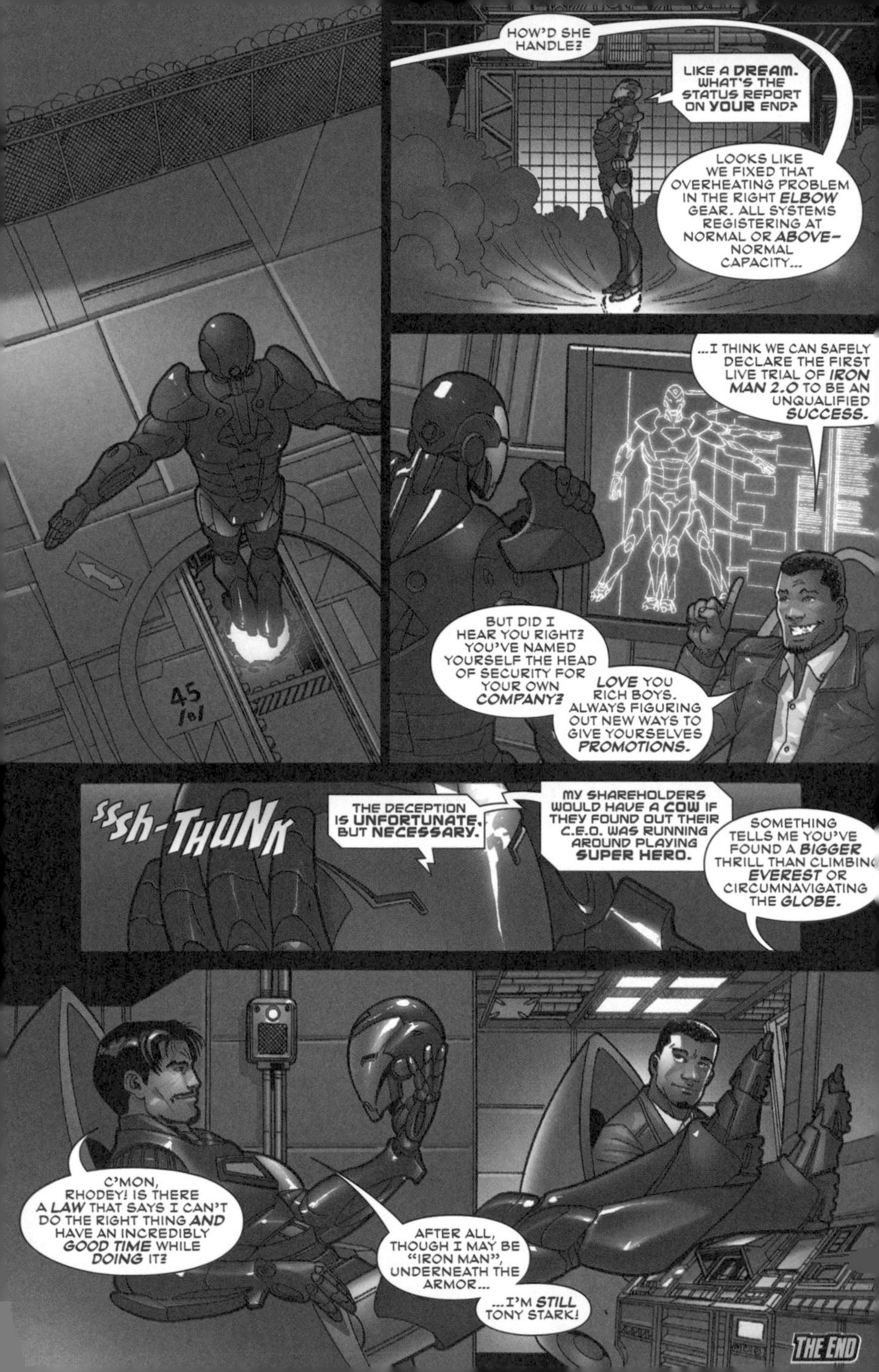

HOW'D SHE HANDLE?
LIKE A **DREAM.** WHAT'S THE STATUS REPORT ON **YOUR** END?
LOOKS LIKE WE FIXED THAT OVERHEATING PROBLEM IN THE RIGHT ***ELBOW*** GEAR. ALL SYSTEMS REGISTERING AT NORMAL OR ***ABOVE***-NORMAL CAPACITY...
...I THINK WE CAN SAFELY DECLARE THE FIRST LIVE TRIAL OF ***IRON MAN 2.0*** TO BE AN UNQUALIFIED ***SUCCESS.***
45 /01
BUT DID I HEAR YOU RIGHT? YOU'VE NAMED YOURSELF THE HEAD OF SECURITY FOR YOUR OWN ***COMPANY?***
LOVE YOU RICH BOYS. ALWAYS FIGURING OUT NEW WAYS TO GIVE YOURSELVES ***PROMOTIONS.***
SSSH-THUNK
THE DECEPTION IS **UNFORTUNATE,** BUT **NECESSARY.**
MY SHAREHOLDERS WOULD HAVE A **COW** IF THEY FOUND OUT THEIR C.E.O. WAS RUNNING AROUND PLAYING **SUPER HERO.**
SOMETHING TELLS ME YOU'VE FOUND A ***BIGGER*** THRILL THAN CLIMBING ***EVEREST*** OR CIRCUMNAVIGATING THE ***GLOBE.***
C'MON, RHODEY! IS THERE A ***LAW*** THAT SAYS I CAN'T DO THE RIGHT THING ***AND*** HAVE AN INCREDIBLY ***GOOD TIME*** WHILE ***DOING*** IT?
AFTER ALL, THOUGH I MAY BE "IRON MAN", UNDERNEATH THE ARMOR...
...I'M ***STILL*** TONY STARK!
THE END

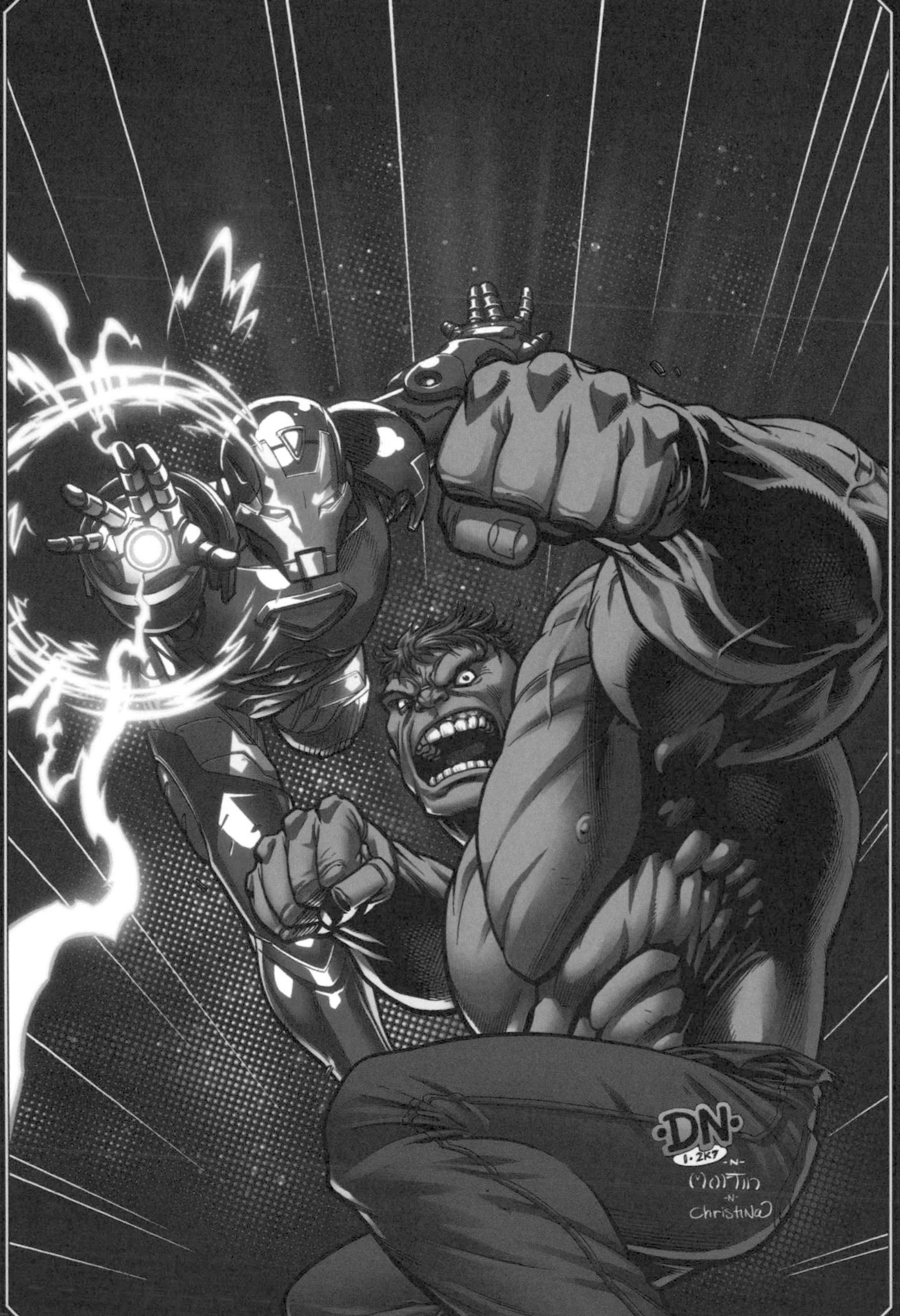
DN
1·2K7
-N-
Martin
-N-
Christina

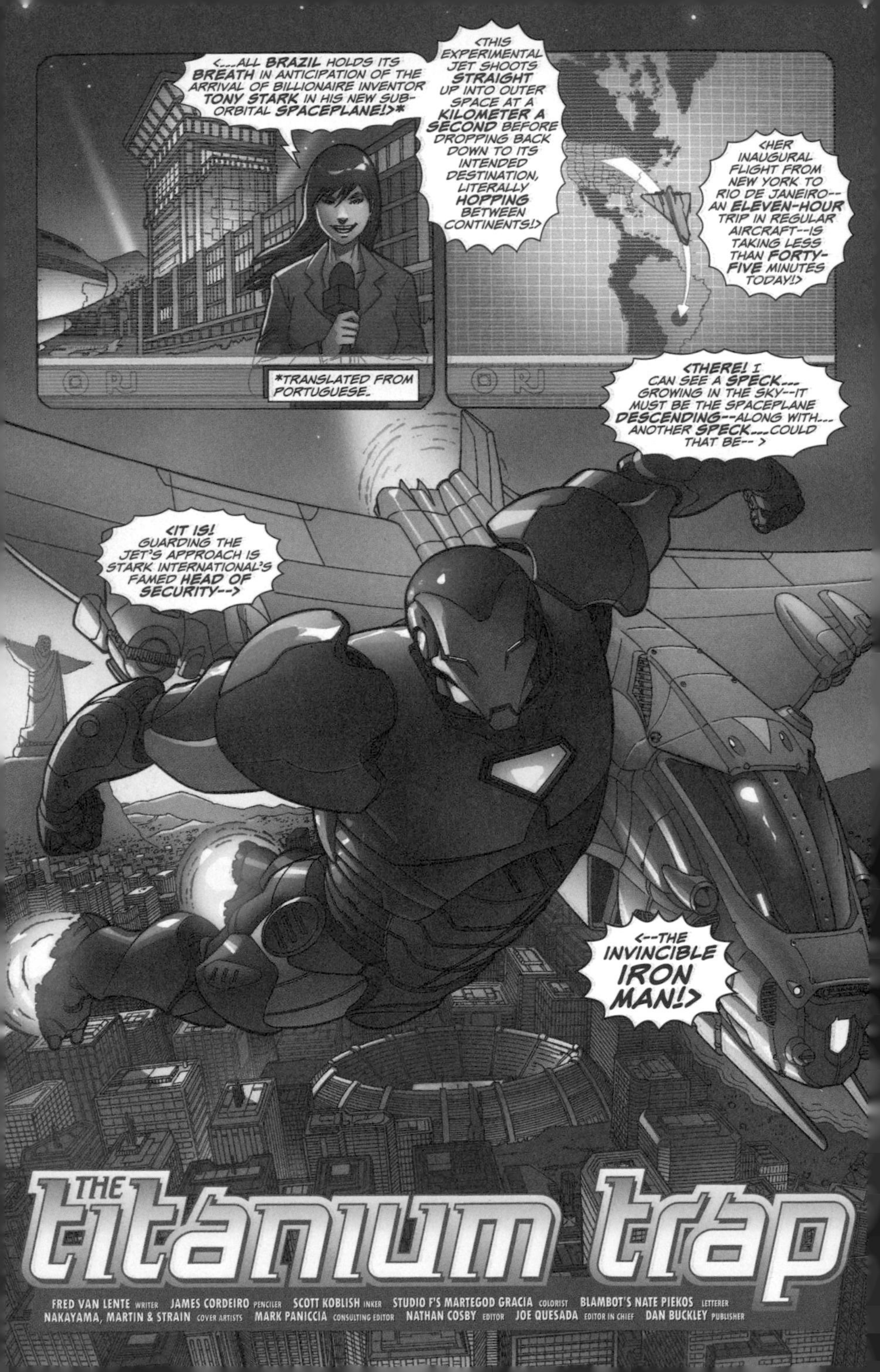
<...ALL BRAZIL HOLDS ITS BREATH IN ANTICIPATION OF THE ARRIVAL OF BILLIONAIRE INVENTOR TONY STARK IN HIS NEW SUB-ORBITAL SPACEPLANE!>*
<THIS EXPERIMENTAL JET SHOOTS STRAIGHT UP INTO OUTER SPACE AT A KILOMETER A SECOND BEFORE DROPPING BACK DOWN TO ITS INTENDED DESTINATION, LITERALLY HOPPING BETWEEN CONTINENTS!>
<HER INAUGURAL FLIGHT FROM NEW YORK TO RIO DE JANEIRO--AN ELEVEN-HOUR TRIP IN REGULAR AIRCRAFT--IS TAKING LESS THAN FORTY-FIVE MINUTES TODAY!>
*TRANSLATED FROM PORTUGUESE.
<THERE! I CAN SEE A SPECK--GROWING IN THE SKY--IT MUST BE THE SPACEPLANE DESCENDING--ALONG WITH...ANOTHER SPECK...COULD THAT BE-- >
<IT IS! GUARDING THE JET'S APPROACH IS STARK INTERNATIONAL'S FAMED HEAD OF SECURITY-->
<--THE INVINCIBLE IRON MAN!>
THE titanium trap
FRED VAN LENTE WRITER JAMES CORDEIRO PENCILER SCOTT KOBLISH INKER STUDIO F'S MARTEGOD GRACIA COLORIST BLAMBOT'S NATE PIEKOS LETTERER
NAKAYAMA, MARTIN & STRAIN COVER ARTISTS MARK PANICCIA CONSULTING EDITOR NATHAN COSBY EDITOR JOE QUESADA EDITOR IN CHIEF DAN BUCKLEY PUBLISHER

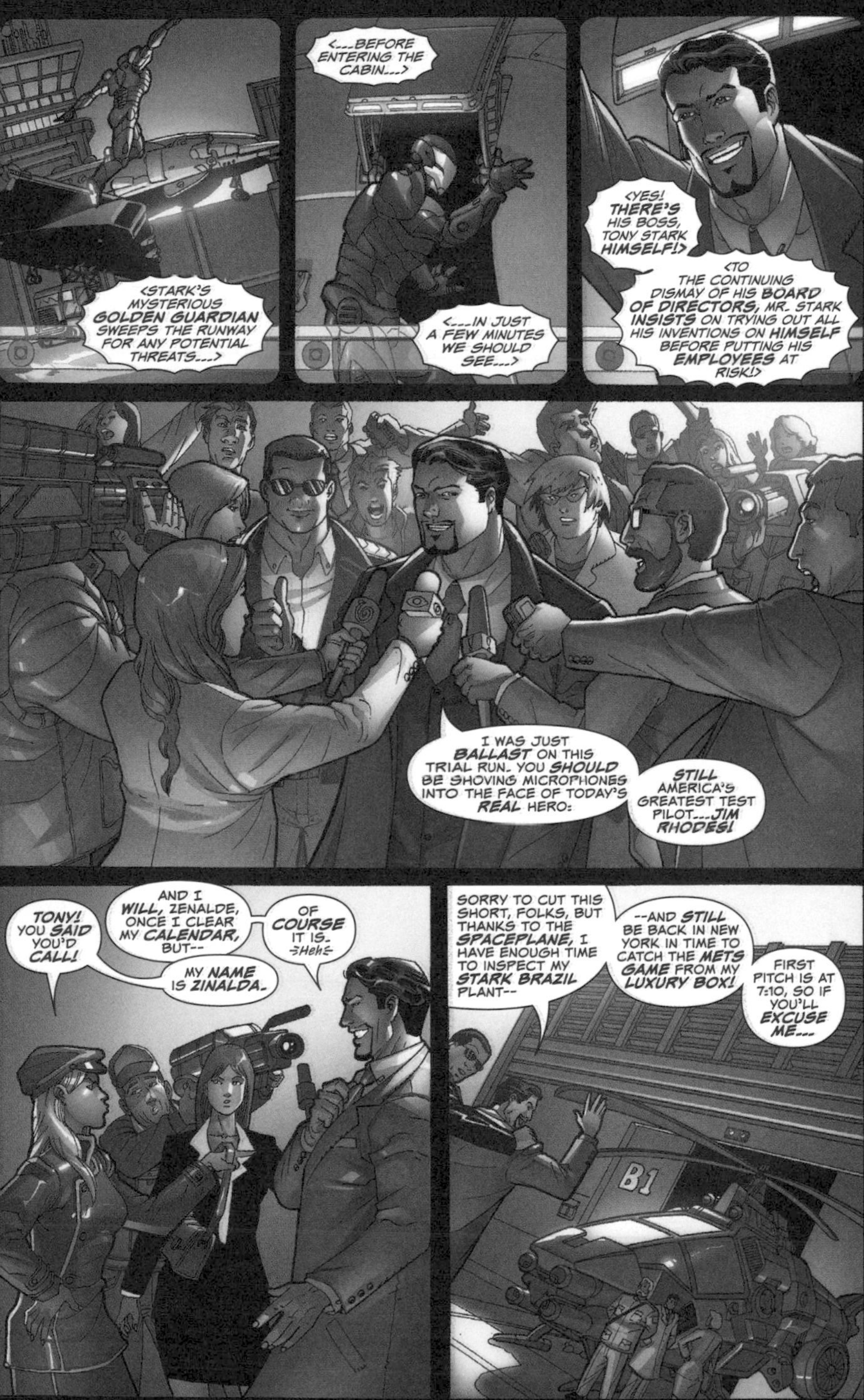
<STARK'S MYSTERIOUS GOLDEN GUARDIAN SWEEPS THE RUNWAY FOR ANY POTENTIAL THREATS--->
<---BEFORE ENTERING THE CABIN--->
<---IN JUST A FEW MINUTES WE SHOULD SEE--->
<YES! THERE'S HIS BOSS, TONY STARK HIMSELF!>
<TO THE CONTINUING DISMAY OF HIS BOARD OF DIRECTORS, MR. STARK INSISTS ON TRYING OUT ALL HIS INVENTIONS ON HIMSELF BEFORE PUTTING HIS EMPLOYEES AT RISK!>
I WAS JUST BALLAST ON THIS TRIAL RUN. YOU SHOULD BE SHOVING MICROPHONES INTO THE FACE OF TODAY'S REAL HERO:
STILL AMERICA'S GREATEST TEST PILOT---JIM RHODES!
TONY! YOU SAID YOU'D CALL!
AND I WILL, ZENALDE, ONCE I CLEAR MY CALENDAR, BUT--
MY NAME IS ZINALDA.
OF COURSE IT IS. Heh
SORRY TO CUT THIS SHORT, FOLKS, BUT THANKS TO THE SPACEPLANE, I HAVE ENOUGH TIME TO INSPECT MY STARK BRAZIL PLANT--
--AND STILL BE BACK IN NEW YORK IN TIME TO CATCH THE METS GAME FROM MY LUXURY BOX!
FIRST PITCH IS AT 7:10, SO IF YOU'LL EXCUSE ME---
B1

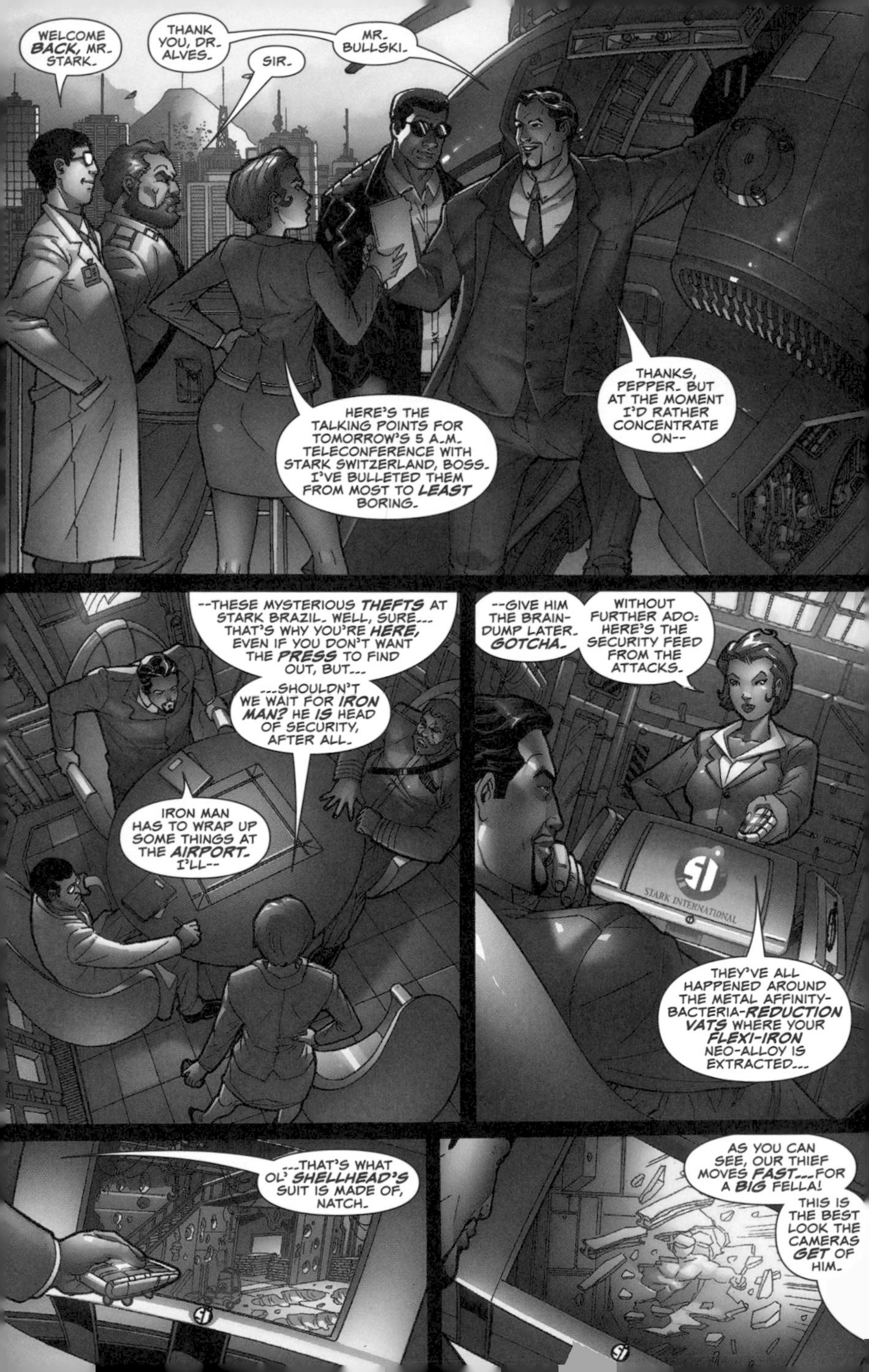
WELCOME BACK, MR. STARK.
THANK YOU, DR. ALVES.
SIR.
MR. BULLSKI.
HERE'S THE TALKING POINTS FOR TOMORROW'S 5 A.M. TELECONFERENCE WITH STARK SWITZERLAND, BOSS. I'VE BULLETED THEM FROM MOST TO LEAST BORING.
THANKS, PEPPER. BUT AT THE MOMENT I'D RATHER CONCENTRATE ON--
--THESE MYSTERIOUS THEFTS AT STARK BRAZIL. WELL, SURE... THAT'S WHY YOU'RE HERE, EVEN IF YOU DON'T WANT THE PRESS TO FIND OUT, BUT...
...SHOULDN'T WE WAIT FOR IRON MAN? HE IS HEAD OF SECURITY, AFTER ALL.
IRON MAN HAS TO WRAP UP SOME THINGS AT THE AIRPORT. I'LL--
--GIVE HIM THE BRAIN-DUMP LATER. GOTCHA.
WITHOUT FURTHER ADO: HERE'S THE SECURITY FEED FROM THE ATTACKS.
STARK INTERNATIONAL
THEY'VE ALL HAPPENED AROUND THE METAL AFFINITY-BACTERIA-REDUCTION VATS WHERE YOUR FLEXI-IRON NEO-ALLOY IS EXTRACTED...
...THAT'S WHAT OL' SHELLHEAD'S SUIT IS MADE OF, NATCH.
AS YOU CAN SEE, OUR THIEF MOVES FAST...FOR A BIG FELLA!
THIS IS THE BEST LOOK THE CAMERAS GET OF HIM.

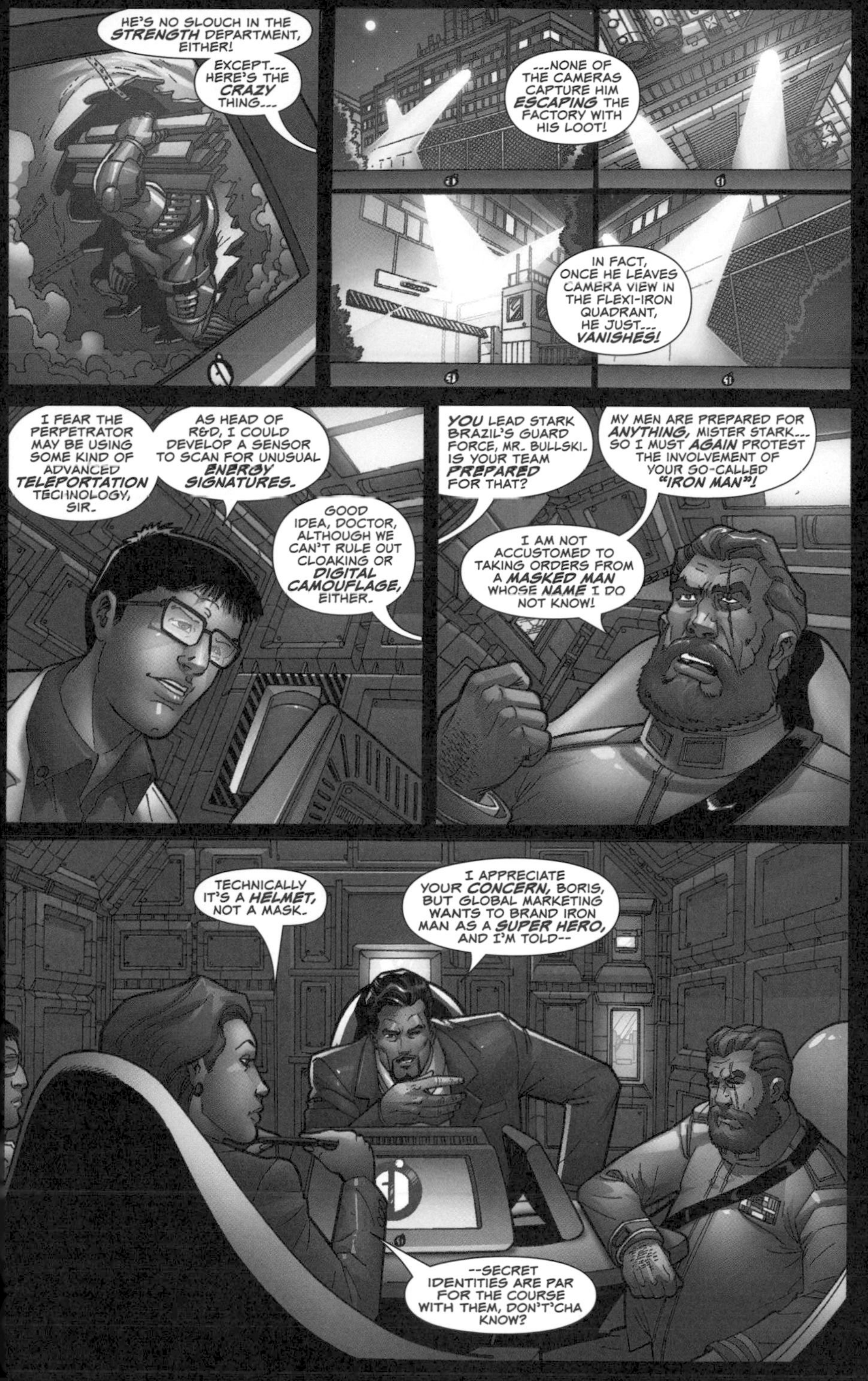
HE'S NO SLOUCH IN THE STRENGTH DEPARTMENT, EITHER!
EXCEPT... HERE'S THE CRAZY THING...
...NONE OF THE CAMERAS CAPTURE HIM ESCAPING THE FACTORY WITH HIS LOOT!
IN FACT, ONCE HE LEAVES CAMERA VIEW IN THE FLEXI-IRON QUADRANT, HE JUST... VANISHES!
I FEAR THE PERPETRATOR MAY BE USING SOME KIND OF ADVANCED TELEPORTATION TECHNOLOGY, SIR.
AS HEAD OF R&D, I COULD DEVELOP A SENSOR TO SCAN FOR UNUSUAL ENERGY SIGNATURES.
GOOD IDEA, DOCTOR, ALTHOUGH WE CAN'T RULE OUT CLOAKING OR DIGITAL CAMOUFLAGE, EITHER.
YOU LEAD STARK BRAZIL'S GUARD FORCE, MR. BULLSKI. IS YOUR TEAM PREPARED FOR THAT?
MY MEN ARE PREPARED FOR ANYTHING, MISTER STARK... SO I MUST AGAIN PROTEST THE INVOLVEMENT OF YOUR SO-CALLED "IRON MAN"!
I AM NOT ACCUSTOMED TO TAKING ORDERS FROM A MASKED MAN WHOSE NAME I DO NOT KNOW!
TECHNICALLY IT'S A HELMET, NOT A MASK.
I APPRECIATE YOUR CONCERN, BORIS, BUT GLOBAL MARKETING WANTS TO BRAND IRON MAN AS A SUPER HERO, AND I'M TOLD--
--SECRET IDENTITIES ARE PAR FOR THE COURSE WITH THEM, DON'T'CHA KNOW?

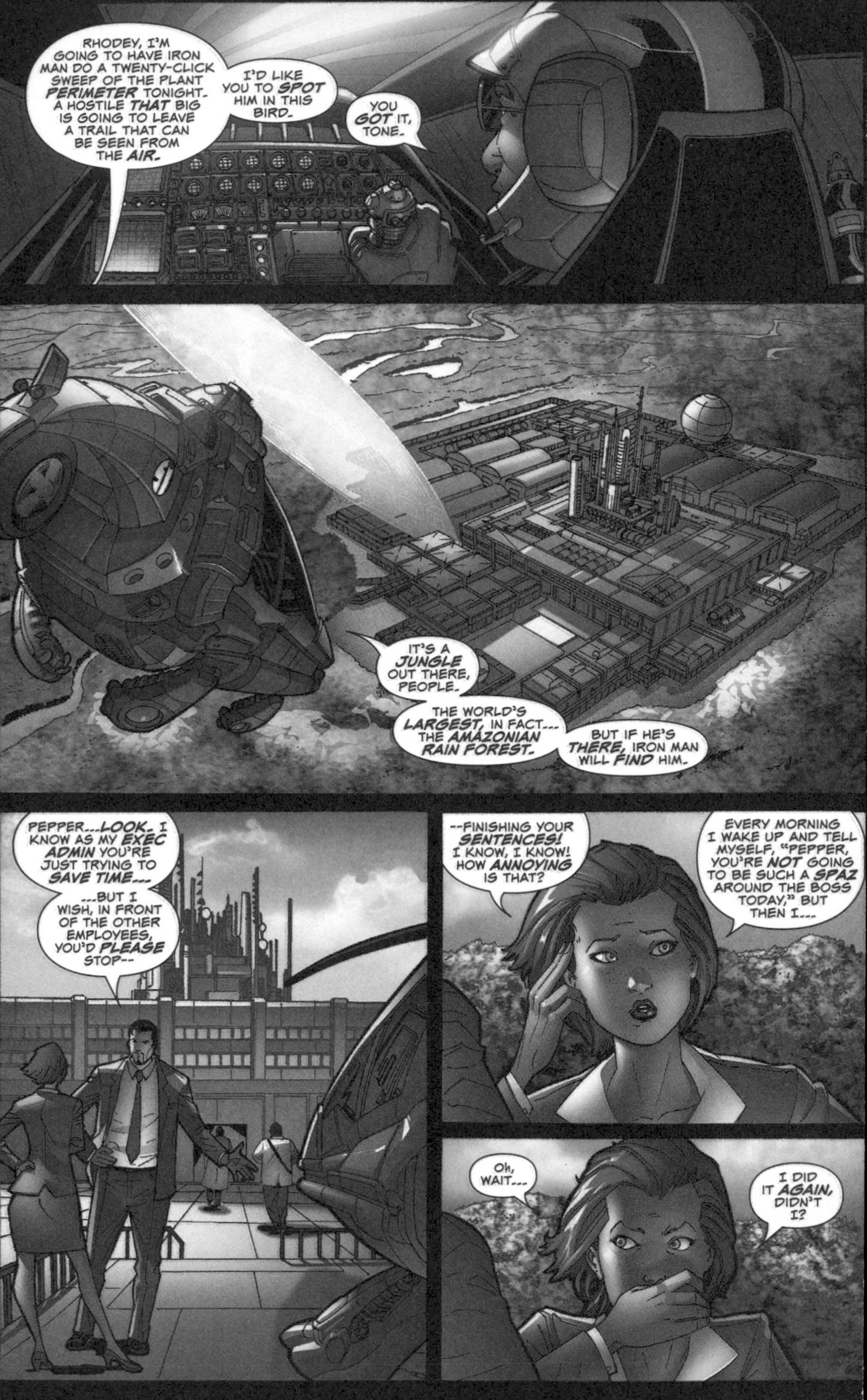
RHODEY, I'M GOING TO HAVE IRON MAN DO A TWENTY-CLICK SWEEP OF THE PLANT PERIMETER TONIGHT. A HOSTILE THAT BIG IS GOING TO LEAVE A TRAIL THAT CAN BE SEEN FROM THE AIR.
I'D LIKE YOU TO SPOT HIM IN THIS BIRD.
YOU GOT IT, TONE.
IT'S A JUNGLE OUT THERE, PEOPLE.
THE WORLD'S LARGEST, IN FACT... THE AMAZONIAN RAIN FOREST.
BUT IF HE'S THERE, IRON MAN WILL FIND HIM.
PEPPER...LOOK. I KNOW AS MY EXEC ADMIN YOU'RE JUST TRYING TO SAVE TIME...
...BUT I WISH, IN FRONT OF THE OTHER EMPLOYEES, YOU'D PLEASE STOP--
--FINISHING YOUR SENTENCES! I KNOW, I KNOW! HOW ANNOYING IS THAT?
EVERY MORNING I WAKE UP AND TELL MYSELF, "PEPPER, YOU'RE NOT GOING TO BE SUCH A SPAZ AROUND THE BOSS TODAY," BUT THEN I...
Oh, WAIT...
I DID IT AGAIN, DIDN'T I?

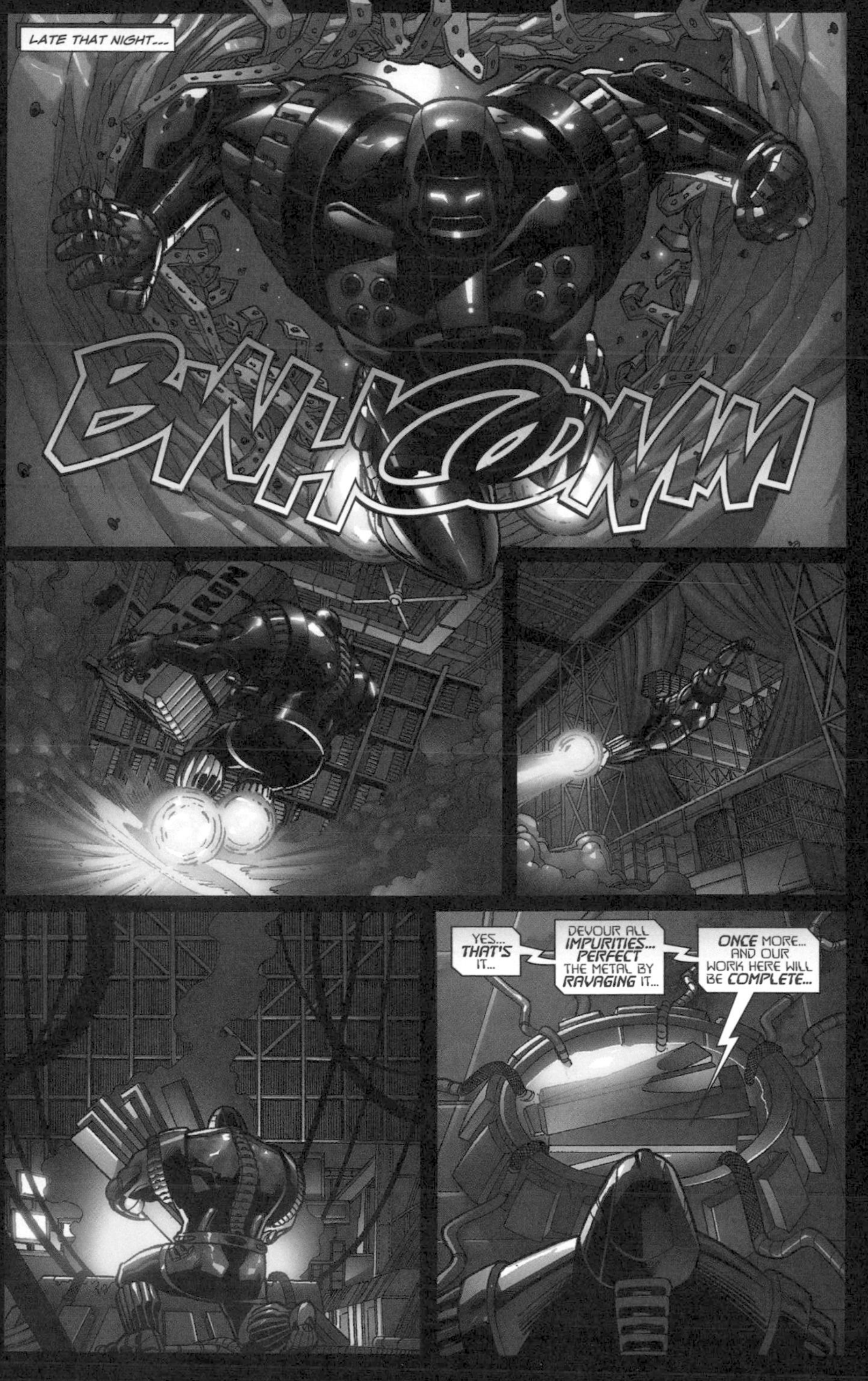
LATE THAT NIGHT...
BWHOOMM
YES... THAT'S IT...
DEVOUR ALL IMPURITIES... PERFECT THE METAL BY RAVAGING IT...
ONCE MORE... AND OUR WORK HERE WILL BE COMPLETE...

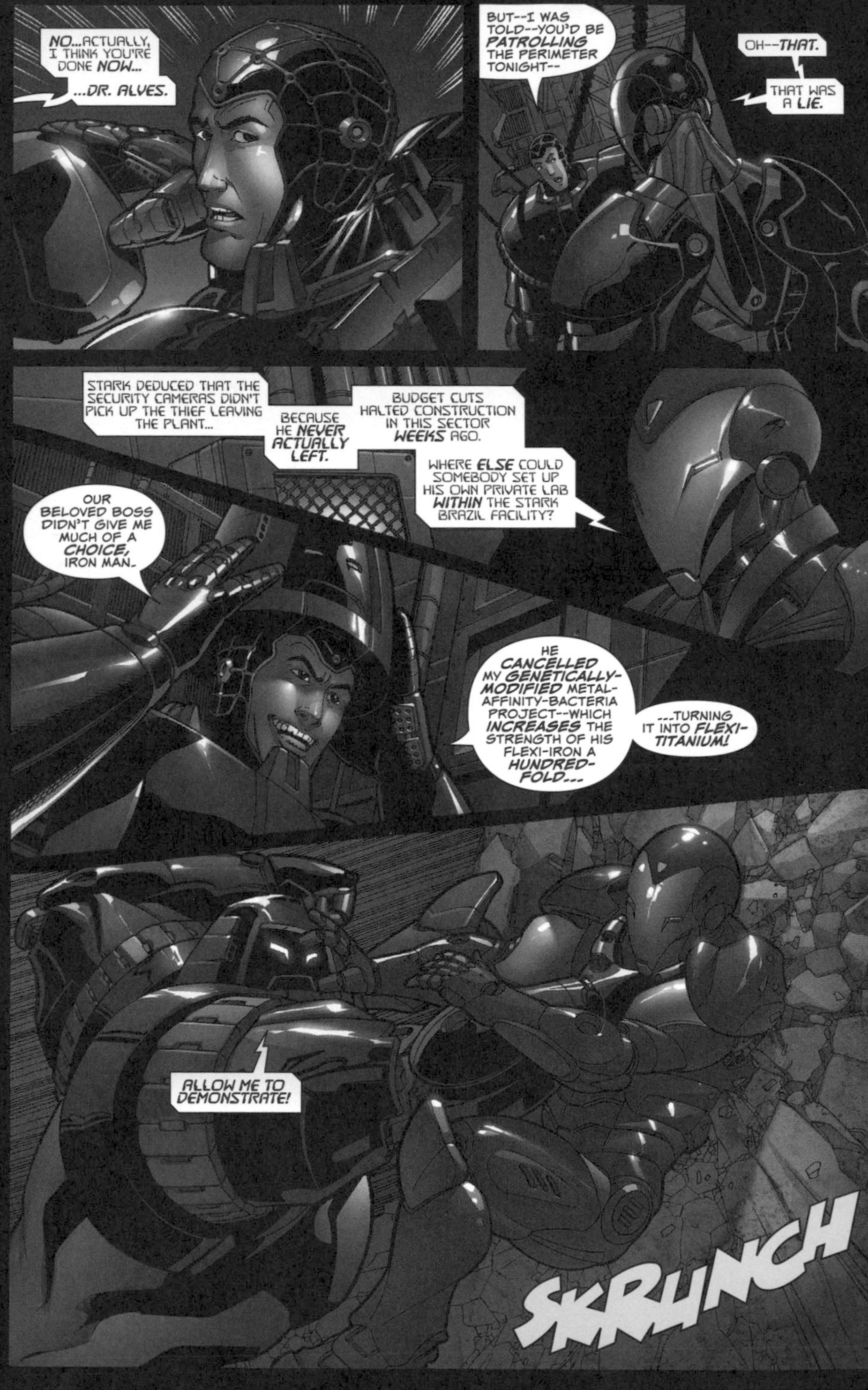
NO...ACTUALLY, I THINK YOU'RE DONE NOW...
...DR. ALVES.
BUT--I WAS TOLD--YOU'D BE PATROLLING THE PERIMETER TONIGHT--
OH--THAT.
THAT WAS A LIE.
STARK DEDUCED THAT THE SECURITY CAMERAS DIDN'T PICK UP THE THIEF LEAVING THE PLANT...
BECAUSE HE NEVER ACTUALLY LEFT.
BUDGET CUTS HALTED CONSTRUCTION IN THIS SECTOR WEEKS AGO.
WHERE ELSE COULD SOMEBODY SET UP HIS OWN PRIVATE LAB WITHIN THE STARK BRAZIL FACILITY?
OUR BELOVED BOSS DIDN'T GIVE ME MUCH OF A CHOICE, IRON MAN.
HE CANCELLED MY GENETICALLY-MODIFIED METAL-AFFINITY-BACTERIA PROJECT--WHICH INCREASES THE STRENGTH OF HIS FLEXI-IRON A HUNDRED-FOLD...
...TURNING IT INTO FLEXI-TITANIUM!
ALLOW ME TO DEMONSTRATE!
SKRUNCH

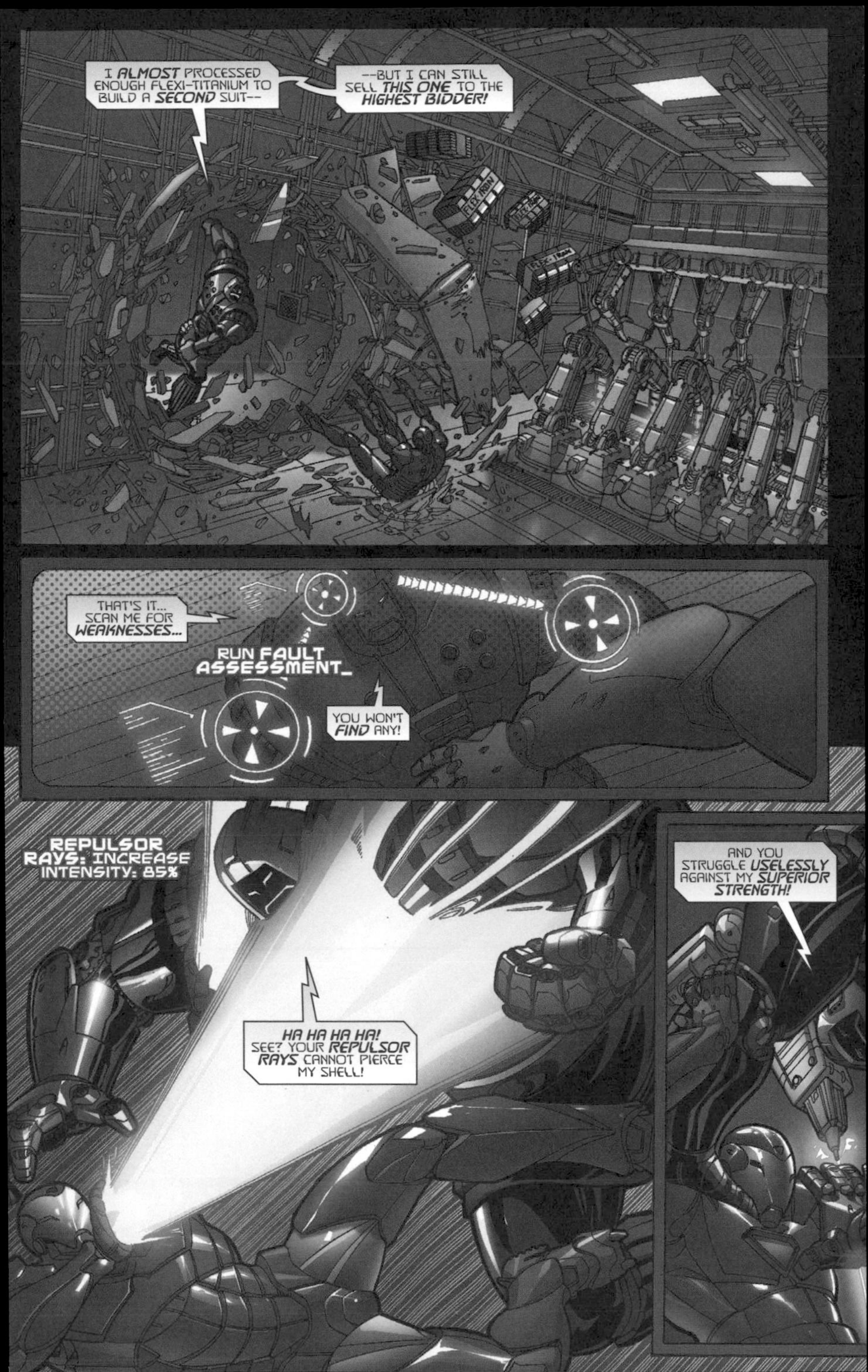

I ALMOST PROCESSED ENOUGH FLEXI-TITANIUM TO BUILD A SECOND SUIT--
--BUT I CAN STILL SELL THIS ONE TO THE HIGHEST BIDDER!
FLEX-IRON
THAT'S IT... SCAN ME FOR WEAKNESSES...
RUN FAULT ASSESSMENT_
YOU WON'T FIND ANY!
REPULSOR RAYS: INCREASE INTENSITY: 85%
HA HA HA HA! SEE? YOUR REPULSOR RAYS CANNOT PIERCE MY SHELL!
AND YOU STRUGGLE USELESSLY AGAINST MY SUPERIOR STRENGTH!

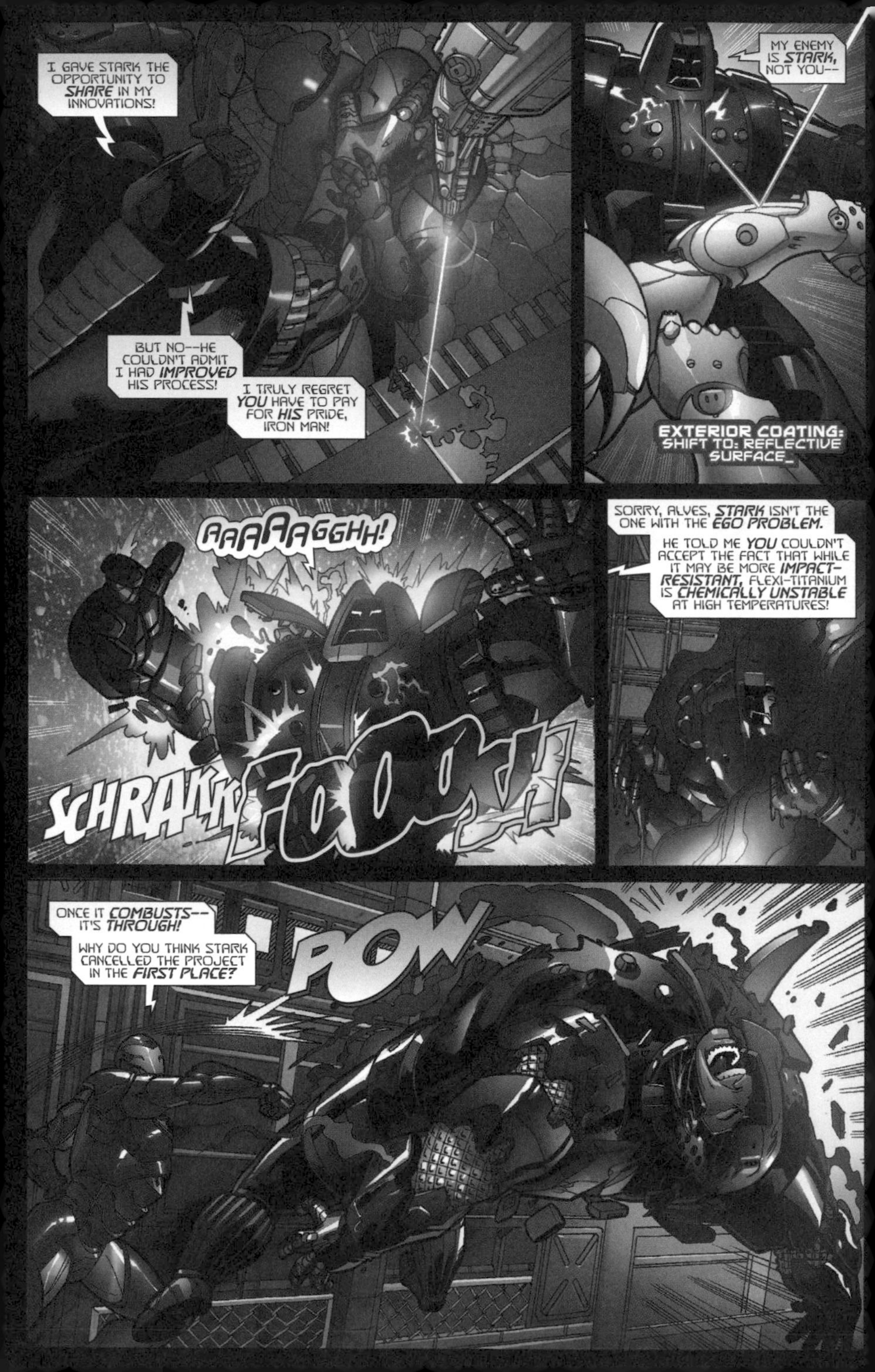
I GAVE STARK THE OPPORTUNITY TO SHARE IN MY INNOVATIONS!
BUT NO--HE COULDN'T ADMIT I HAD IMPROVED HIS PROCESS!
I TRULY REGRET YOU HAVE TO PAY FOR HIS PRIDE, IRON MAN!
MY ENEMY IS STARK, NOT YOU--
EXTERIOR COATING: SHIFT TO: REFLECTIVE SURFACE_
AAAAAGGHH!
SCHRAKKFOOM!!
SORRY, ALVES, STARK ISN'T THE ONE WITH THE EGO PROBLEM.
HE TOLD ME YOU COULDN'T ACCEPT THE FACT THAT WHILE IT MAY BE MORE IMPACT-RESISTANT, FLEXI-TITANIUM IS CHEMICALLY UNSTABLE AT HIGH TEMPERATURES!
ONCE IT COMBUSTS-- IT'S THROUGH!
WHY DO YOU THINK STARK CANCELLED THE PROJECT IN THE FIRST PLACE?
POW

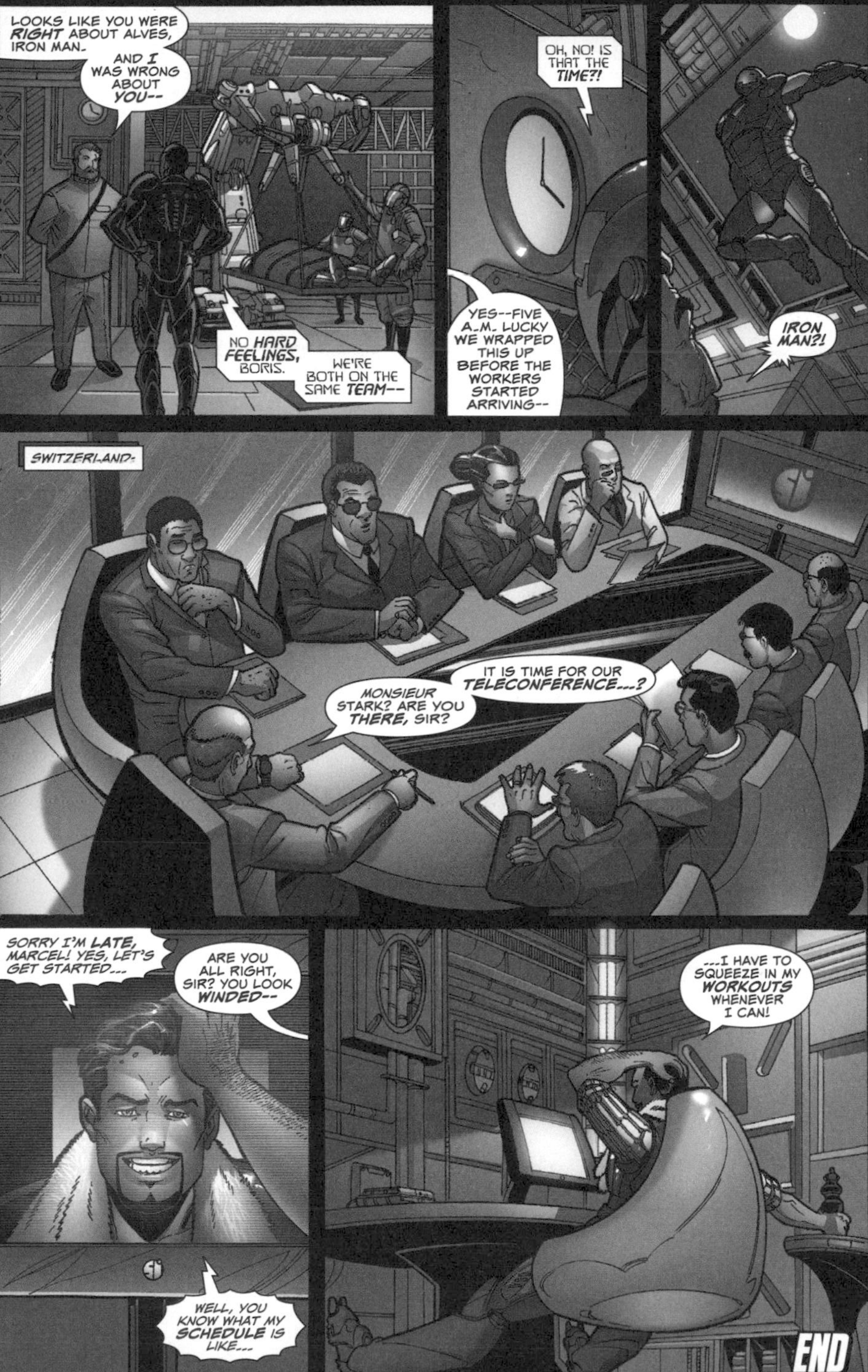
LOOKS LIKE YOU WERE RIGHT ABOUT ALVES, IRON MAN.
AND I WAS WRONG ABOUT YOU--
NO HARD FEELINGS, BORIS.
WE'RE BOTH ON THE SAME TEAM--
OH, NO! IS THAT THE TIME?!
YES--FIVE A.M. LUCKY WE WRAPPED THIS UP BEFORE THE WORKERS STARTED ARRIVING--
IRON MAN?!
SWITZERLAND:
MONSIEUR STARK? ARE YOU THERE, SIR?
IT IS TIME FOR OUR TELECONFERENCE...?
SORRY I'M LATE, MARCEL! YES, LET'S GET STARTED...
ARE YOU ALL RIGHT, SIR? YOU LOOK WINDED--
WELL, YOU KNOW WHAT MY SCHEDULE IS LIKE...
...I HAVE TO SQUEEZE IN MY WORKOUTS WHENEVER I CAN!
END

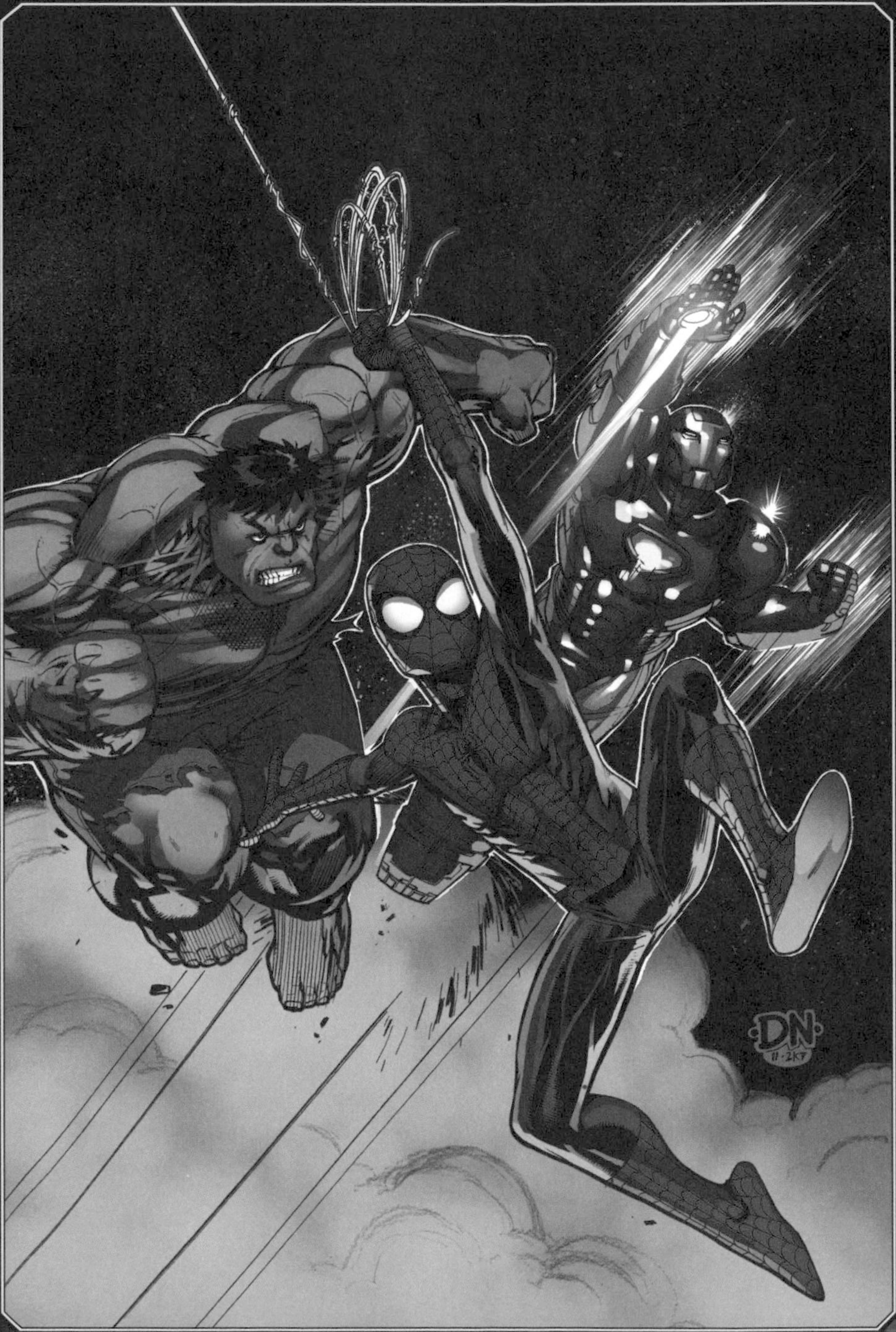

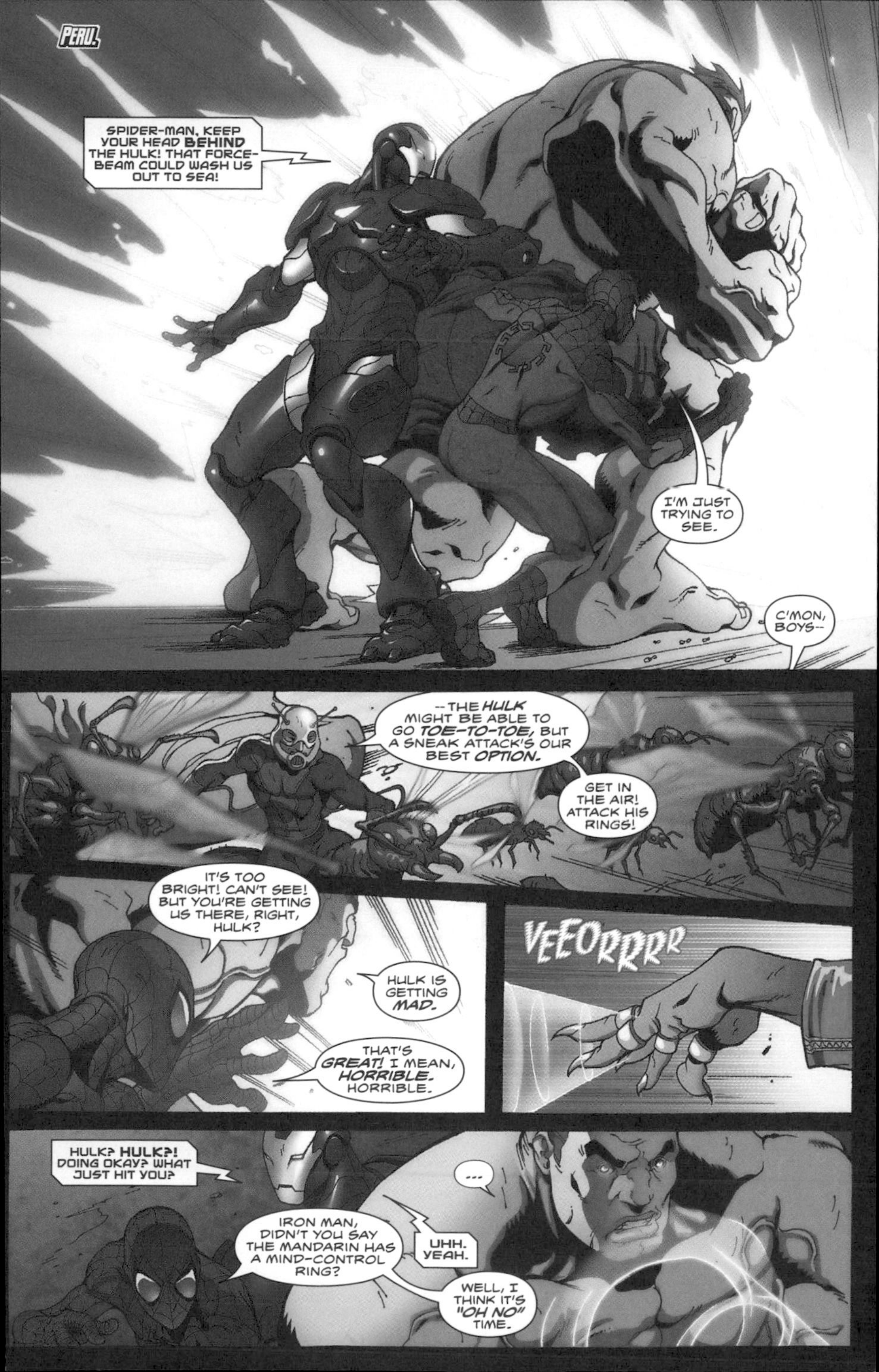
PERU.
SPIDER-MAN, KEEP YOUR HEAD BEHIND THE HULK! THAT FORCE-BEAM COULD WASH US OUT TO SEA!
I'M JUST TRYING TO SEE.
C'MON, BOYS--
--THE HULK MIGHT BE ABLE TO GO TOE-TO-TOE, BUT A SNEAK ATTACK'S OUR BEST OPTION.
GET IN THE AIR! ATTACK HIS RINGS!
IT'S TOO BRIGHT! CAN'T SEE! BUT YOU'RE GETTING US THERE, RIGHT, HULK?
HULK IS GETTING MAD.
THAT'S GREAT! I MEAN, HORRIBLE. HORRIBLE.
VEEORRRR
HULK? HULK?! DOING OKAY? WHAT JUST HIT YOU?
...
IRON MAN, DIDN'T YOU SAY THE MANDARIN HAS A MIND-CONTROL RING?
UHH. YEAH.
WELL, I THINK IT'S "OH NO" TIME.

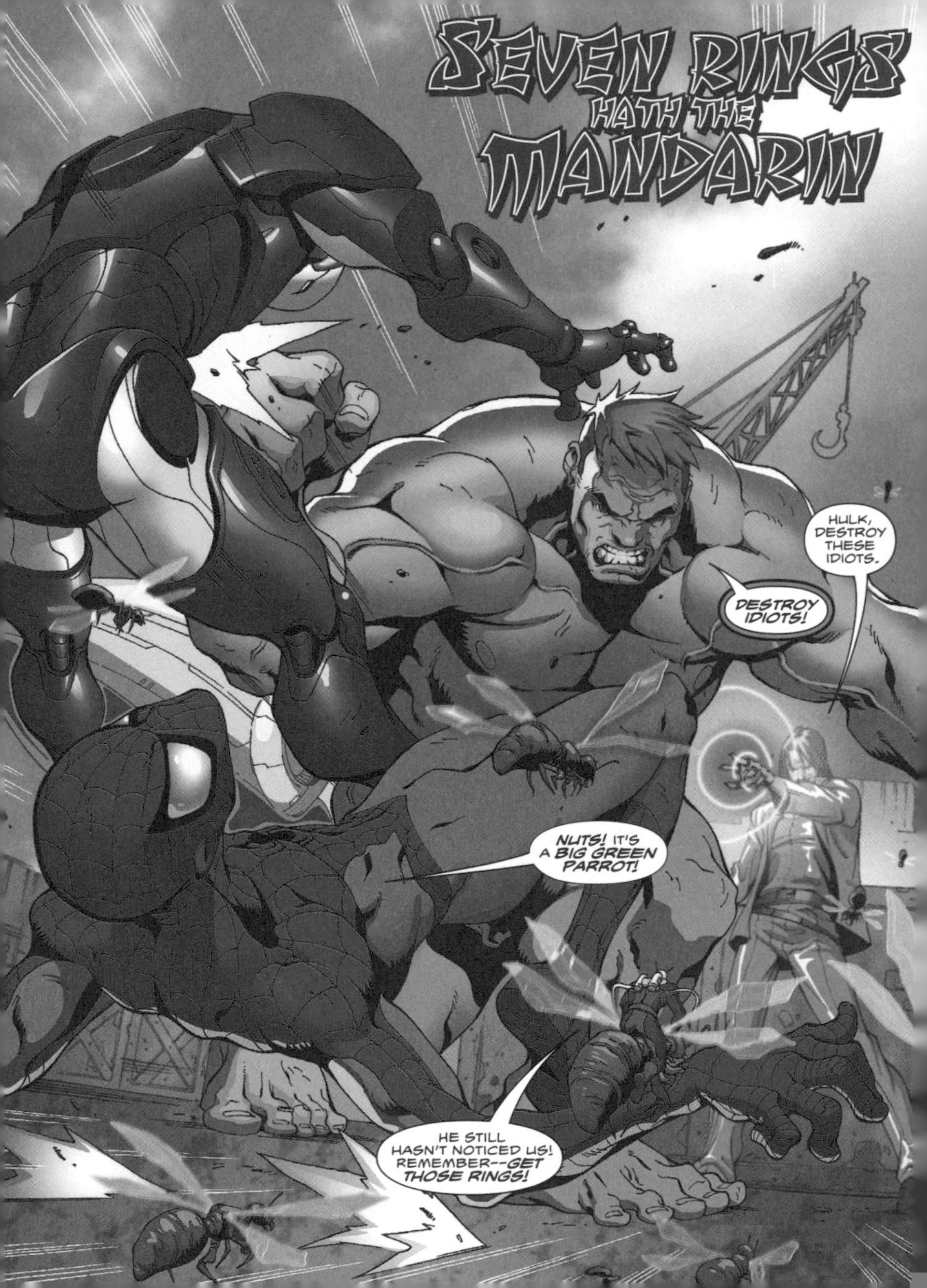
SEVEN RINGS HATH THE MANDARIN
HULK, DESTROY THESE IDIOTS.
DESTROY IDIOTS!
NUTS! IT'S A BIG GREEN PARROT!
HE STILL HASN'T NOTICED US! REMEMBER--GET THOSE RINGS!

WHO DESIGNED THIS DELIGHTFUL DISPLAY OF DARING DISTINCTION? NONE OTHER THAN
AMOROUS AUTHORS–JEFF PARKER & PAUL TOBIN! PENCIL PURVEYOR–ALVIN LEE!
INK EMBELLISHER–TERRY PALLOT! COLOR CREATOR–WILFREDO QUINTANA!
WORD WRANGLER–NATE PIEKOS! COVER CRAFTERS–NAKAYAMA & STRAIN!
PLEASANT PRODUCER–RICH GINTER! ELEGANT EDITORS–NATHAN COSBY & MARK PANICCIA!
JOE QUESADA–THE CHIEF OF ALL EDITORS! AND PIOUS PUBLISHER–DAN BUCKLEY!

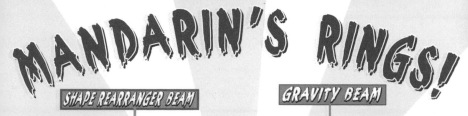

MANDARIN'S RINGS!

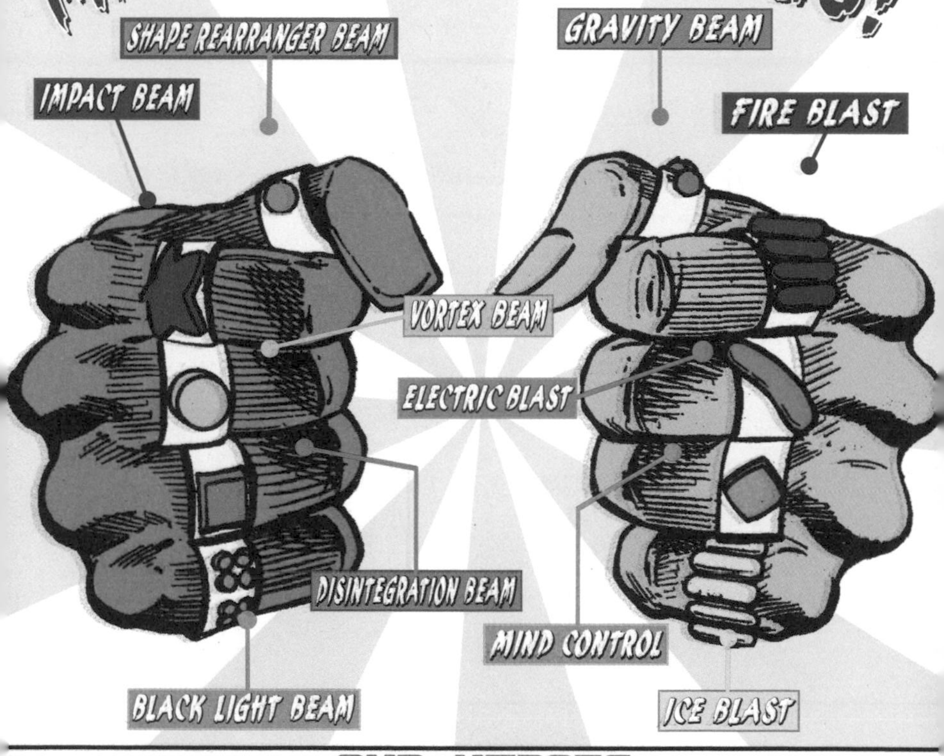
SHAPE REARRANGER BEAM
IMPACT BEAM
GRAVITY BEAM
FIRE BLAST
VORTEX BEAM
ELECTRIC BLAST
DISINTEGRATION BEAM
MIND CONTROL
BLACK LIGHT BEAM
ICE BLAST

OUR HEROES!

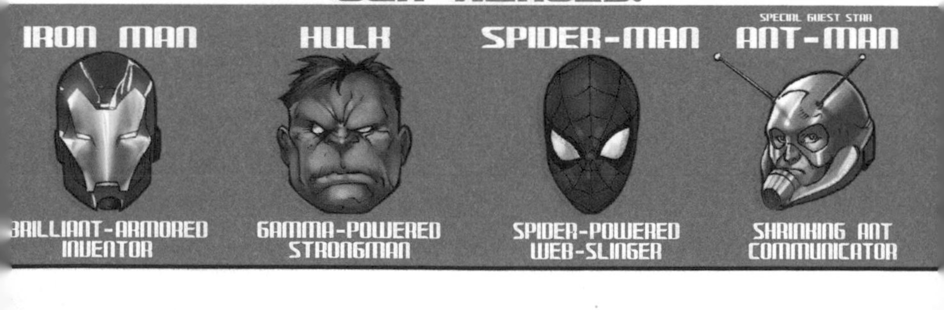
IRON MAN
HULK
SPIDER-MAN
SPECIAL GUEST STAR
ANT-MAN
BRILLIANT-ARMORED INVENTOR
GAMMA-POWERED STRONGMAN
SPIDER-POWERED WEB-SLINGER
SHRINKING ANT COMMUNICATOR

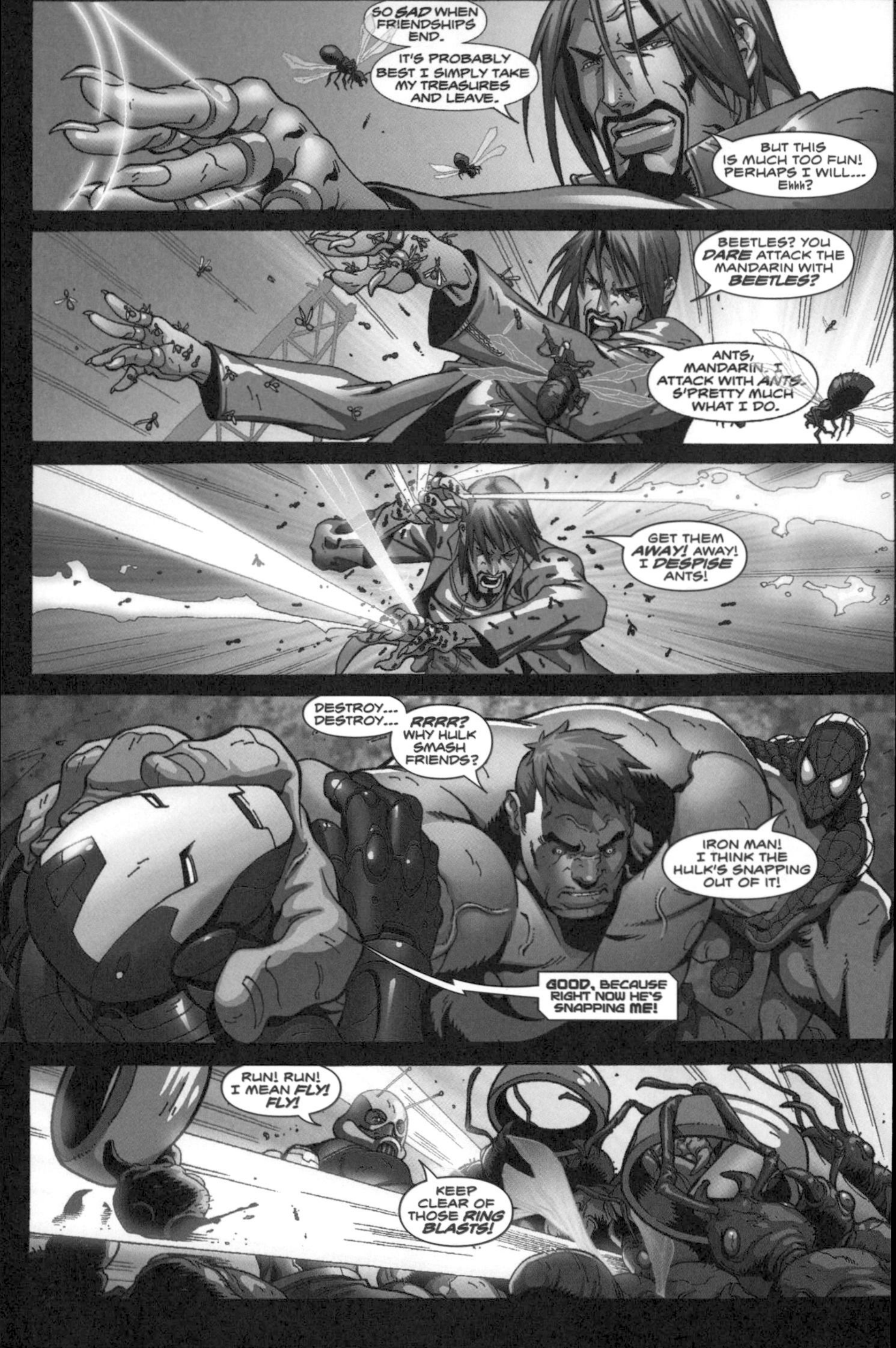
SO SAD WHEN FRIENDSHIPS END.
IT'S PROBABLY BEST I SIMPLY TAKE MY TREASURES AND LEAVE.
BUT THIS IS MUCH TOO FUN! PERHAPS I WILL... Ehhh?
BEETLES? YOU DARE ATTACK THE MANDARIN WITH BEETLES?
ANTS, MANDARIN. I ATTACK WITH ANTS. S'PRETTY MUCH WHAT I DO.
GET THEM AWAY! AWAY! I DESPISE ANTS!
DESTROY... DESTROY...
RRRR? WHY HULK SMASH FRIENDS?
IRON MAN! I THINK THE HULK'S SNAPPING OUT OF IT!
GOOD, BECAUSE RIGHT NOW HE'S SNAPPING ME!
RUN! RUN! I MEAN FLY! FLY!
KEEP CLEAR OF THOSE RING BLASTS!

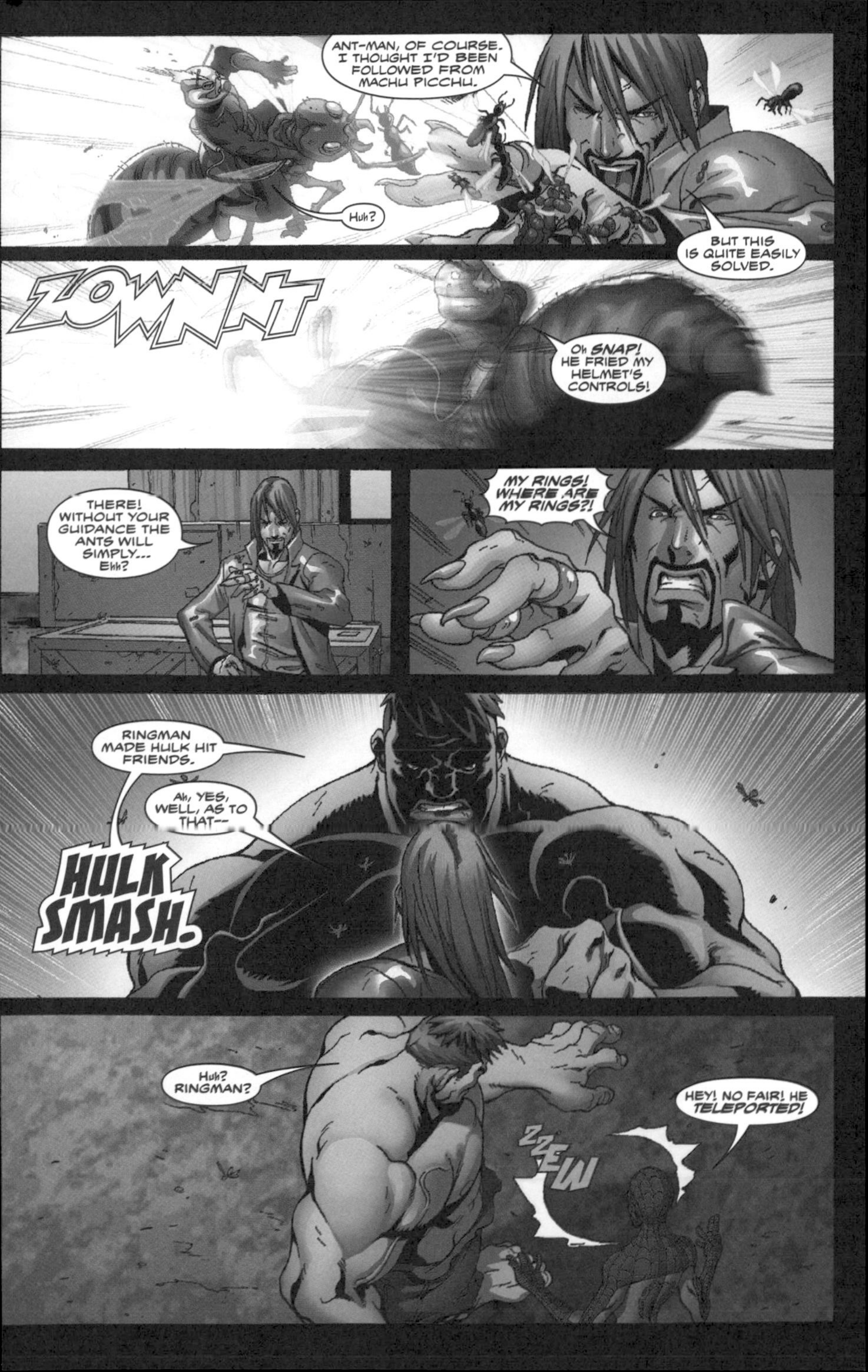
ANT-MAN, OF COURSE. I THOUGHT I'D BEEN FOLLOWED FROM MACHU PICCHU.
Huh?
BUT THIS IS QUITE EASILY SOLVED.
ZOWNT
Oh SNAP! HE FRIED MY HELMET'S CONTROLS!
THERE! WITHOUT YOUR GUIDANCE THE ANTS WILL SIMPLY--- Ehh?
MY RINGS! WHERE ARE MY RINGS?!
RINGMAN MADE HULK HIT FRIENDS.
Ah, YES, WELL, AS TO THAT--
HULK SMASH.
Huh? RINGMAN?
ZZEW
HEY! NO FAIR! HE TELEPORTED!

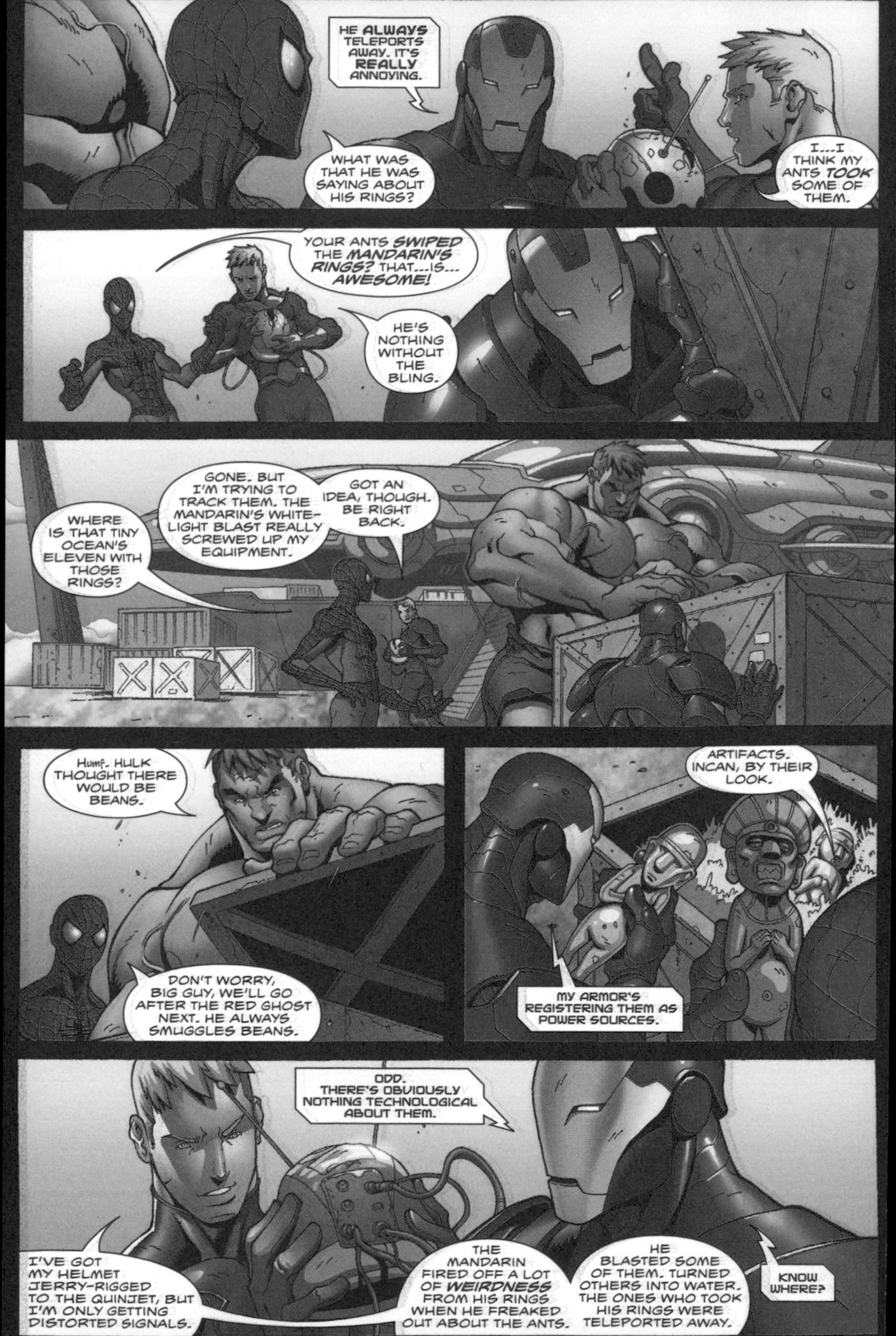
HE ALWAYS TELEPORTS AWAY. IT'S REALLY ANNOYING.
WHAT WAS THAT HE WAS SAYING ABOUT HIS RINGS?
I...I THINK MY ANTS TOOK SOME OF THEM.
YOUR ANTS SWIPED THE MANDARIN'S RINGS? THAT...IS... AWESOME!
HE'S NOTHING WITHOUT THE BLING.
WHERE IS THAT TINY OCEAN'S ELEVEN WITH THOSE RINGS?
GONE. BUT I'M TRYING TO TRACK THEM. THE MANDARIN'S WHITE-LIGHT BLAST REALLY SCREWED UP MY EQUIPMENT.
GOT AN IDEA, THOUGH. BE RIGHT BACK.
Hump. HULK THOUGHT THERE WOULD BE BEANS.
DON'T WORRY, BIG GUY, WE'LL GO AFTER THE RED GHOST NEXT. HE ALWAYS SMUGGLES BEANS.
ARTIFACTS. INCAN, BY THEIR LOOK.
MY ARMOR'S REGISTERING THEM AS POWER SOURCES.
ODD. THERE'S OBVIOUSLY NOTHING TECHNOLOGICAL ABOUT THEM.
I'VE GOT MY HELMET JERRY-RIGGED TO THE QUINJET, BUT I'M ONLY GETTING DISTORTED SIGNALS.
THE MANDARIN FIRED OFF A LOT OF WEIRDNESS FROM HIS RINGS WHEN HE FREAKED OUT ABOUT THE ANTS.
HE BLASTED SOME OF THEM. TURNED OTHERS INTO WATER. THE ONES WHO TOOK HIS RINGS WERE TELEPORTED AWAY.
KNOW WHERE?

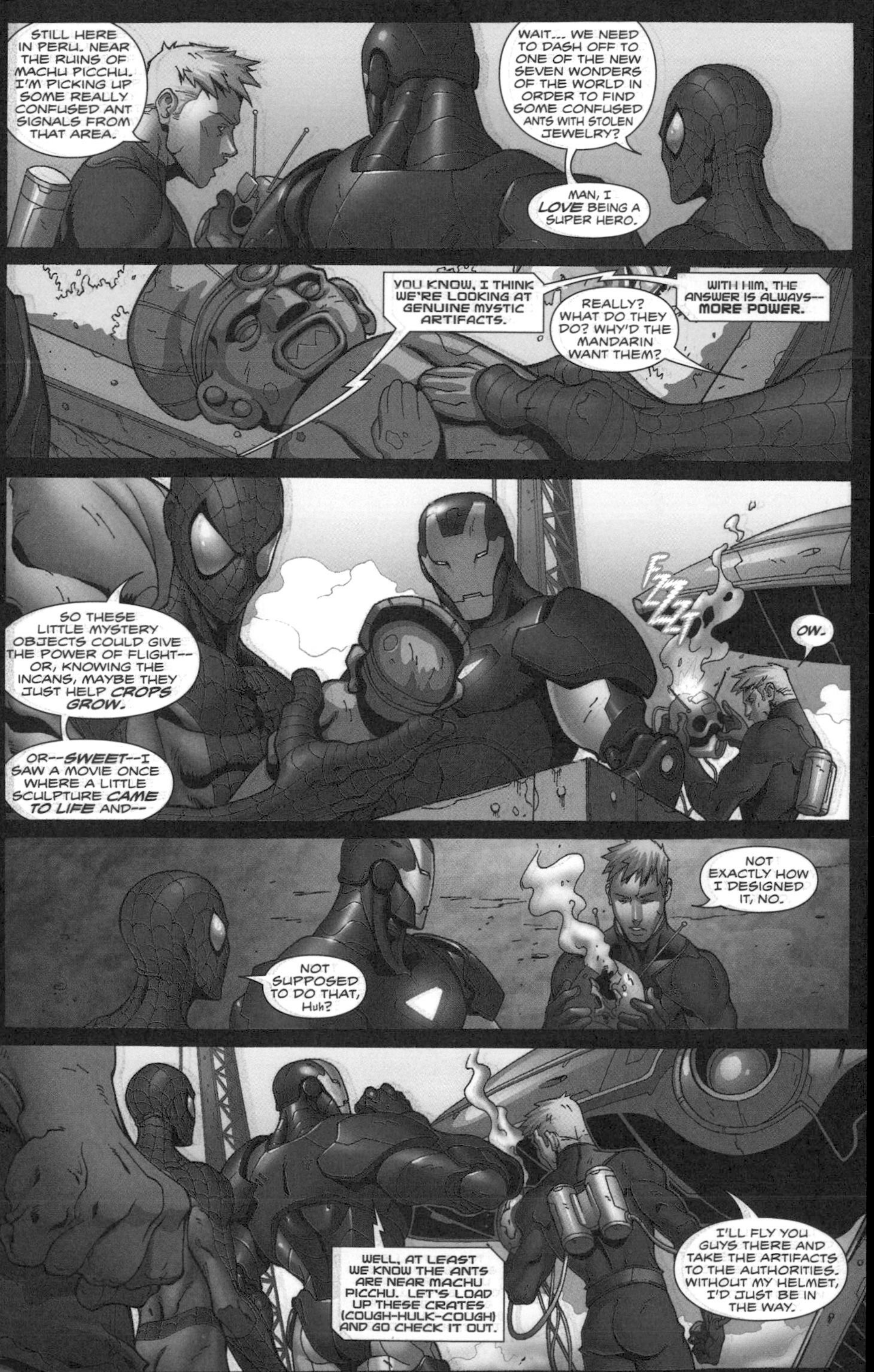

STILL HERE IN PERU. NEAR THE RUINS OF MACHU PICCHU. I'M PICKING UP SOME REALLY CONFUSED ANT SIGNALS FROM THAT AREA.
WAIT... WE NEED TO DASH OFF TO ONE OF THE NEW SEVEN WONDERS OF THE WORLD IN ORDER TO FIND SOME CONFUSED ANTS WITH STOLEN JEWELRY?
MAN, I LOVE BEING A SUPER HERO.
YOU KNOW, I THINK WE'RE LOOKING AT GENUINE MYSTIC ARTIFACTS.
REALLY? WHAT DO THEY DO? WHY'D THE MANDARIN WANT THEM?
WITH HIM, THE ANSWER IS ALWAYS-- MORE POWER.
SO THESE LITTLE MYSTERY OBJECTS COULD GIVE THE POWER OF FLIGHT-- OR, KNOWING THE INCANS, MAYBE THEY JUST HELP CROPS GROW.
OR--SWEET--I SAW A MOVIE ONCE WHERE A LITTLE SCULPTURE CAME TO LIFE AND--
FZZZT
OW.
NOT SUPPOSED TO DO THAT, HUH?
NOT EXACTLY HOW I DESIGNED IT, NO.
WELL, AT LEAST WE KNOW THE ANTS ARE NEAR MACHU PICCHU. LET'S LOAD UP THESE CRATES (COUGH-HULK-COUGH) AND GO CHECK IT OUT.
I'LL FLY YOU GUYS THERE AND TAKE THE ARTIFACTS TO THE AUTHORITIES. WITHOUT MY HELMET, I'D JUST BE IN THE WAY.

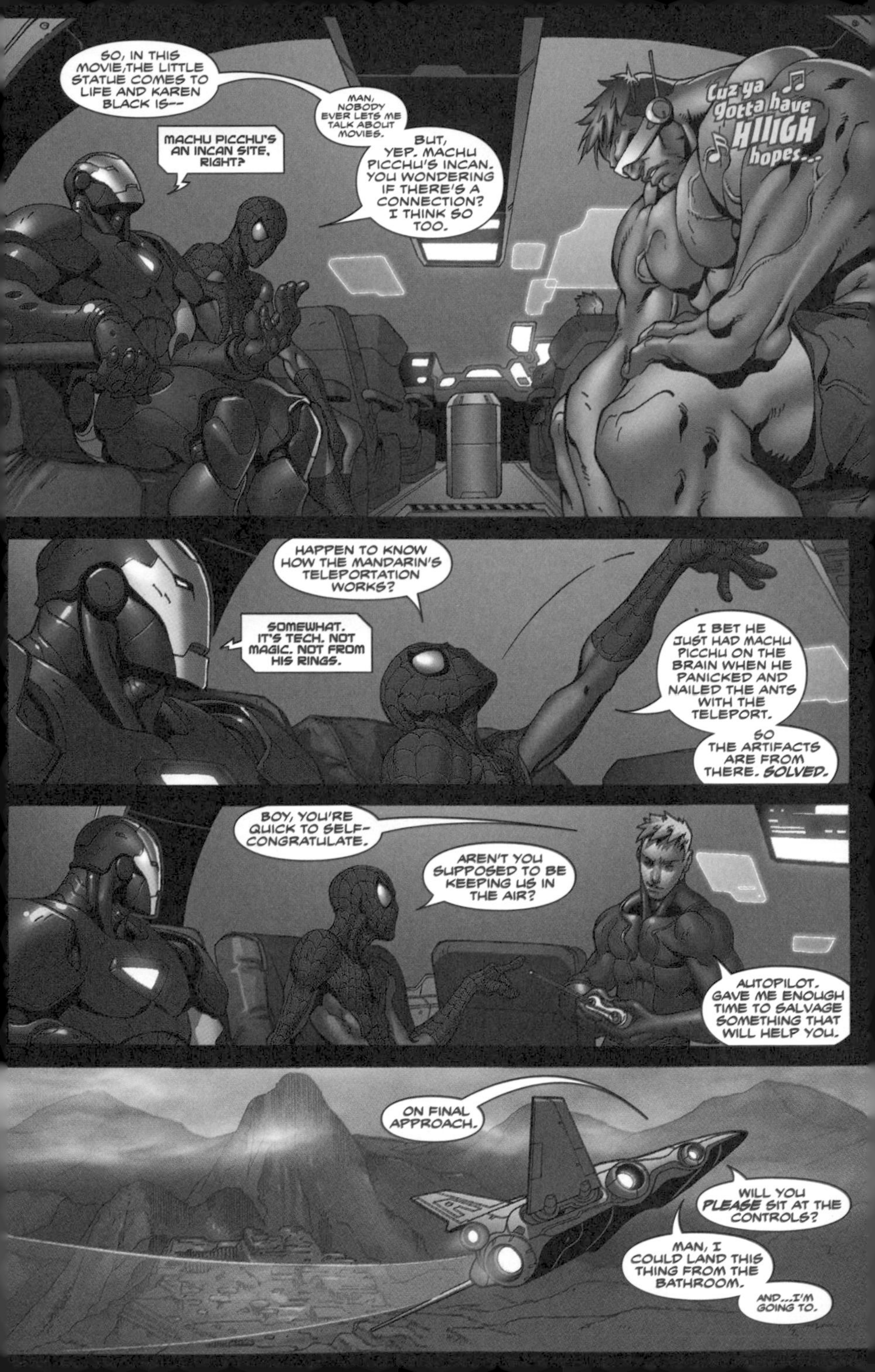
SO, IN THIS MOVIE, THE LITTLE STATUE COMES TO LIFE AND KAREN BLACK IS--
MAN, NOBODY EVER LETS ME TALK ABOUT MOVIES.
MACHU PICCHU'S AN INCAN SITE, RIGHT?
BUT, YEP. MACHU PICCHU'S INCAN. YOU WONDERING IF THERE'S A CONNECTION? I THINK SO TOO.
Cuz ya gotta have HIIIGH hopes...
HAPPEN TO KNOW HOW THE MANDARIN'S TELEPORTATION WORKS?
SOMEWHAT. IT'S TECH. NOT MAGIC. NOT FROM HIS RINGS.
I BET HE JUST HAD MACHU PICCHU ON THE BRAIN WHEN HE PANICKED AND NAILED THE ANTS WITH THE TELEPORT.
SO THE ARTIFACTS ARE FROM THERE. SOLVED.
BOY, YOU'RE QUICK TO SELF-CONGRATULATE.
AREN'T YOU SUPPOSED TO BE KEEPING US IN THE AIR?
AUTOPILOT. GAVE ME ENOUGH TIME TO SALVAGE SOMETHING THAT WILL HELP YOU.
ON FINAL APPROACH.
WILL YOU PLEASE SIT AT THE CONTROLS?
MAN, I COULD LAND THIS THING FROM THE BATHROOM.
AND...I'M GOING TO.

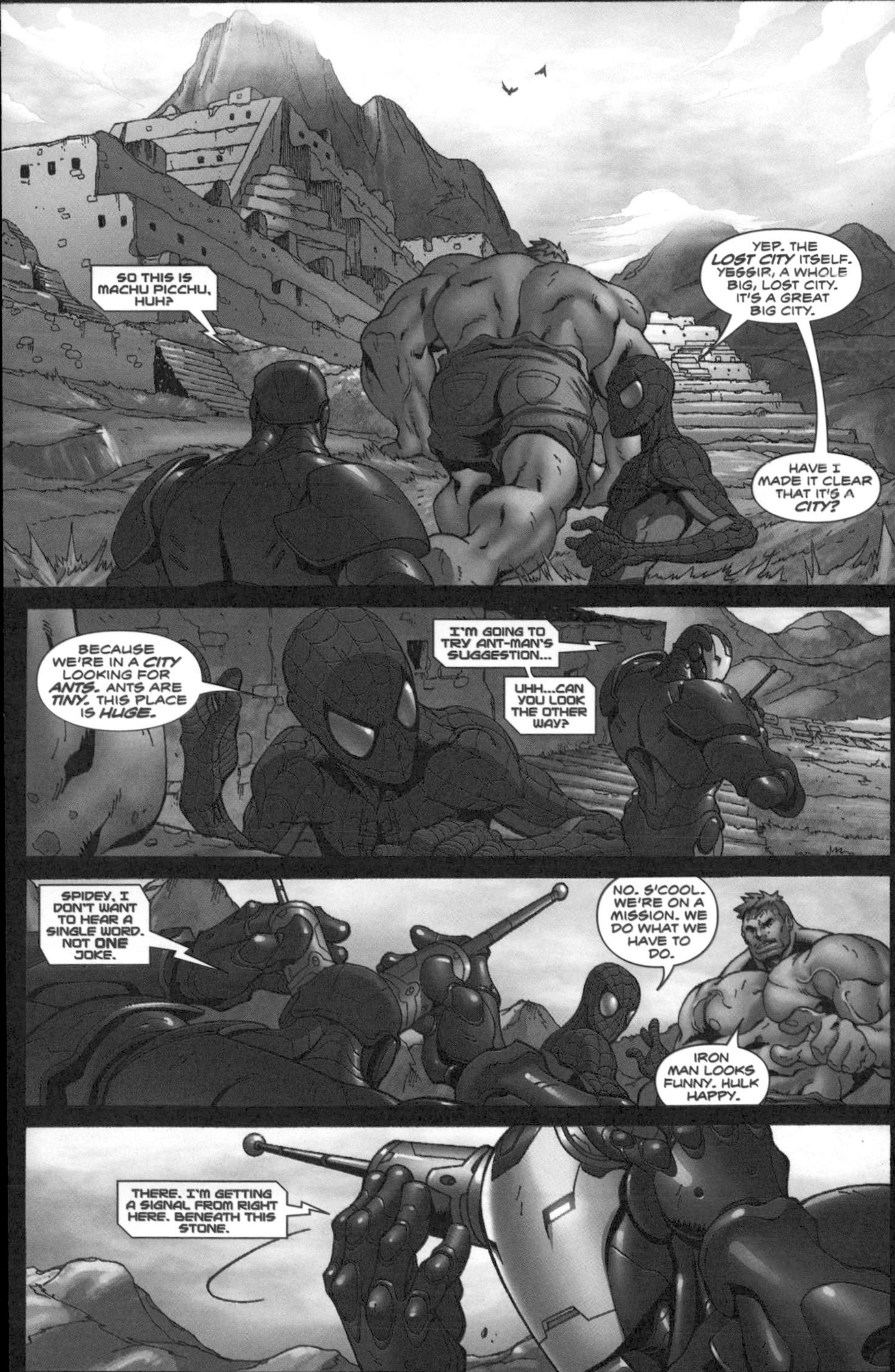
SO THIS IS MACHU PICCHU, HUH?
YEP. THE LOST CITY ITSELF. YESSIR, A WHOLE BIG, LOST CITY. IT'S A GREAT BIG CITY.
HAVE I MADE IT CLEAR THAT IT'S A CITY?
BECAUSE WE'RE IN A CITY LOOKING FOR ANTS. ANTS ARE TINY. THIS PLACE IS HUGE.
I'M GOING TO TRY ANT-MAN'S SUGGESTION...
UHH...CAN YOU LOOK THE OTHER WAY?
SPIDEY, I DON'T WANT TO HEAR A SINGLE WORD. NOT ONE JOKE.
NO. S'COOL. WE'RE ON A MISSION. WE DO WHAT WE HAVE TO DO.
IRON MAN LOOKS FUNNY. HULK HAPPY.
THERE. I'M GETTING A SIGNAL FROM RIGHT HERE. BENEATH THIS STONE.

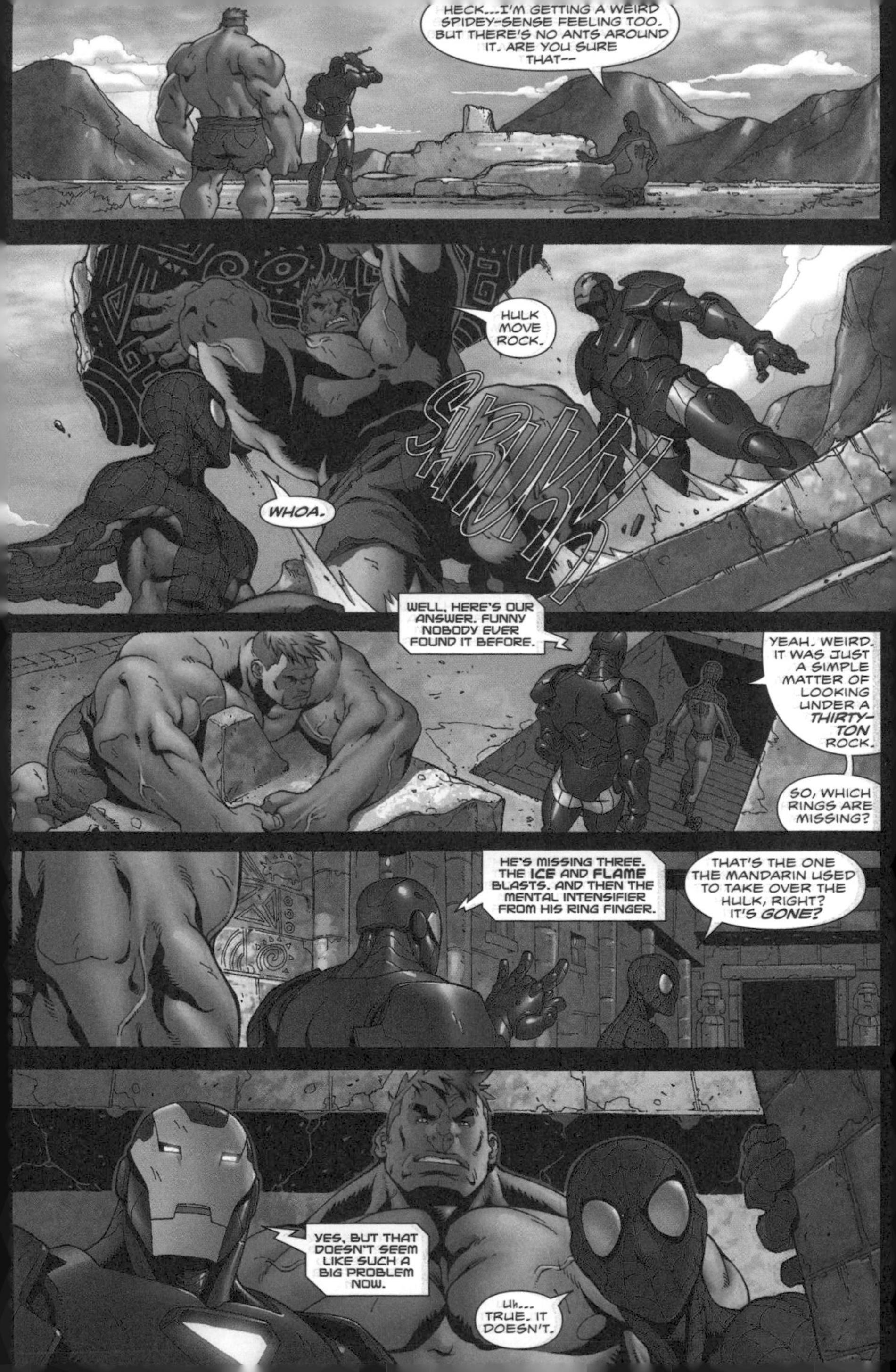
HECK...I'M GETTING A WEIRD SPIDEY-SENSE FEELING TOO. BUT THERE'S NO ANTS AROUND IT. ARE YOU SURE THAT--
HULK MOVE ROCK.
SKRUNCH
WHOA.
WELL, HERE'S OUR ANSWER. FUNNY NOBODY EVER FOUND IT BEFORE.
YEAH. WEIRD. IT WAS JUST A SIMPLE MATTER OF LOOKING UNDER A THIRTY-TON ROCK.
SO, WHICH RINGS ARE MISSING?
HE'S MISSING THREE. THE ICE AND FLAME BLASTS. AND THEN THE MENTAL INTENSIFIER FROM HIS RING FINGER.
THAT'S THE ONE THE MANDARIN USED TO TAKE OVER THE HULK, RIGHT? IT'S GONE?
YES, BUT THAT DOESN'T SEEM LIKE SUCH A BIG PROBLEM NOW.
Uh... TRUE. IT DOESN'T.

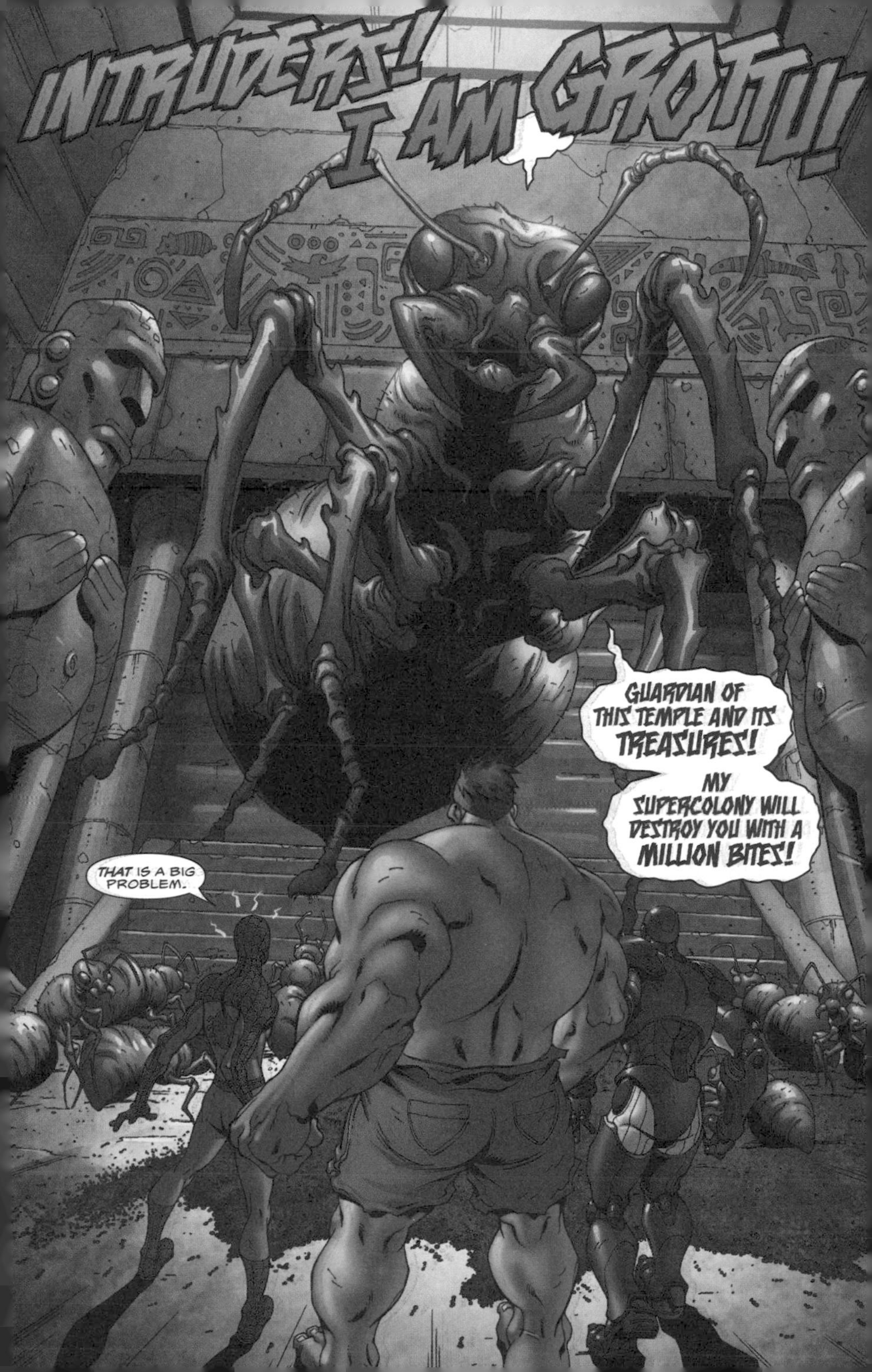
INTRUDERS! I AM GROTTU!
GUARDIAN OF THIS TEMPLE AND ITS TREASURES!
MY SUPERCOLONY WILL DESTROY YOU WITH A MILLION BITES!
THAT IS A BIG PROBLEM.

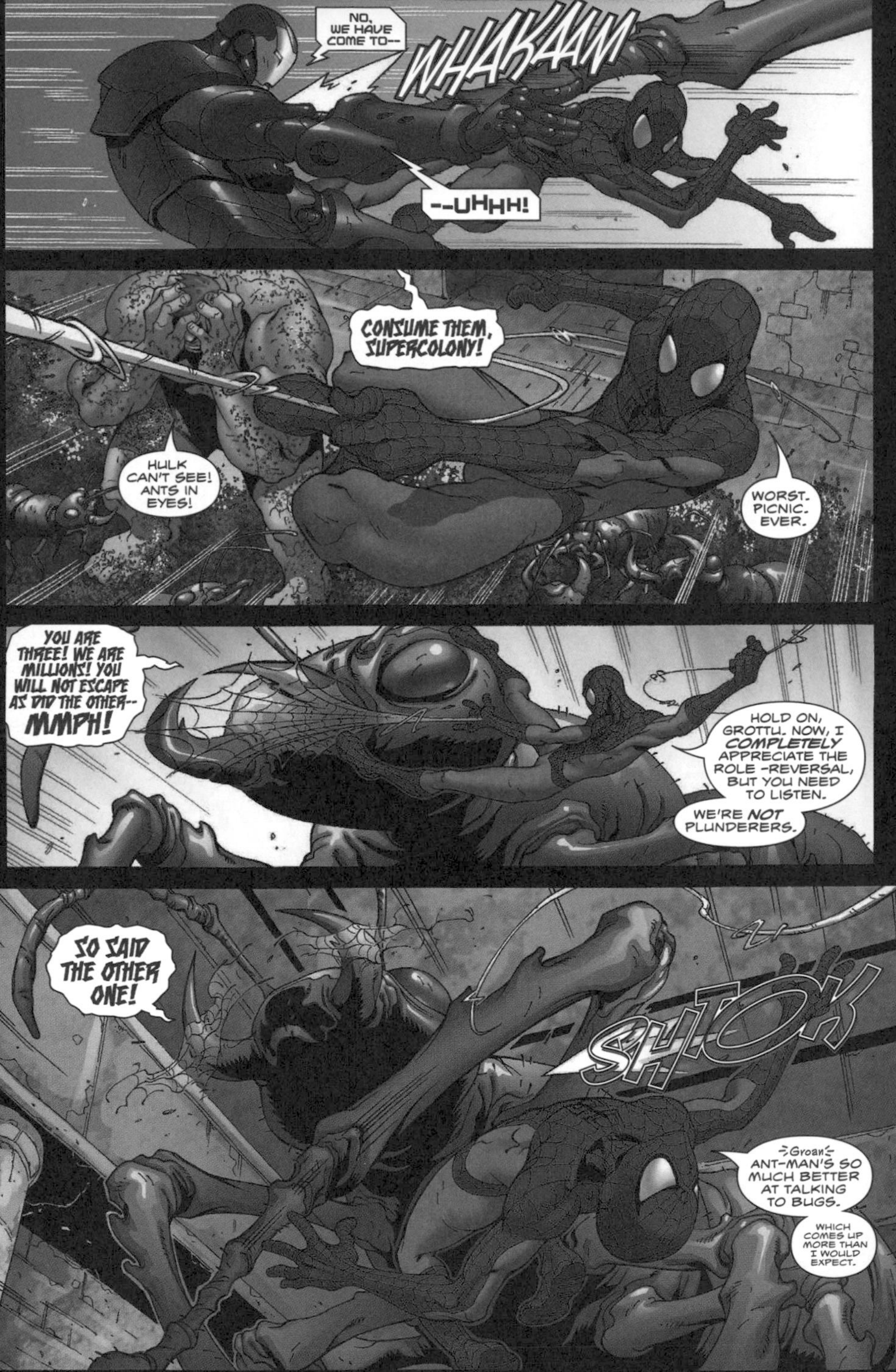
NO, WE HAVE COME TO--
WHAKAAM
--UHHH!
CONSUME THEM, SUPERCOLONY!
HULK CAN'T SEE! ANTS IN EYES!
WORST. PICNIC. EVER.
YOU ARE THREE! WE ARE MILLIONS! YOU WILL NOT ESCAPE AS DID THE OTHER-- MMPH!
HOLD ON, GROTTU. NOW, I COMPLETELY APPRECIATE THE ROLE-REVERSAL, BUT YOU NEED TO LISTEN.
WE'RE NOT PLUNDERERS.
SO SAID THE OTHER ONE!
SHTOK
-Groan- ANT-MAN'S SO MUCH BETTER AT TALKING TO BUGS.
WHICH COMES UP MORE THAN I WOULD EXPECT.

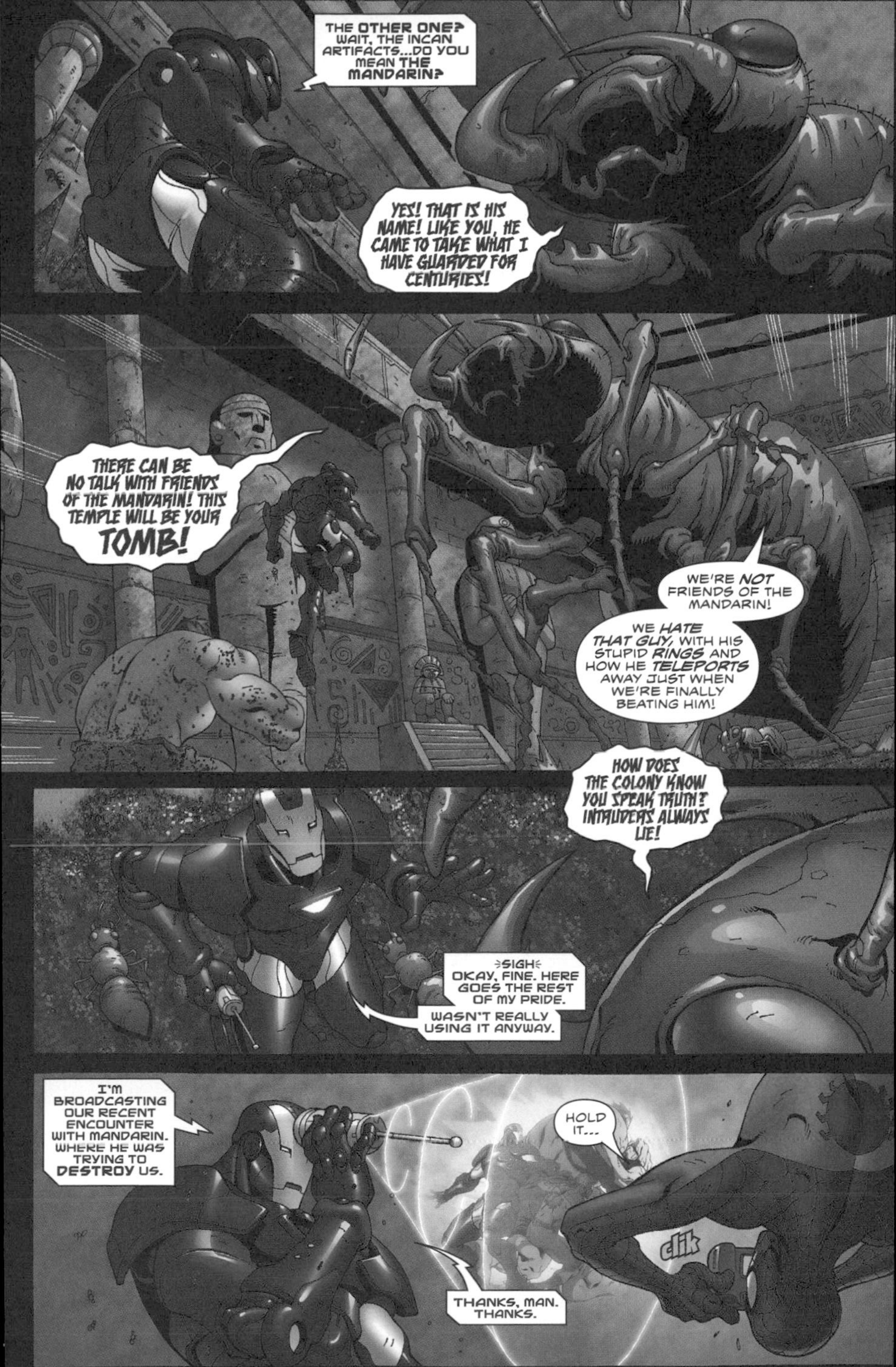
THE OTHER ONE? WAIT, THE INCAN ARTIFACTS...DO YOU MEAN THE MANDARIN?
YES! THAT IS HIS NAME! LIKE YOU, HE CAME TO TAKE WHAT I HAVE GUARDED FOR CENTURIES!
THERE CAN BE NO TALK WITH FRIENDS OF THE MANDARIN! THIS TEMPLE WILL BE YOUR TOMB!
WE'RE NOT FRIENDS OF THE MANDARIN!
WE HATE THAT GUY, WITH HIS STUPID RINGS AND HOW HE TELEPORTS AWAY JUST WHEN WE'RE FINALLY BEATING HIM!
HOW DOES THE COLONY KNOW YOU SPEAK TRUTH? INTRUDERS ALWAYS LIE!
SIGH OKAY, FINE. HERE GOES THE REST OF MY PRIDE.
WASN'T REALLY USING IT ANYWAY.
I'M BROADCASTING OUR RECENT ENCOUNTER WITH MANDARIN. WHERE HE WAS TRYING TO DESTROY US.
HOLD IT...
CLIK
THANKS, MAN. THANKS.

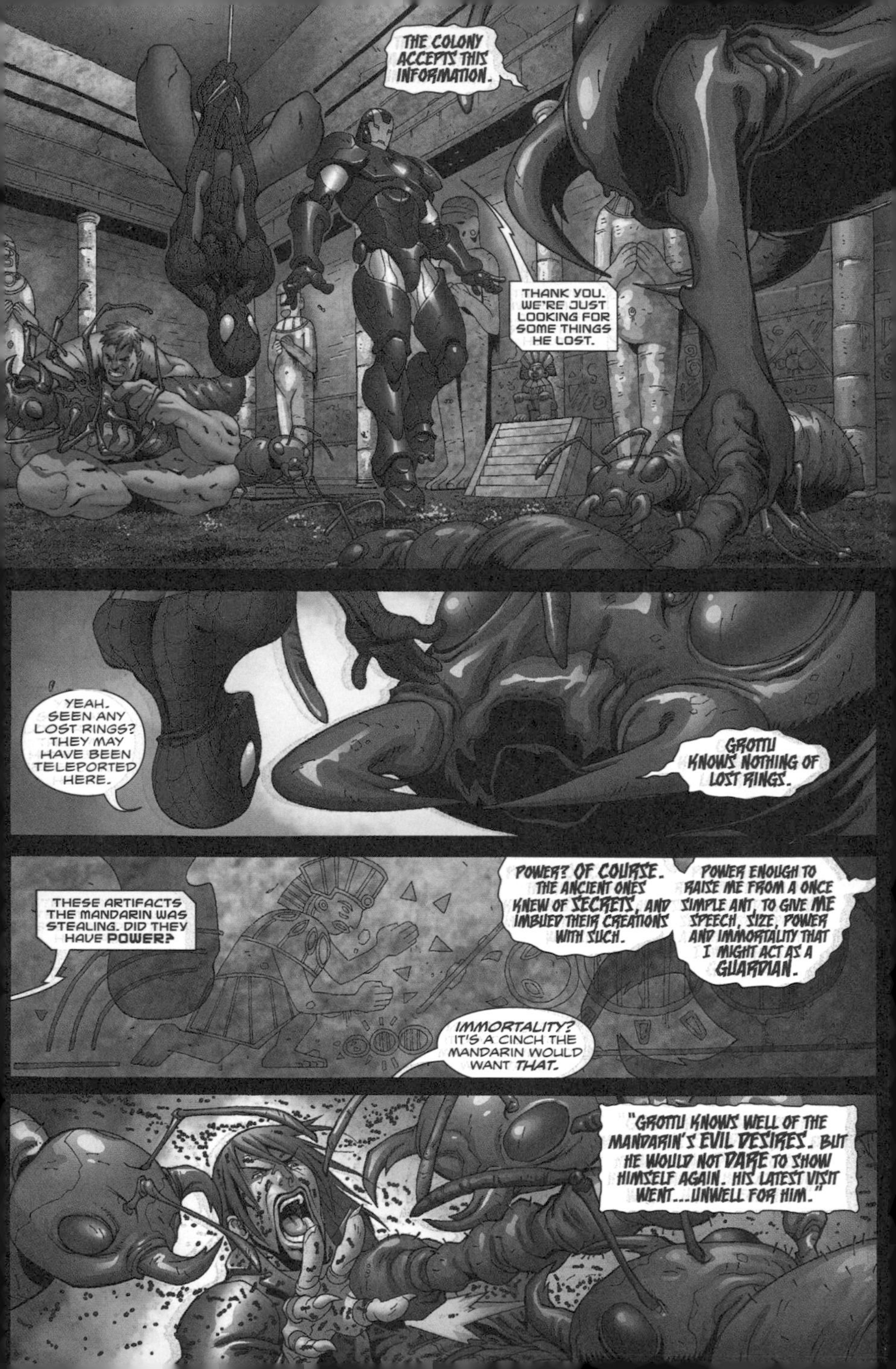
THE COLONY ACCEPTS THIS INFORMATION.
THANK YOU. WE'RE JUST LOOKING FOR SOME THINGS HE LOST.
YEAH. SEEN ANY LOST RINGS? THEY MAY HAVE BEEN TELEPORTED HERE.
GROTTU KNOWS NOTHING OF LOST RINGS.
THESE ARTIFACTS THE MANDARIN WAS STEALING. DID THEY HAVE POWER?
POWER? OF COURSE. THE ANCIENT ONES KNEW OF SECRETS, AND IMBUED THEIR CREATIONS WITH SUCH.
POWER ENOUGH TO RAISE ME FROM A ONCE SIMPLE ANT, TO GIVE ME SPEECH, SIZE, POWER AND IMMORTALITY THAT I MIGHT ACT AS A GUARDIAN.
IMMORTALITY? IT'S A CINCH THE MANDARIN WOULD WANT THAT.
"GROTTU KNOWS WELL OF THE MANDARIN'S EVIL DESIRES. BUT HE WOULD NOT DARE TO SHOW HIMSELF AGAIN. HIS LATEST VISIT WENT...UNWELL FOR HIM."

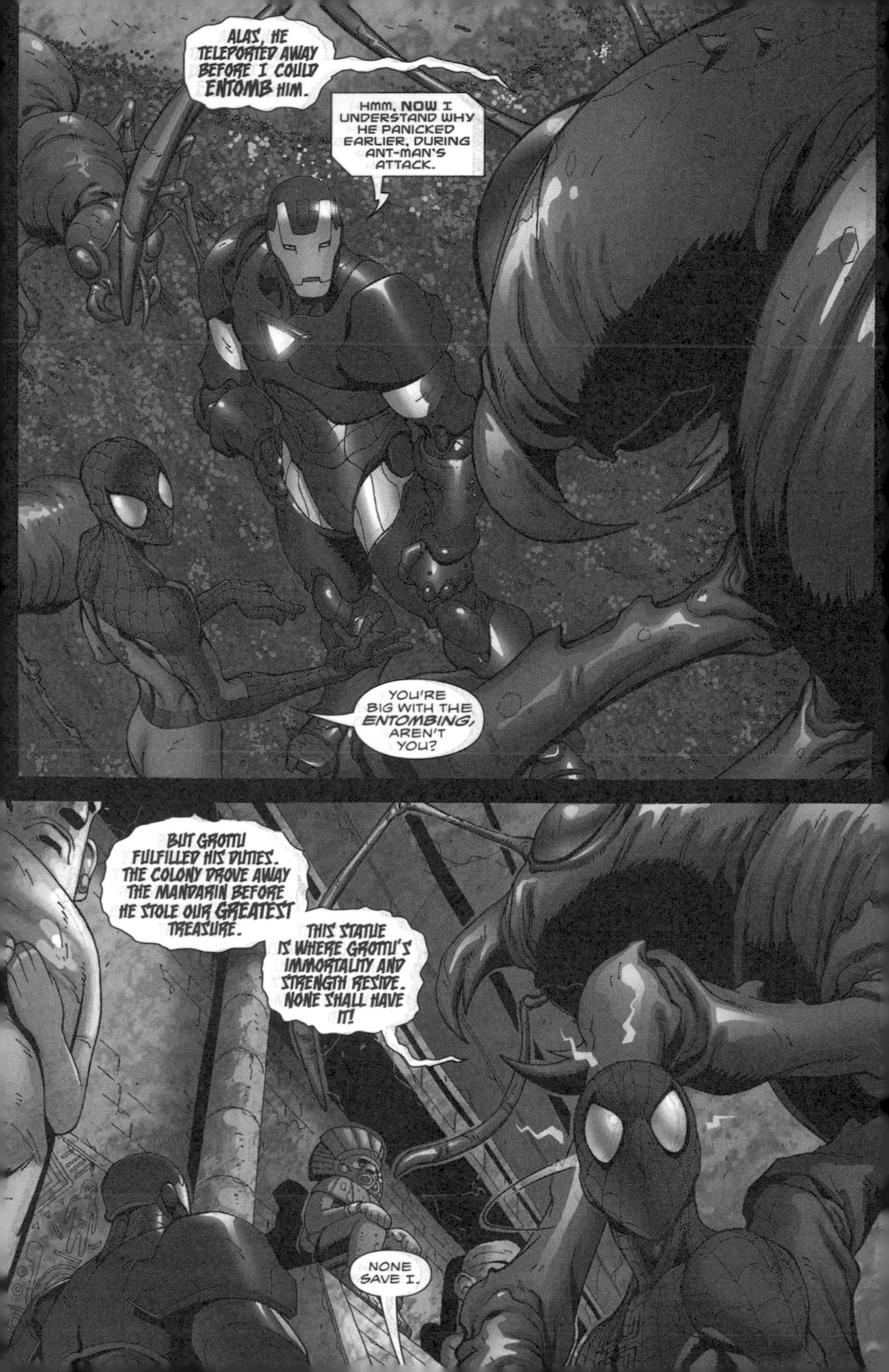
ALAS, HE TELEPORTED AWAY BEFORE I COULD ENTOMB HIM.
HMM, NOW I UNDERSTAND WHY HE PANICKED EARLIER, DURING ANT-MAN'S ATTACK.
YOU'RE BIG WITH THE ENTOMBING, AREN'T YOU?
BUT GROTTU FULFILLED HIS DUTIES. THE COLONY DROVE AWAY THE MANDARIN BEFORE HE STOLE OUR GREATEST TREASURE.
THIS STATUE IS WHERE GROTTU'S IMMORTALITY AND STRENGTH RESIDE. NONE SHALL HAVE IT!
NONE SAVE I.

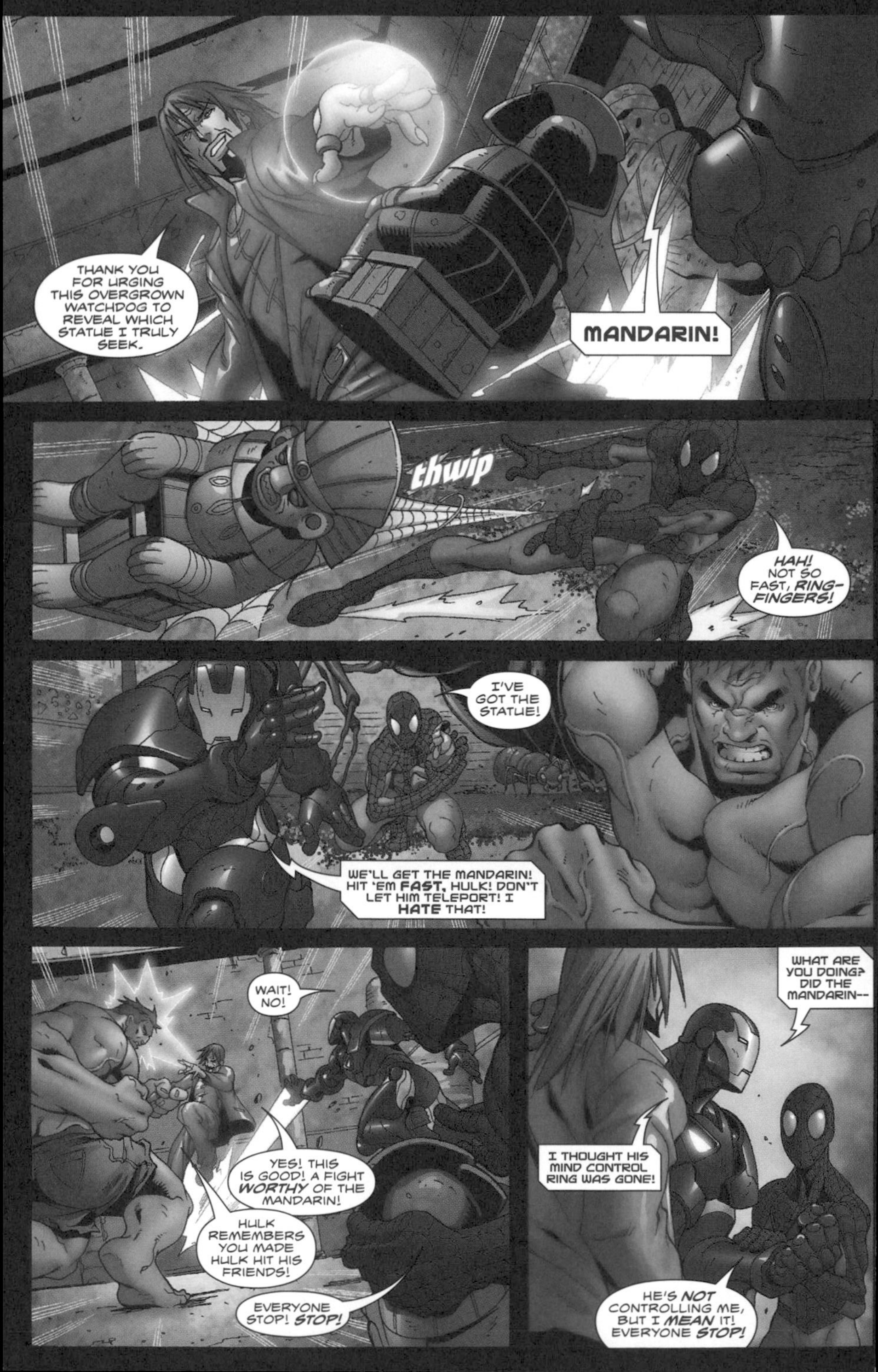
THANK YOU FOR URGING THIS OVERGROWN WATCHDOG TO REVEAL WHICH STATUE I TRULY SEEK.
MANDARIN!
thwip
HAH! NOT SO FAST, RING-FINGERS!
I'VE GOT THE STATUE!
WE'LL GET THE MANDARIN! HIT 'EM FAST, HULK! DON'T LET HIM TELEPORT! I HATE THAT!
WAIT! NO!
YES! THIS IS GOOD! A FIGHT WORTHY OF THE MANDARIN!
HULK REMEMBERS YOU MADE HULK HIT HIS FRIENDS!
EVERYONE STOP! STOP!
WHAT ARE YOU DOING? DID THE MANDARIN--
I THOUGHT HIS MIND CONTROL RING WAS GONE!
HE'S NOT CONTROLLING ME, BUT I MEAN IT! EVERYONE STOP!

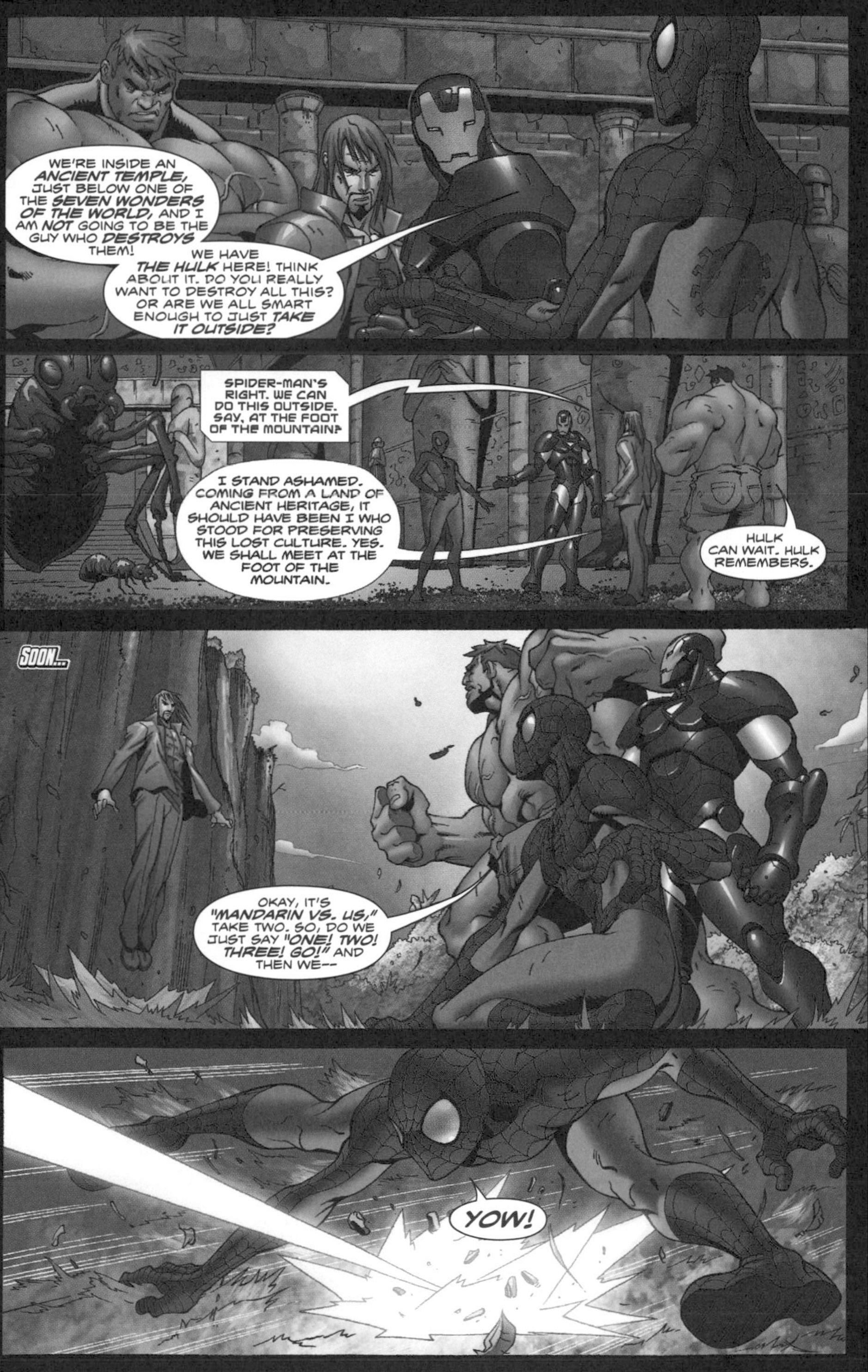
WE'RE INSIDE AN ANCIENT TEMPLE, JUST BELOW ONE OF THE SEVEN WONDERS OF THE WORLD, AND I AM NOT GOING TO BE THE GUY WHO DESTROYS THEM!
WE HAVE THE HULK HERE! THINK ABOUT IT. DO YOU REALLY WANT TO DESTROY ALL THIS? OR ARE WE ALL SMART ENOUGH TO JUST TAKE IT OUTSIDE?
SPIDER-MAN'S RIGHT. WE CAN DO THIS OUTSIDE. SAY, AT THE FOOT OF THE MOUNTAIN?
I STAND ASHAMED. COMING FROM A LAND OF ANCIENT HERITAGE, IT SHOULD HAVE BEEN I WHO STOOD FOR PRESERVING THIS LOST CULTURE. YES. WE SHALL MEET AT THE FOOT OF THE MOUNTAIN.
HULK CAN WAIT. HULK REMEMBERS.
SOON...
OKAY, IT'S "MANDARIN VS. US," TAKE TWO. SO, DO WE JUST SAY "ONE! TWO! THREE! GO!" AND THEN WE--
YOW!

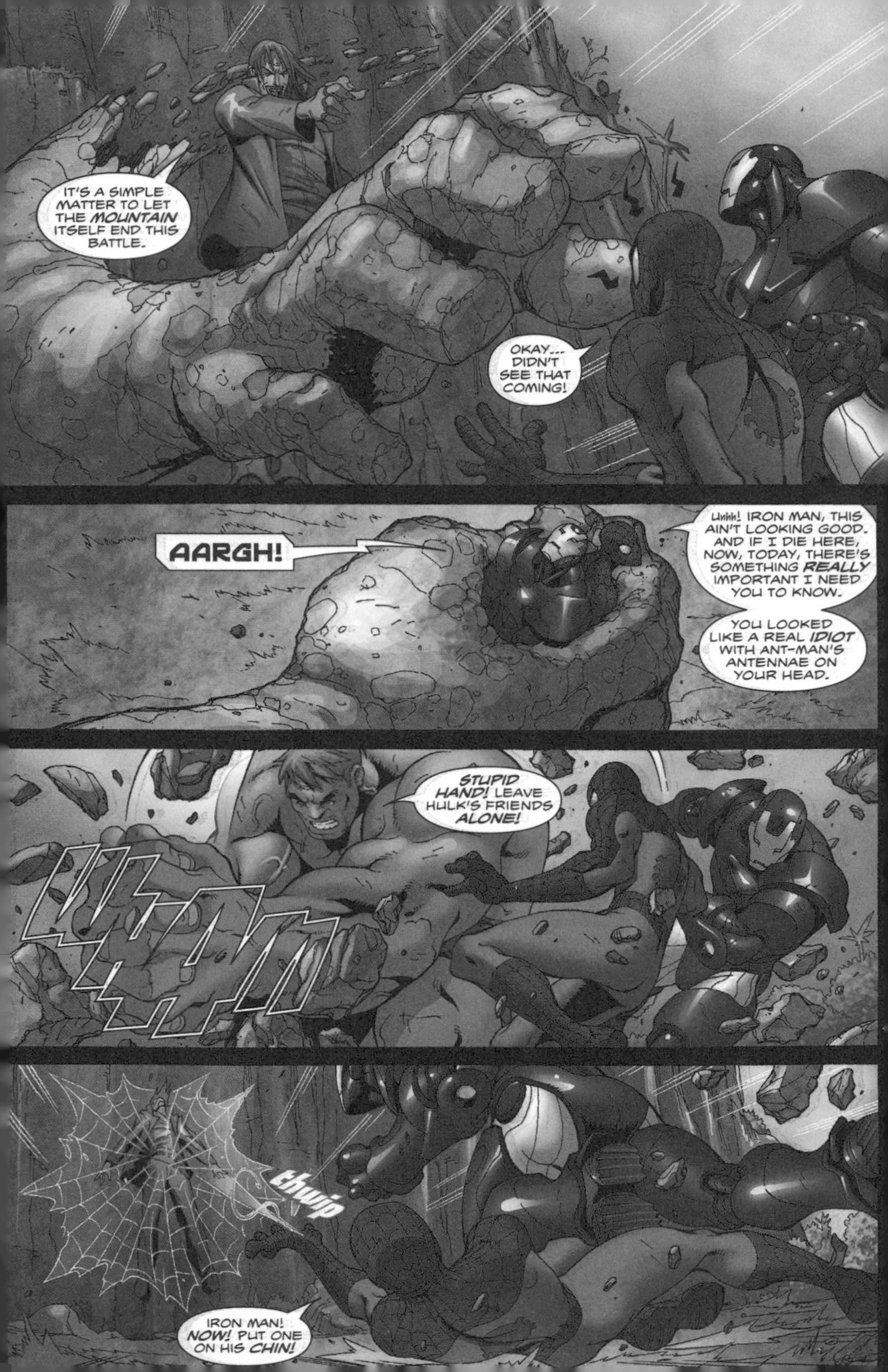
IT'S A SIMPLE MATTER TO LET THE MOUNTAIN ITSELF END THIS BATTLE.
OKAY... DIDN'T SEE THAT COMING!
AARGH!
Unhh! IRON MAN, THIS AIN'T LOOKING GOOD. AND IF I DIE HERE, NOW, TODAY, THERE'S SOMETHING REALLY IMPORTANT I NEED YOU TO KNOW.
YOU LOOKED LIKE A REAL IDIOT WITH ANT-MAN'S ANTENNAE ON YOUR HEAD.
STUPID HAND! LEAVE HULK'S FRIENDS ALONE!
thwip
IRON MAN! NOW! PUT ONE ON HIS CHIN!

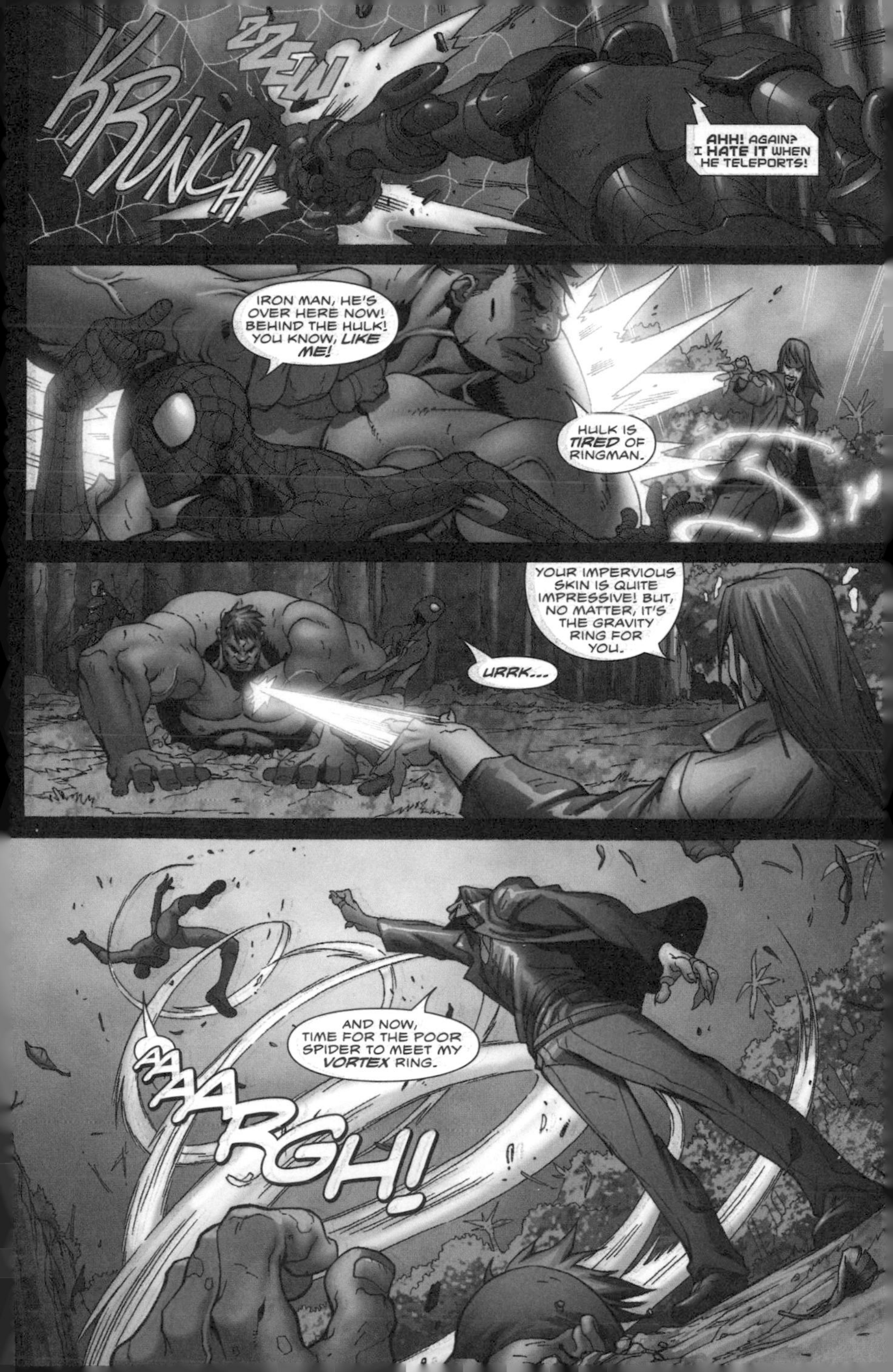

KRUNCH
ZZEW
AHH! AGAIN? I HATE IT WHEN HE TELEPORTS!
IRON MAN, HE'S OVER HERE NOW! BEHIND THE HULK! YOU KNOW, LIKE ME!
HULK IS TIRED OF RINGMAN.
YOUR IMPERVIOUS SKIN IS QUITE IMPRESSIVE! BUT, NO MATTER, IT'S THE GRAVITY RING FOR YOU.
URRK...
AND NOW, TIME FOR THE POOR SPIDER TO MEET MY VORTEX RING.
AAAARGH!

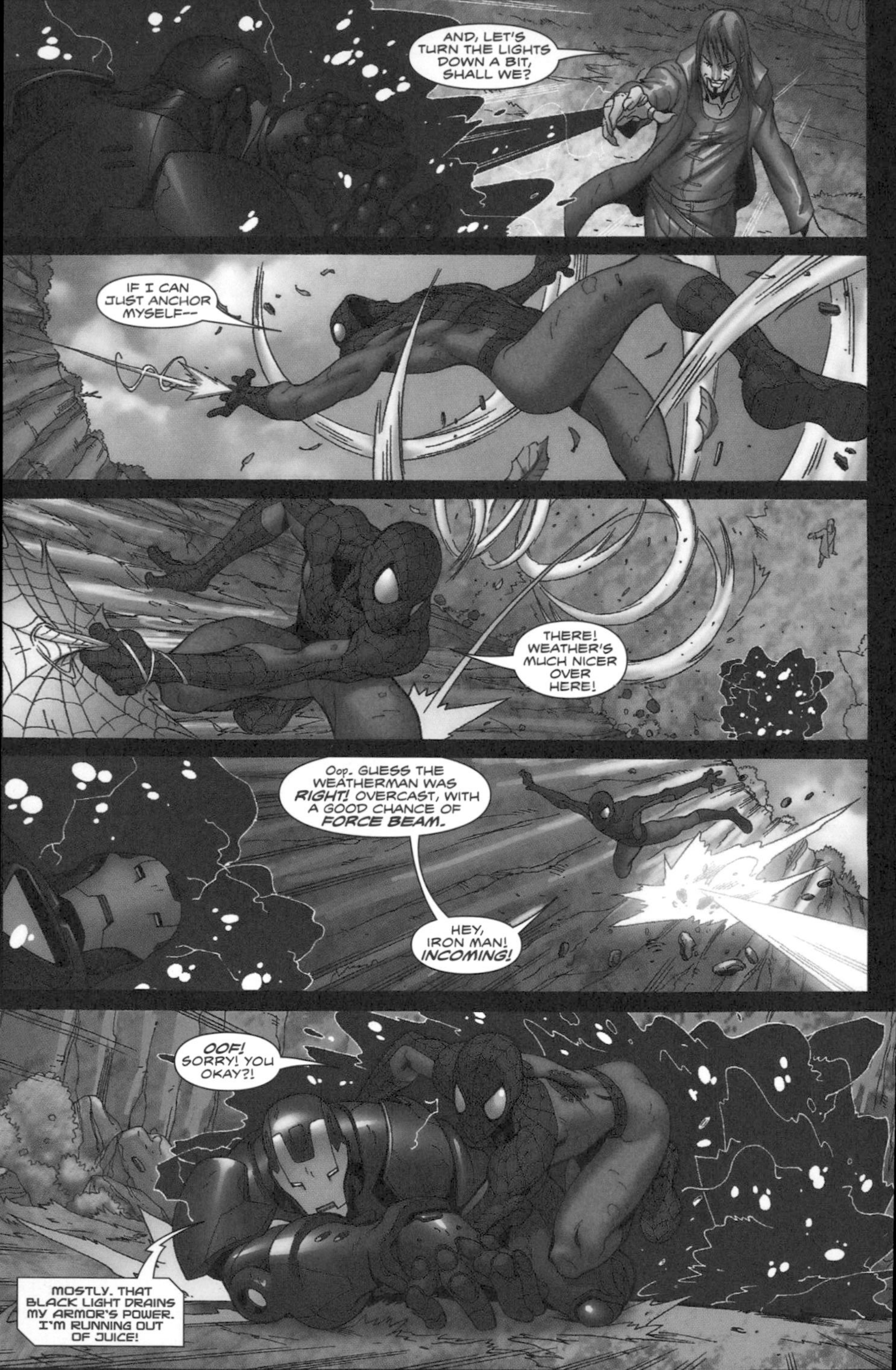
AND, LET'S TURN THE LIGHTS DOWN A BIT, SHALL WE?
IF I CAN JUST ANCHOR MYSELF--
THERE! WEATHER'S MUCH NICER OVER HERE!
Oop. GUESS THE WEATHERMAN WAS RIGHT! OVERCAST, WITH A GOOD CHANCE OF FORCE BEAM.
HEY, IRON MAN! INCOMING!
OOF! SORRY! YOU OKAY?!
MOSTLY. THAT BLACK LIGHT DRAINS MY ARMOR'S POWER. I'M RUNNING OUT OF JUICE!

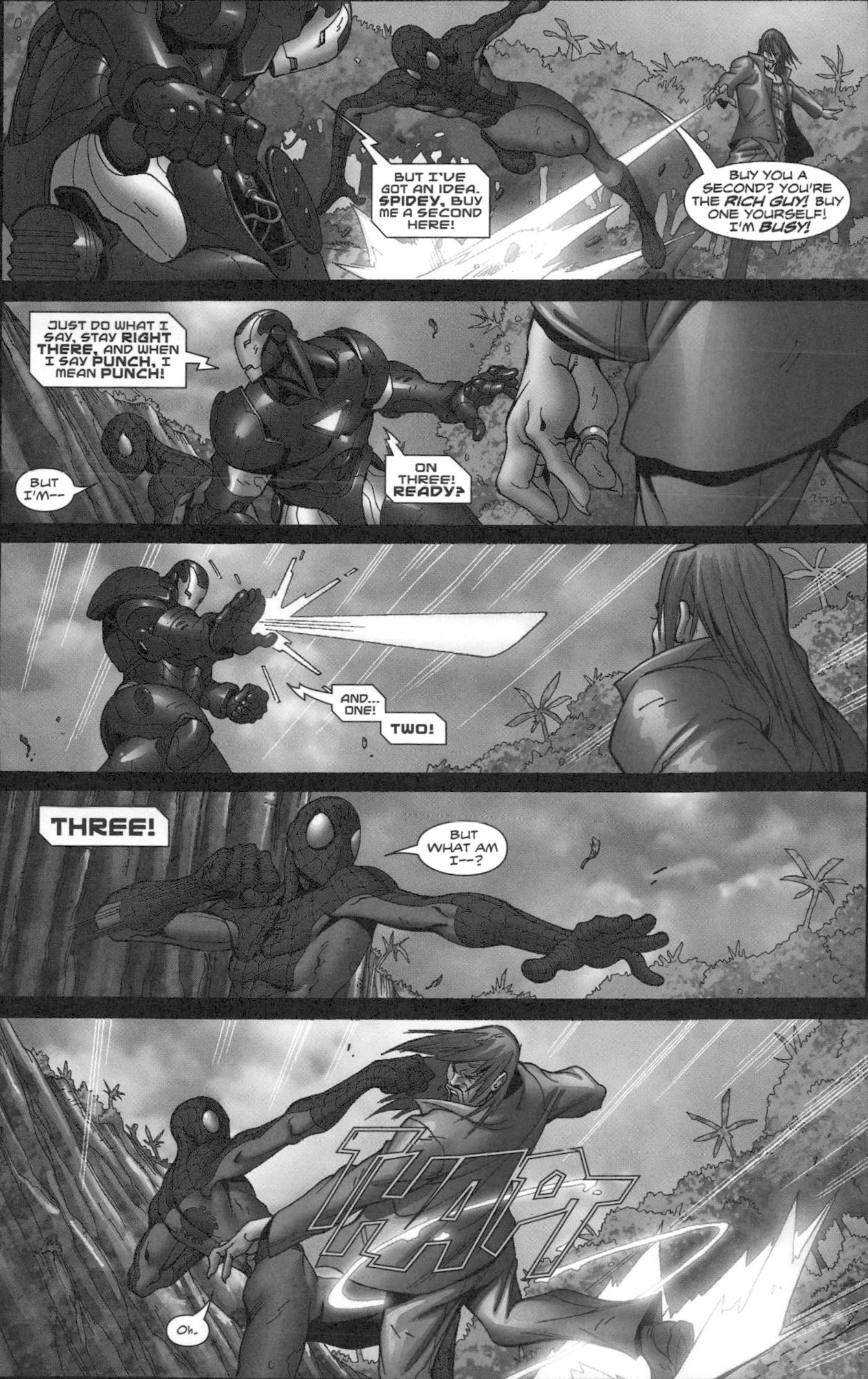
BUT I'VE GOT AN IDEA. SPIDEY, BUY ME A SECOND HERE!
BUY YOU A SECOND? YOU'RE THE RICH GUY! BUY ONE YOURSELF! I'M BUSY!
JUST DO WHAT I SAY, STAY RIGHT THERE, AND WHEN I SAY PUNCH, I MEAN PUNCH!
BUT I'M--
ON THREE! READY?
AND... ONE!
TWO!
THREE!
BUT WHAT AM I--?
THAP
Oh.

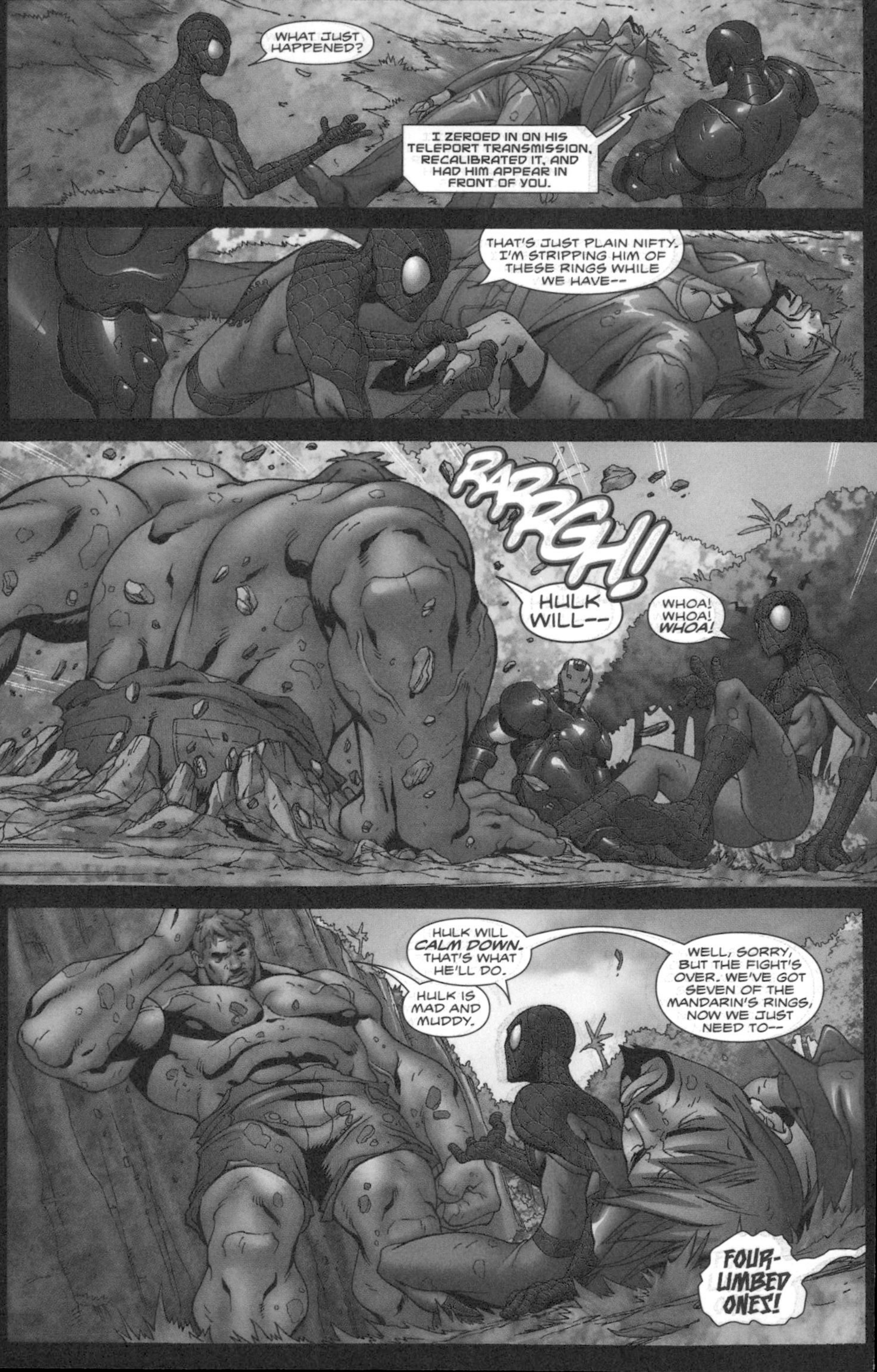
WHAT JUST HAPPENED?
I ZEROED IN ON HIS TELEPORT TRANSMISSION, RECALIBRATED IT, AND HAD HIM APPEAR IN FRONT OF YOU.
THAT'S JUST PLAIN NIFTY. I'M STRIPPING HIM OF THESE RINGS WHILE WE HAVE--
RARRGH!
HULK WILL--
WHOA! WHOA! WHOA!
HULK WILL CALM DOWN. THAT'S WHAT HE'LL DO.
HULK IS MAD AND MUDDY.
WELL, SORRY, BUT THE FIGHT'S OVER. WE'VE GOT SEVEN OF THE MANDARIN'S RINGS, NOW WE JUST NEED TO--
FOUR-LIMBED ONES!

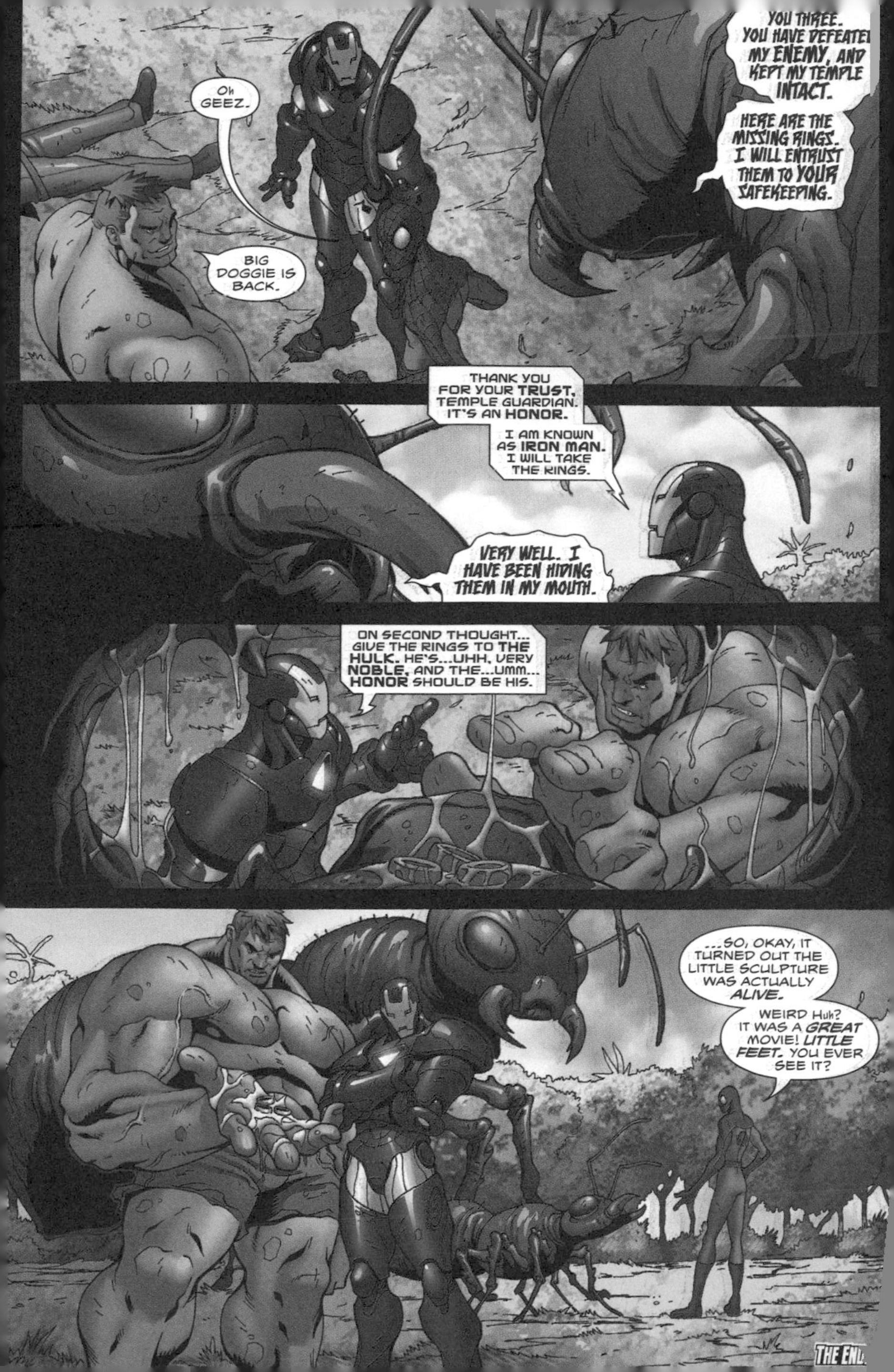
YOU THREE. YOU HAVE DEFEATED MY ENEMY, AND KEPT MY TEMPLE INTACT.
HERE ARE THE MISSING RINGS. I WILL ENTRUST THEM TO YOUR SAFEKEEPING.
Oh GEEZ.
BIG DOGGIE IS BACK.
THANK YOU FOR YOUR TRUST, TEMPLE GUARDIAN. IT'S AN HONOR.
I AM KNOWN AS IRON MAN. I WILL TAKE THE RINGS.
VERY WELL. I HAVE BEEN HIDING THEM IN MY MOUTH.
ON SECOND THOUGHT... GIVE THE RINGS TO THE HULK. HE'S...UHH, VERY NOBLE, AND THE...UMM... HONOR SHOULD BE HIS.
...SO, OKAY, IT TURNED OUT THE LITTLE SCULPTURE WAS ACTUALLY ALIVE.
WEIRD Huh? IT WAS A GREAT MOVIE! LITTLE FEET. YOU EVER SEE IT?
THE END.

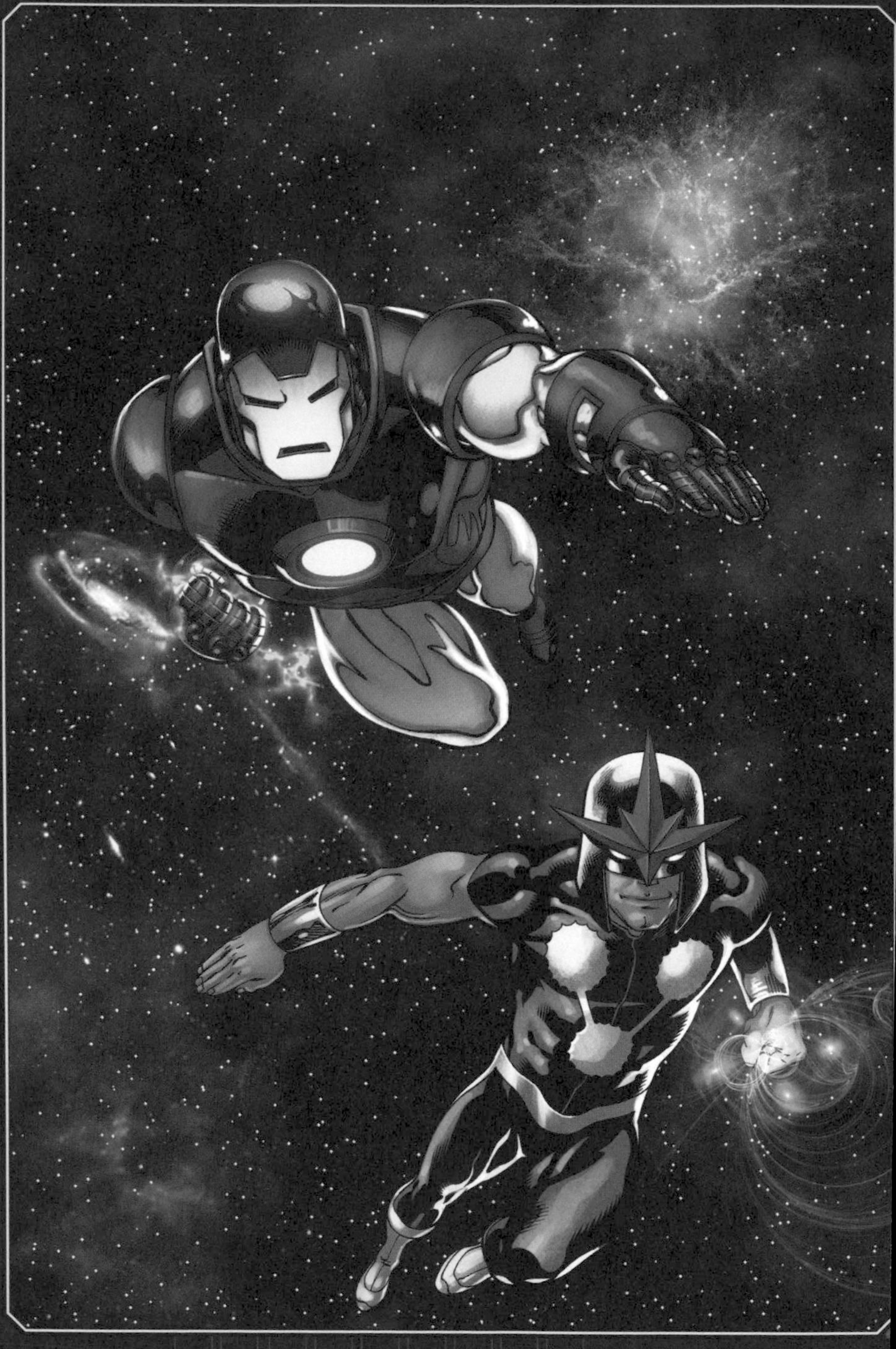

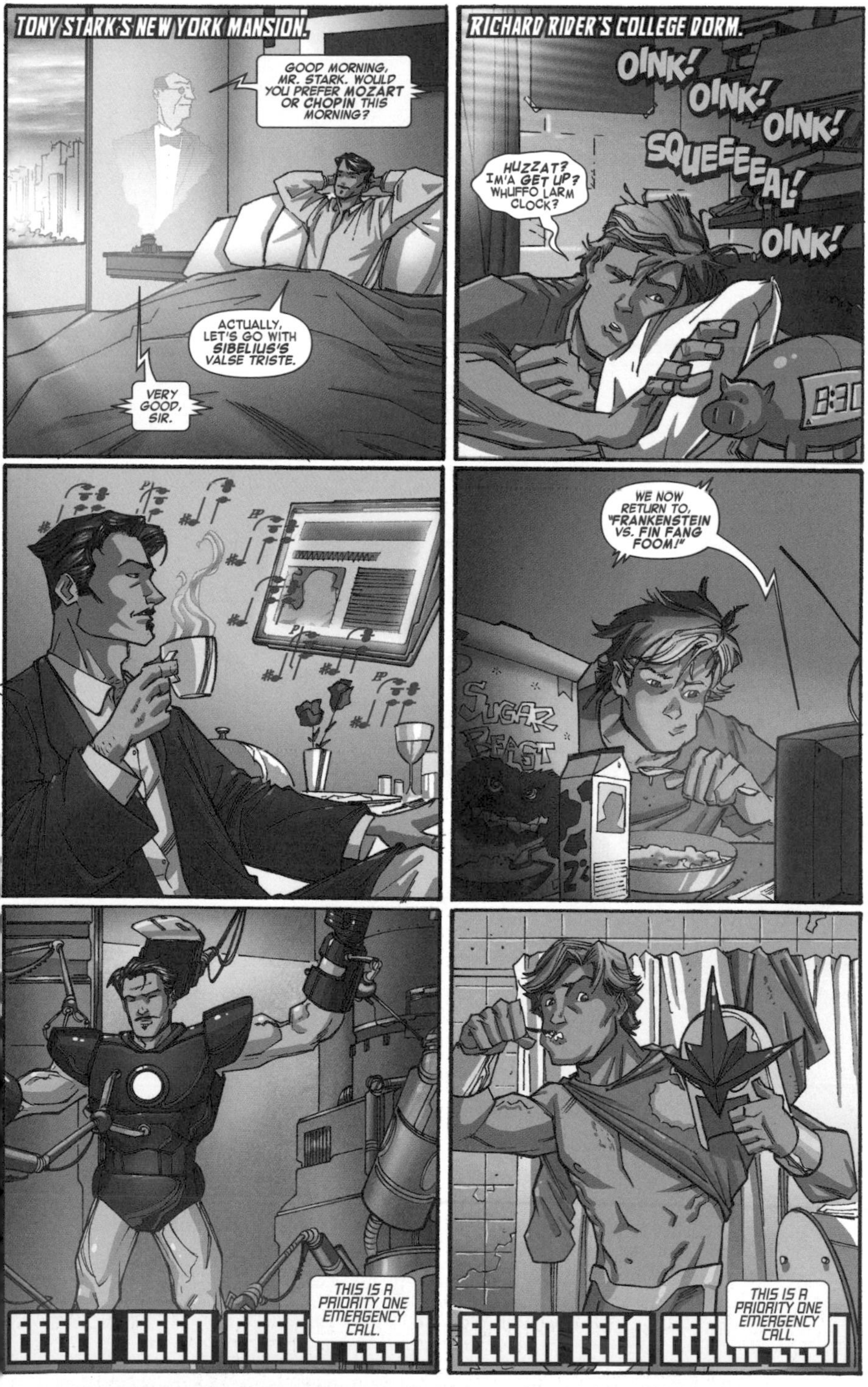
TONY STARK'S NEW YORK MANSION.
GOOD MORNING, MR. STARK. WOULD YOU PREFER MOZART OR CHOPIN THIS MORNING?
ACTUALLY, LET'S GO WITH SIBELIUS'S VALSE TRISTE.
VERY GOOD, SIR.
RICHARD RIDER'S COLLEGE DORM.
OINK! OINK! OINK!
SQUEEEEEAL!
OINK!
HUZZAT? IM'A GET UP? WHUFFO LARM CLOCK?
8:30
WE NOW RETURN TO, "FRANKENSTEIN VS. FIN FANG FOOM!"
SUGAR BEAST
2%
THIS IS A PRIORITY ONE EMERGENCY CALL.
EEEEN EEEN EEEE
THIS IS A PRIORITY ONE EMERGENCY CALL.
EEEEN EEEN EEEE

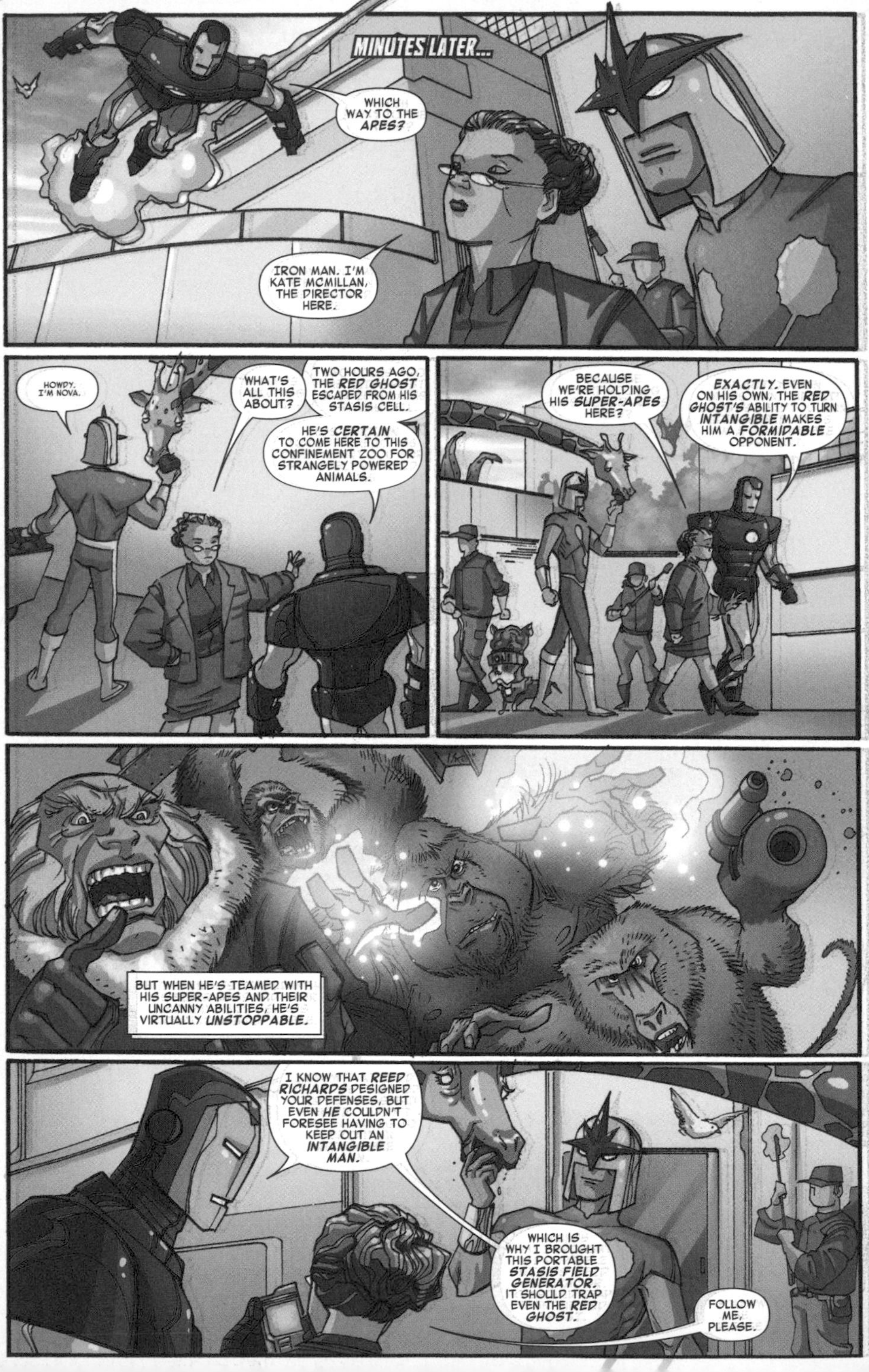
MINUTES LATER...
WHICH WAY TO THE APES?
IRON MAN. I'M KATE MCMILLAN, THE DIRECTOR HERE.
HOWDY. I'M NOVA.
WHAT'S ALL THIS ABOUT?
TWO HOURS AGO, THE RED GHOST ESCAPED FROM HIS STASIS CELL.
HE'S CERTAIN TO COME HERE TO THIS CONFINEMENT ZOO FOR STRANGELY POWERED ANIMALS.
BECAUSE WE'RE HOLDING HIS SUPER-APES HERE?
EXACTLY. EVEN ON HIS OWN, THE RED GHOST'S ABILITY TO TURN INTANGIBLE MAKES HIM A FORMIDABLE OPPONENT.
BUT WHEN HE'S TEAMED WITH HIS SUPER-APES AND THEIR UNCANNY ABILITIES, HE'S VIRTUALLY UNSTOPPABLE.
I KNOW THAT REED RICHARDS DESIGNED YOUR DEFENSES, BUT EVEN HE COULDN'T FORESEE HAVING TO KEEP OUT AN INTANGIBLE MAN.
WHICH IS WHY I BROUGHT THIS PORTABLE STASIS FIELD GENERATOR. IT SHOULD TRAP EVEN THE RED GHOST.
FOLLOW ME, PLEASE.

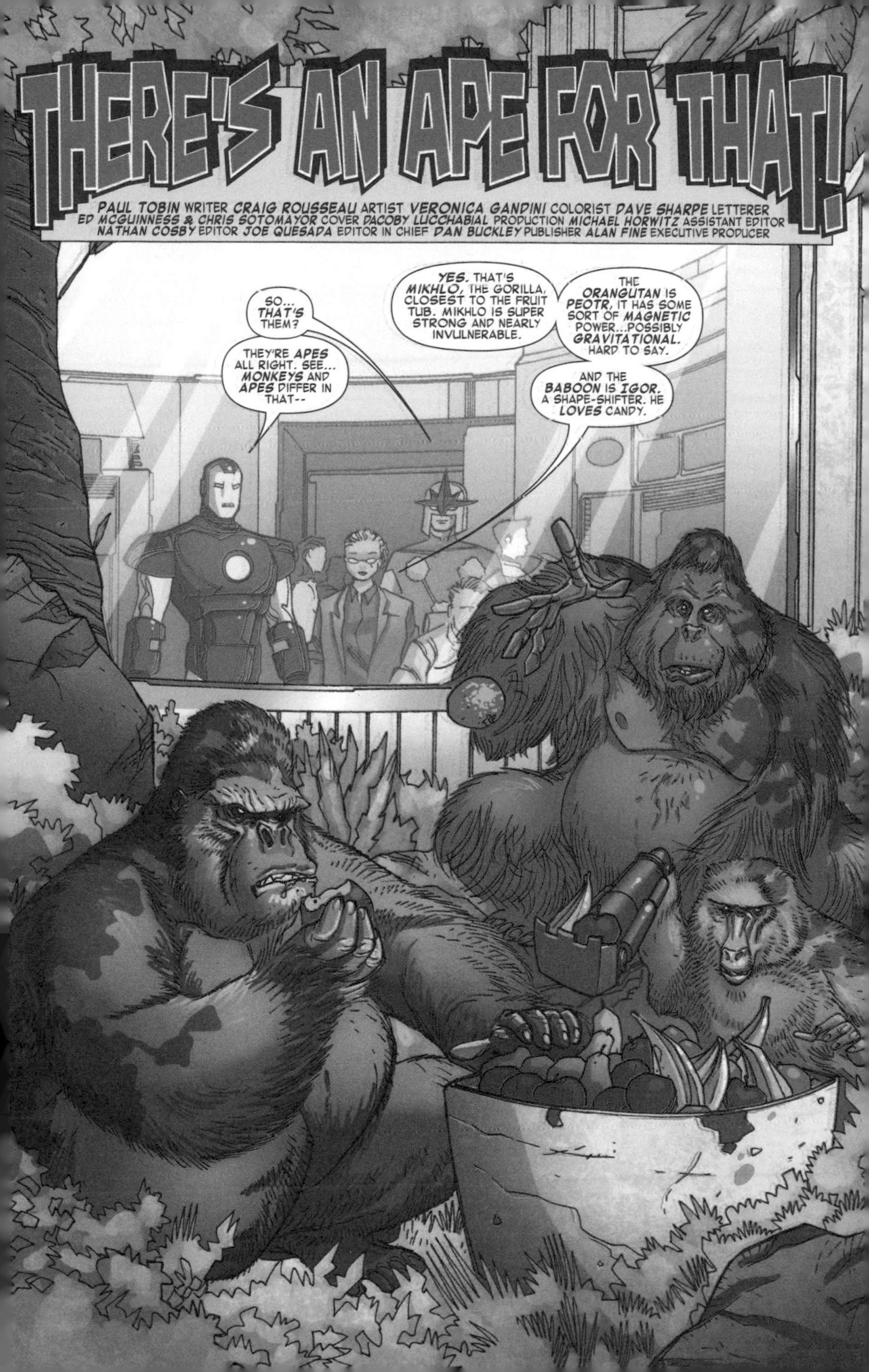
THERE'S AN APE FOR THAT!
PAUL TOBIN WRITER CRAIG ROUSSEAU ARTIST VERONICA GANDINI COLORIST DAVE SHARPE LETTERER
ED MCGUINNESS & CHRIS SOTOMAYOR COVER DACOBY LUCCHABIAL PRODUCTION MICHAEL HORWITZ ASSISTANT EDITOR
NATHAN COSBY EDITOR JOE QUESADA EDITOR IN CHIEF DAN BUCKLEY PUBLISHER ALAN FINE EXECUTIVE PRODUCER
SO... THAT'S THEM?
THEY'RE APES ALL RIGHT. SEE... MONKEYS AND APES DIFFER IN THAT--
YES. THAT'S MIKHLO, THE GORILLA, CLOSEST TO THE FRUIT TUB. MIKHLO IS SUPER STRONG AND NEARLY INVULNERABLE.
THE ORANGUTAN IS PEOTR, IT HAS SOME SORT OF MAGNETIC POWER...POSSIBLY GRAVITATIONAL. HARD TO SAY.
AND THE BABOON IS IGOR. A SHAPE-SHIFTER. HE LOVES CANDY.

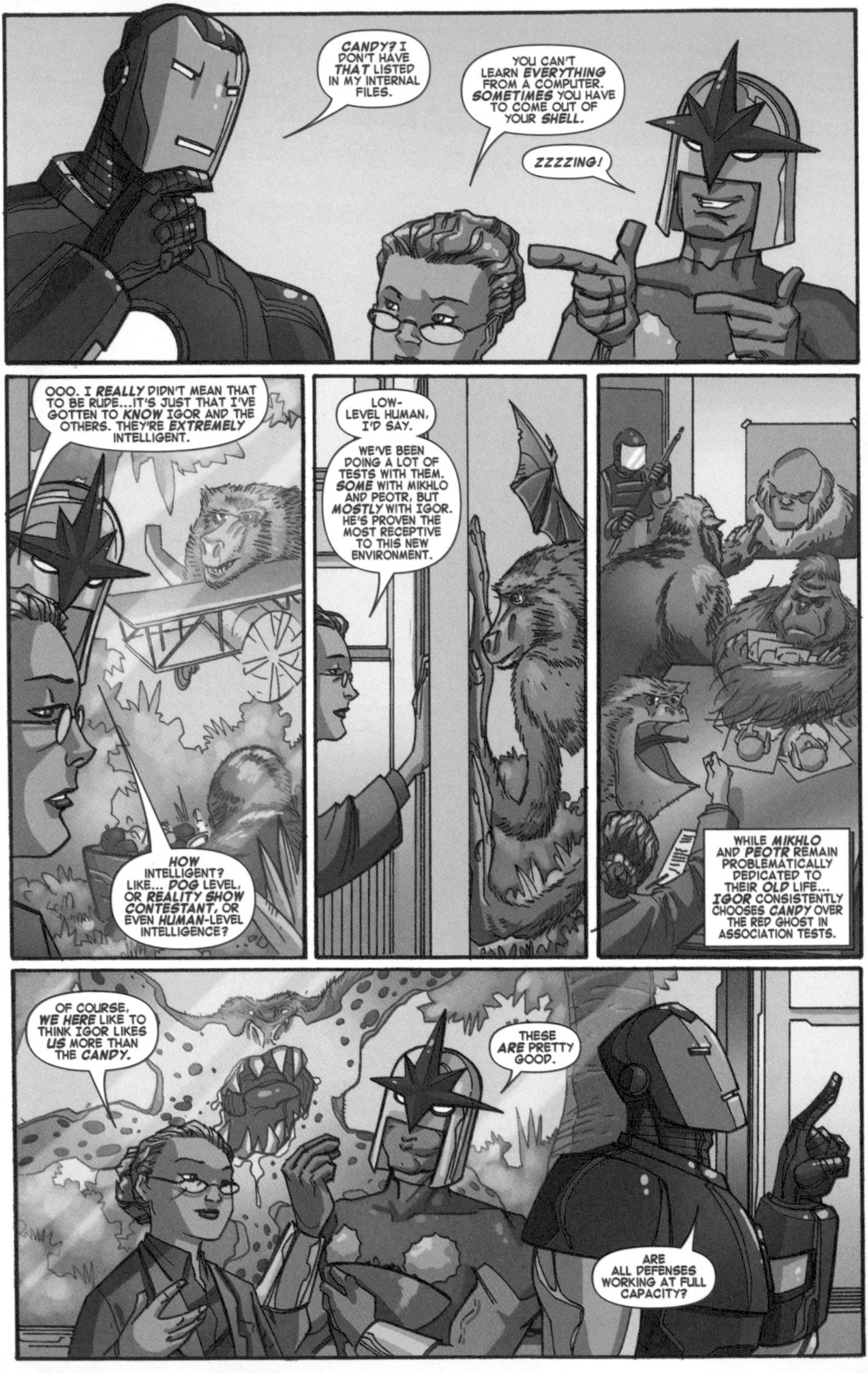
CANDY? I DON'T HAVE THAT LISTED IN MY INTERNAL FILES.
YOU CAN'T LEARN EVERYTHING FROM A COMPUTER. SOMETIMES YOU HAVE TO COME OUT OF YOUR SHELL.
ZZZZING!
OOO. I REALLY DIDN'T MEAN THAT TO BE RUDE...IT'S JUST THAT I'VE GOTTEN TO KNOW IGOR AND THE OTHERS. THEY'RE EXTREMELY INTELLIGENT.
HOW INTELLIGENT? LIKE... DOG LEVEL, OR REALITY SHOW CONTESTANT, OR EVEN HUMAN-LEVEL INTELLIGENCE?
LOW-LEVEL HUMAN, I'D SAY.
WE'VE BEEN DOING A LOT OF TESTS WITH THEM. SOME WITH MIKHLO AND PEOTR, BUT MOSTLY WITH IGOR. HE'S PROVEN THE MOST RECEPTIVE TO THIS NEW ENVIRONMENT.
WHILE MIKHLO AND PEOTR REMAIN PROBLEMATICALLY DEDICATED TO THEIR OLD LIFE... IGOR CONSISTENTLY CHOOSES CANDY OVER THE RED GHOST IN ASSOCIATION TESTS.
OF COURSE, WE HERE LIKE TO THINK IGOR LIKES US MORE THAN THE CANDY.
THESE ARE PRETTY GOOD.
ARE ALL DEFENSES WORKING AT FULL CAPACITY?

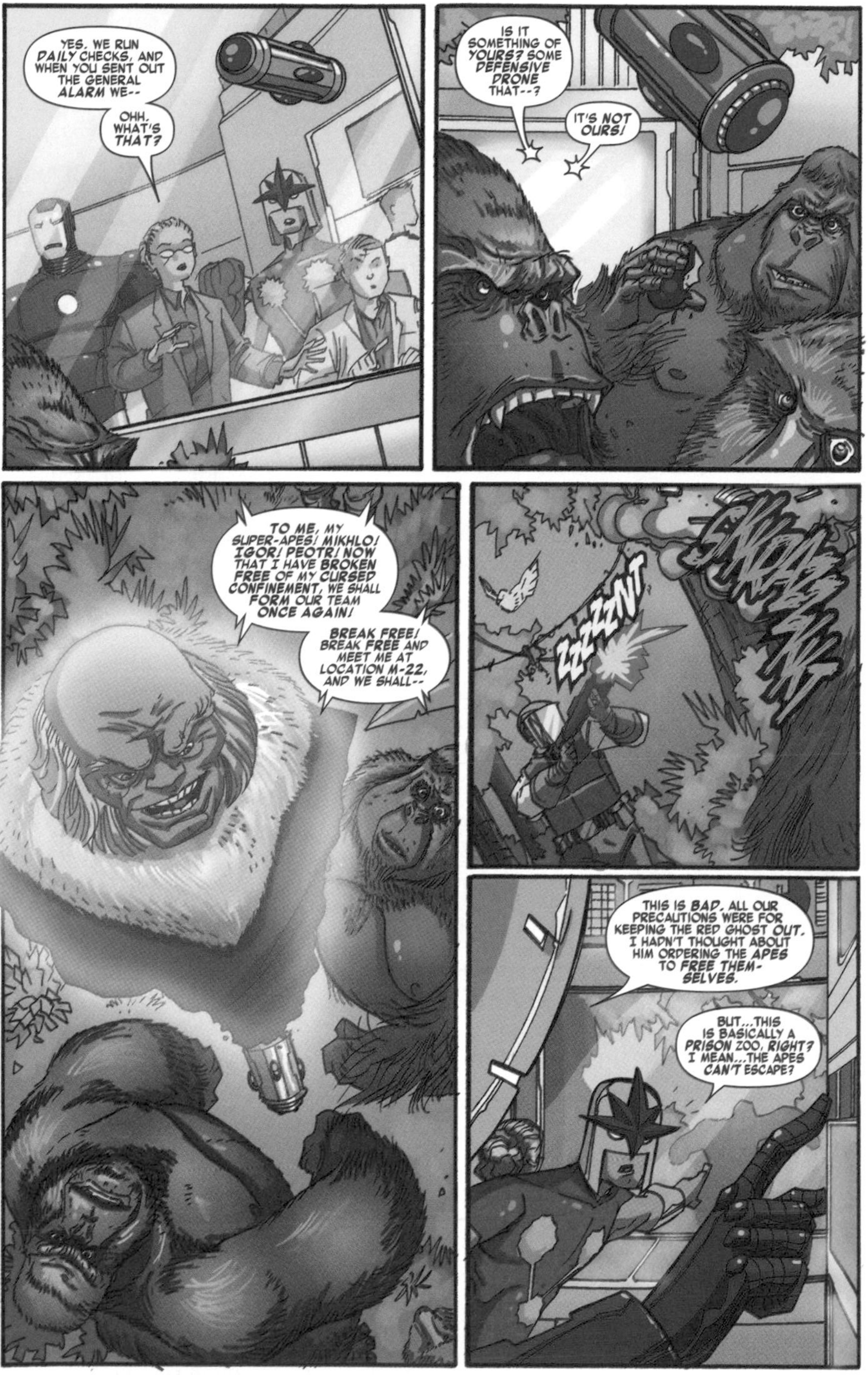
YES, WE RUN DAILY CHECKS, AND WHEN YOU SENT OUT THE GENERAL ALARM WE--
OHH. WHAT'S THAT?
IS IT SOMETHING OF YOURS? SOME DEFENSIVE DRONE THAT--?
IT'S NOT OURS!
TO ME, MY SUPER-APES! MIKHLO! IGOR! PEOTR! NOW THAT I HAVE BROKEN FREE OF MY CURSED CONFINEMENT, WE SHALL FORM OUR TEAM ONCE AGAIN!
BREAK FREE! BREAK FREE AND MEET ME AT LOCATION M-22, AND WE SHALL--
ZZZZZNT
SKRAKAKK
THIS IS BAD. ALL OUR PRECAUTIONS WERE FOR KEEPING THE RED GHOST OUT. I HADN'T THOUGHT ABOUT HIM ORDERING THE APES TO FREE THEM-SELVES.
BUT...THIS IS BASICALLY A PRISON ZOO, RIGHT? I MEAN...THE APES CAN'T ESCAPE?

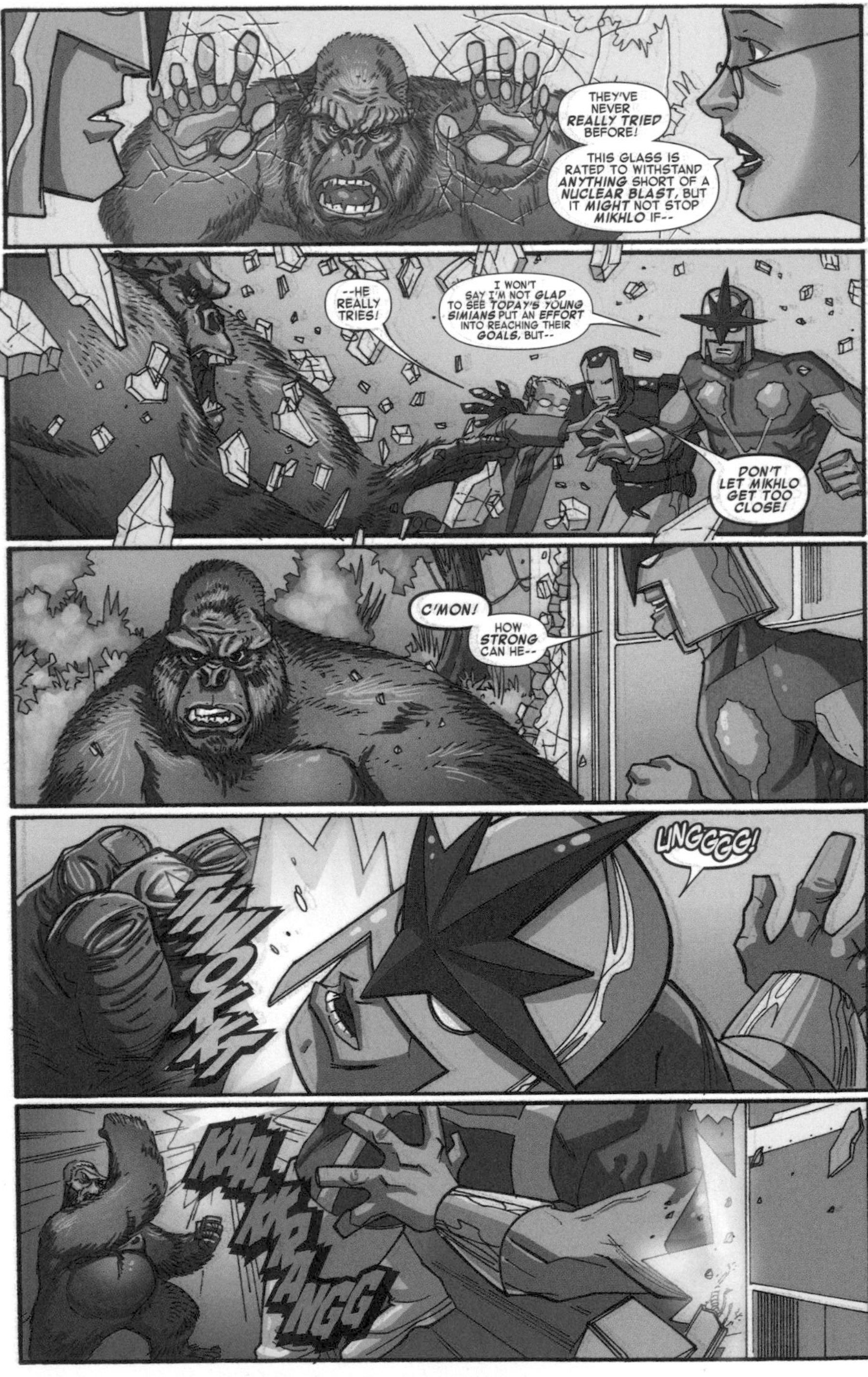
THEY'VE NEVER REALLY TRIED BEFORE!
THIS GLASS IS RATED TO WITHSTAND ANYTHING SHORT OF A NUCLEAR BLAST, BUT IT MIGHT NOT STOP MIKHLO IF--
--HE REALLY TRIES!
I WON'T SAY I'M NOT GLAD TO SEE TODAY'S YOUNG SIMIANS PUT AN EFFORT INTO REACHING THEIR GOALS, BUT--
DON'T LET MIKHLO GET TOO CLOSE!
C'MON!
HOW STRONG CAN HE--
UNGGGG!
THWOKKT
KAA-KRRANGG

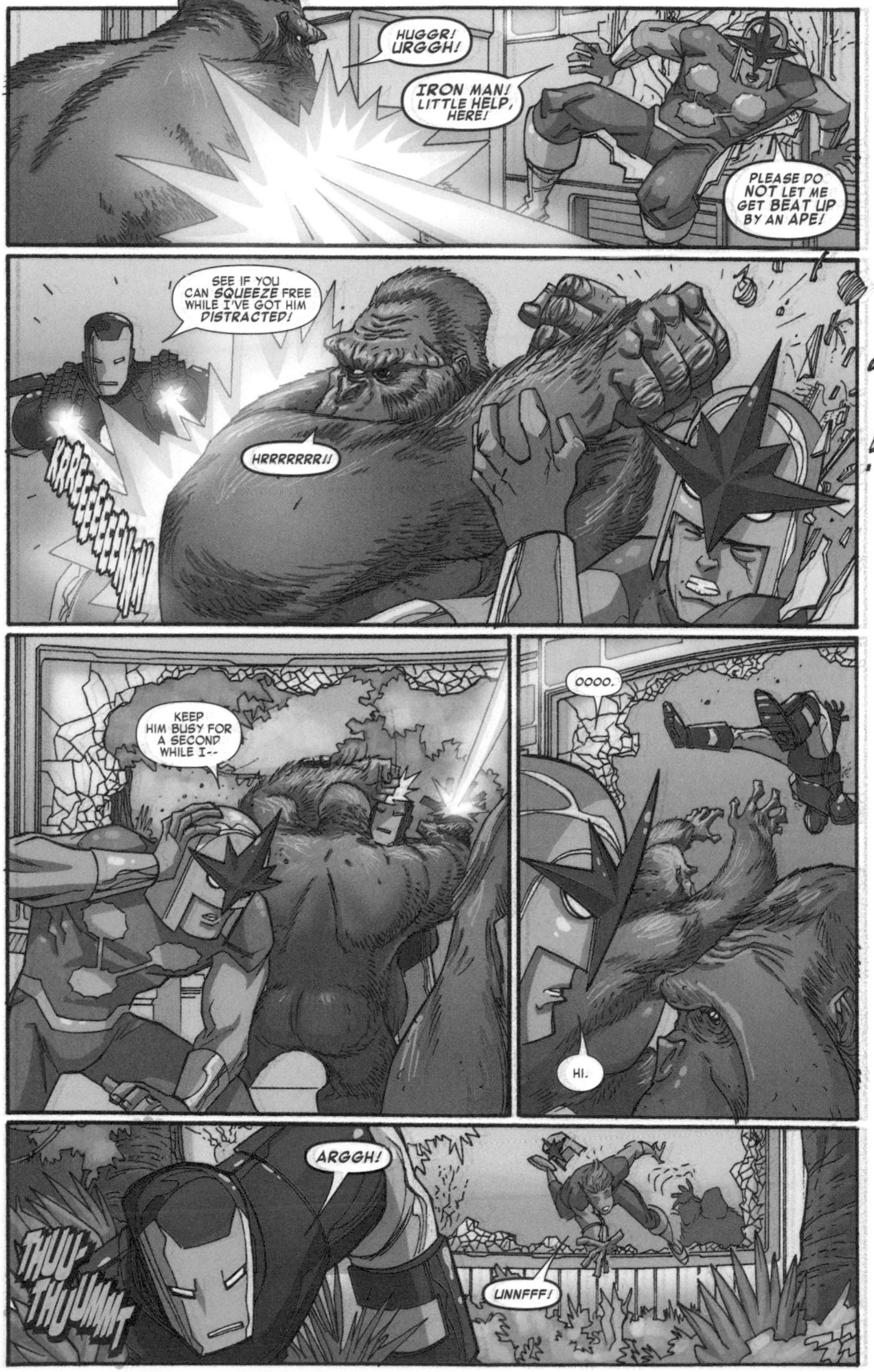
HUGGR! URGGH!
IRON MAN! LITTLE HELP, HERE!
PLEASE DO NOT LET ME GET BEAT UP BY AN APE!
SEE IF YOU CAN SQUEEZE FREE WHILE I'VE GOT HIM DISTRACTED!
KRREEEEEEEENNN
HRRRRRRR!!
KEEP HIM BUSY FOR A SECOND WHILE I--
OOOO.
HI.
ARGGH!
THUU-THUUMMT
UNNFFF!

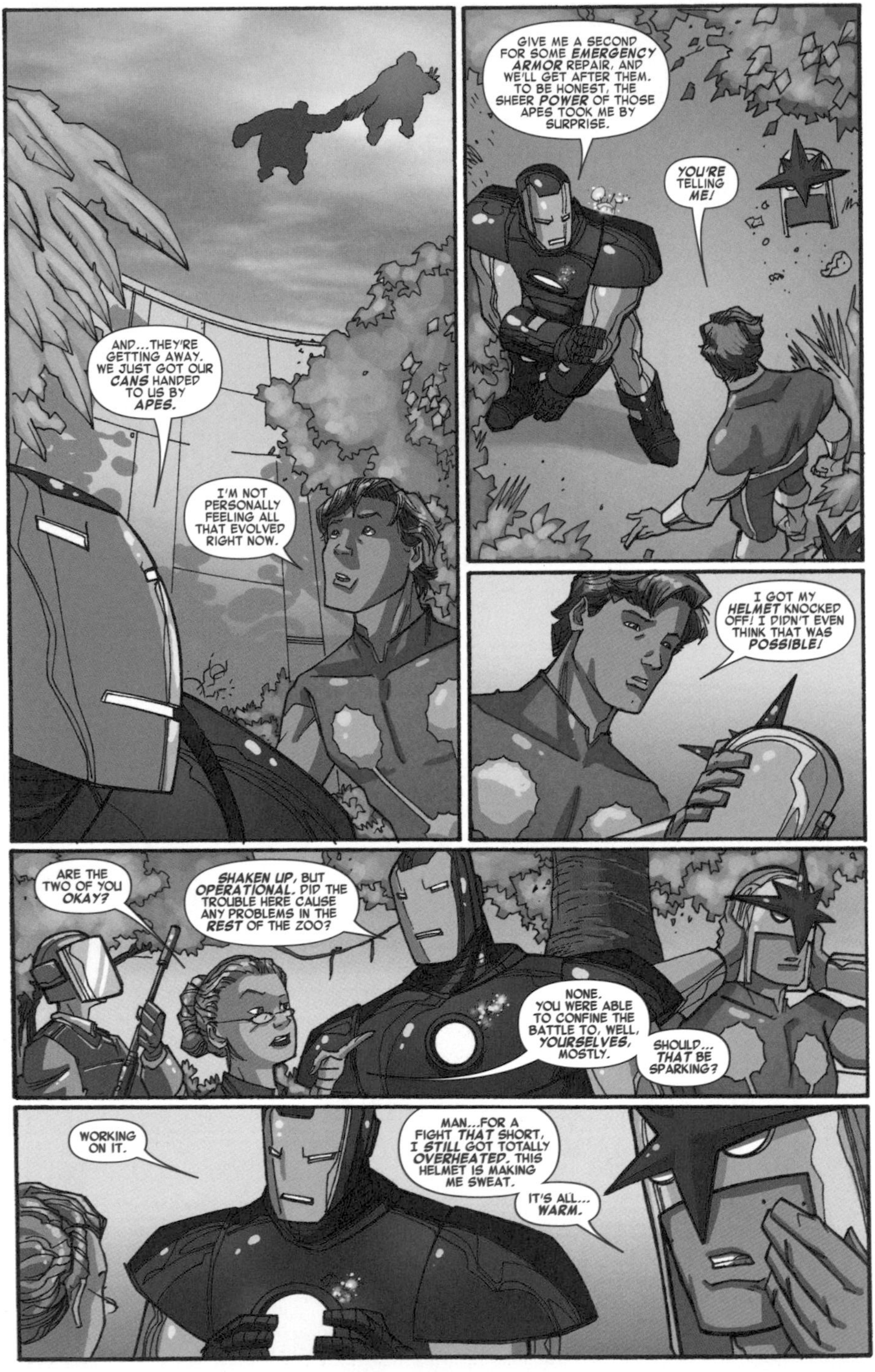
AND...THEY'RE GETTING AWAY. WE JUST GOT OUR CANS HANDED TO US BY APES.
I'M NOT PERSONALLY FEELING ALL THAT EVOLVED RIGHT NOW.
GIVE ME A SECOND FOR SOME EMERGENCY ARMOR REPAIR, AND WE'LL GET AFTER THEM. TO BE HONEST, THE SHEER POWER OF THOSE APES TOOK ME BY SURPRISE.
YOU'RE TELLING ME!
I GOT MY HELMET KNOCKED OFF! I DIDN'T EVEN THINK THAT WAS POSSIBLE!
ARE THE TWO OF YOU OKAY?
SHAKEN UP, BUT OPERATIONAL. DID THE TROUBLE HERE CAUSE ANY PROBLEMS IN THE REST OF THE ZOO?
NONE. YOU WERE ABLE TO CONFINE THE BATTLE TO, WELL, YOURSELVES, MOSTLY.
SHOULD... THAT BE SPARKING?
WORKING ON IT.
MAN...FOR A FIGHT THAT SHORT, I STILL GOT TOTALLY OVERHEATED. THIS HELMET IS MAKING ME SWEAT.
IT'S ALL... WARM.

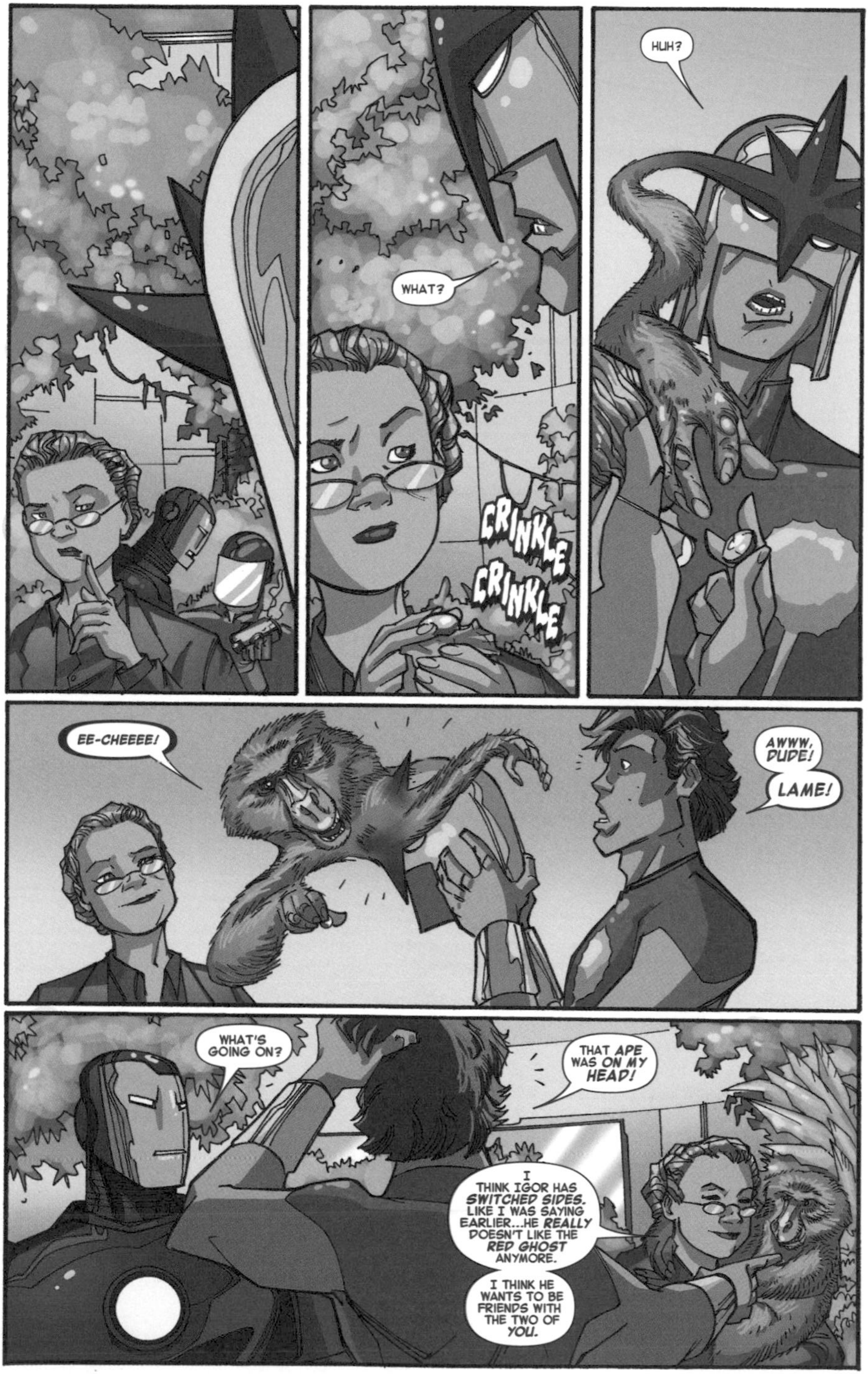
WHAT?
CRINKLE CRINKLE
HUH?
EE-CHEEEE!
AWWW, DUDE!
LAME!
WHAT'S GOING ON?
THAT APE WAS ON MY HEAD!
I THINK IGOR HAS SWITCHED SIDES. LIKE I WAS SAYING EARLIER...HE REALLY DOESN'T LIKE THE RED GHOST ANYMORE.
I THINK HE WANTS TO BE FRIENDS WITH THE TWO OF YOU.

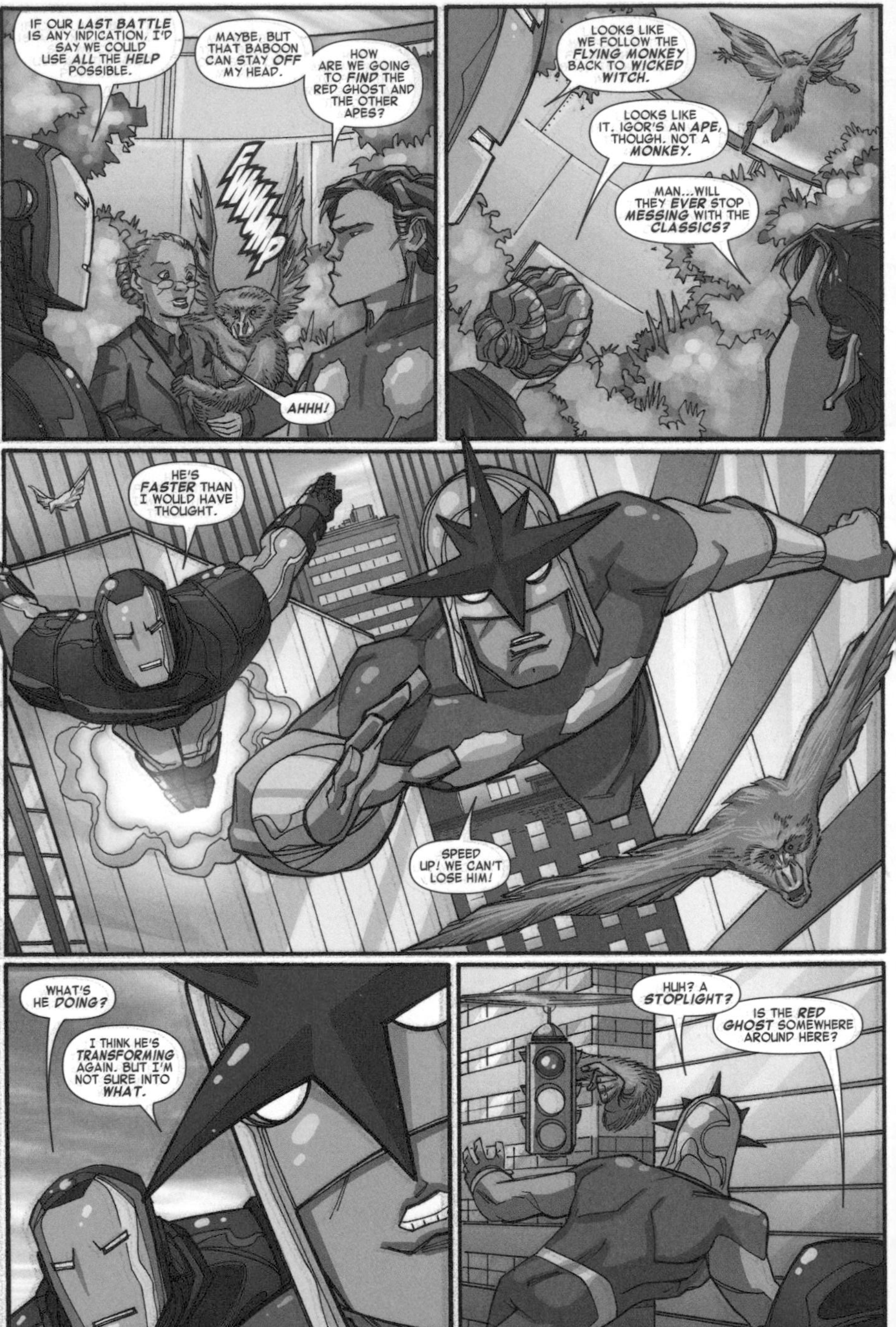
IF OUR LAST BATTLE IS ANY INDICATION, I'D SAY WE COULD USE ALL THE HELP POSSIBLE.
MAYBE, BUT THAT BABOON CAN STAY OFF MY HEAD.
HOW ARE WE GOING TO FIND THE RED GHOST AND THE OTHER APES?
FWWUMP
AHHH!
LOOKS LIKE WE FOLLOW THE FLYING MONKEY BACK TO WICKED WITCH.
LOOKS LIKE IT. IGOR'S AN APE, THOUGH. NOT A MONKEY.
MAN...WILL THEY EVER STOP MESSING WITH THE CLASSICS?
HE'S FASTER THAN I WOULD HAVE THOUGHT.
SPEED UP! WE CAN'T LOSE HIM!
WHAT'S HE DOING?
I THINK HE'S TRANSFORMING AGAIN. BUT I'M NOT SURE INTO WHAT.
HUH? A STOPLIGHT?
IS THE RED GHOST SOMEWHERE AROUND HERE?

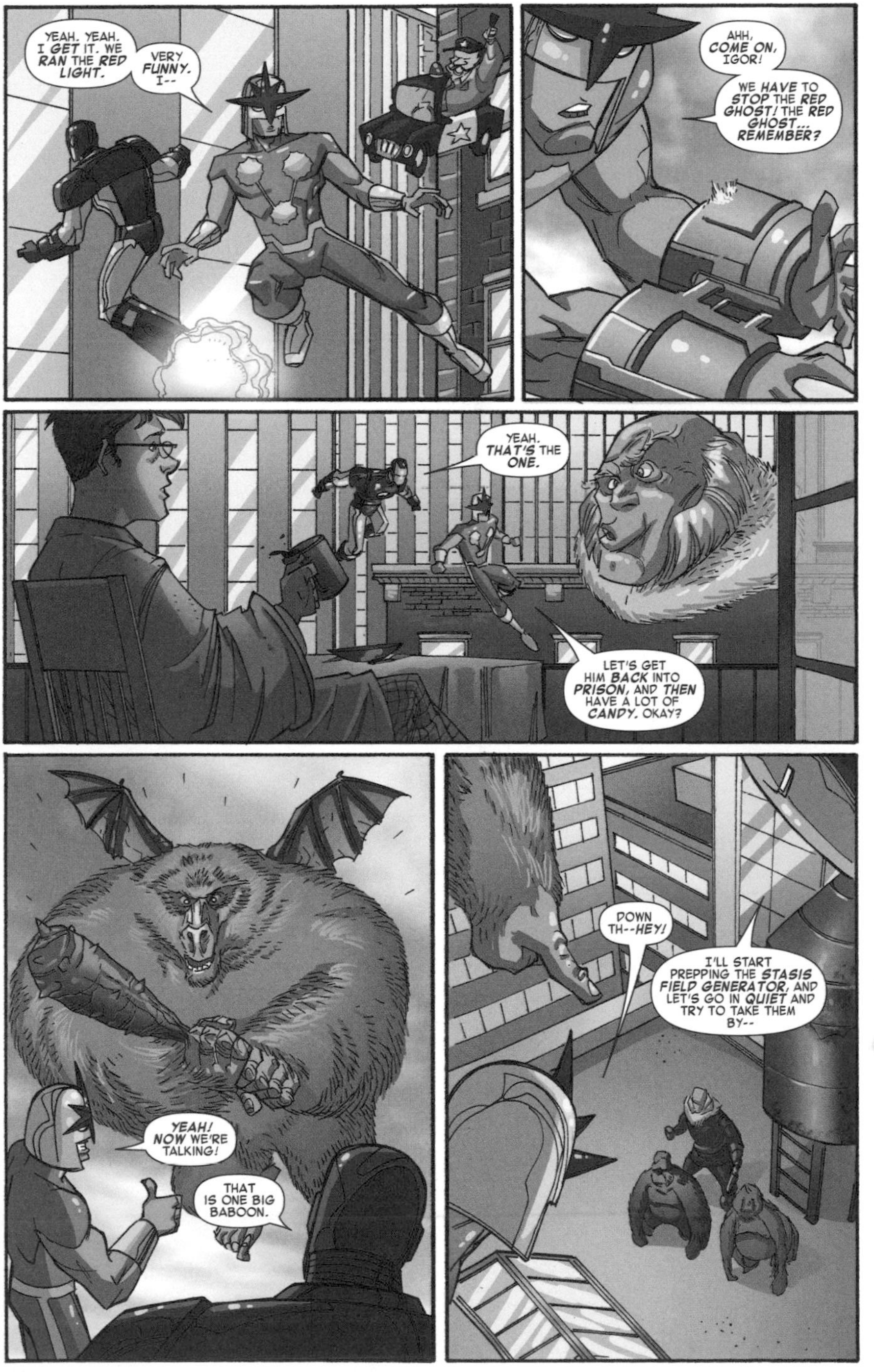
YEAH. YEAH. I GET IT. WE RAN THE RED LIGHT.
VERY FUNNY. I--
AHH, COME ON, IGOR!
WE HAVE TO STOP THE RED GHOST! THE RED GHOST... REMEMBER?
YEAH. THAT'S THE ONE.
LET'S GET HIM BACK INTO PRISON, AND THEN HAVE A LOT OF CANDY. OKAY?
YEAH! NOW WE'RE TALKING!
THAT IS ONE BIG BABOON.
DOWN TH--HEY!
I'LL START PREPPING THE STASIS FIELD GENERATOR, AND LET'S GO IN QUIET AND TRY TO TAKE THEM BY--

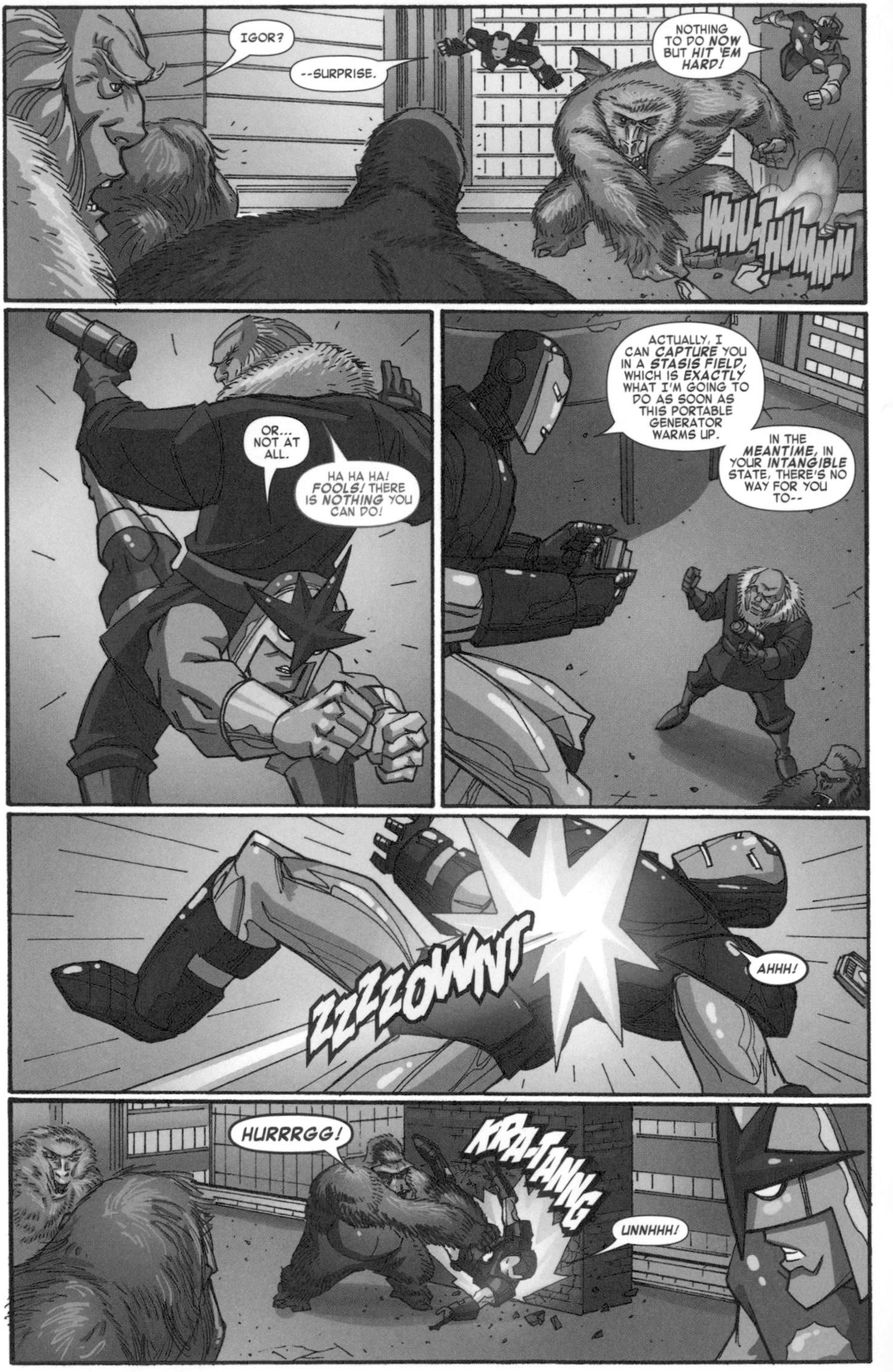
IGOR?
--SURPRISE.
NOTHING TO DO NOW BUT HIT 'EM HARD!
WHU-THUMMM
OR... NOT AT ALL.
HA HA HA! FOOLS! THERE IS NOTHING YOU CAN DO!
ACTUALLY, I CAN CAPTURE YOU IN A STASIS FIELD, WHICH IS EXACTLY WHAT I'M GOING TO DO AS SOON AS THIS PORTABLE GENERATOR WARMS UP.
IN THE MEANTIME, IN YOUR INTANGIBLE STATE, THERE'S NO WAY FOR YOU TO--
ZZZZOWNT
AHHH!
HURRRGG!
KRA-TANNG
UNNHHH!

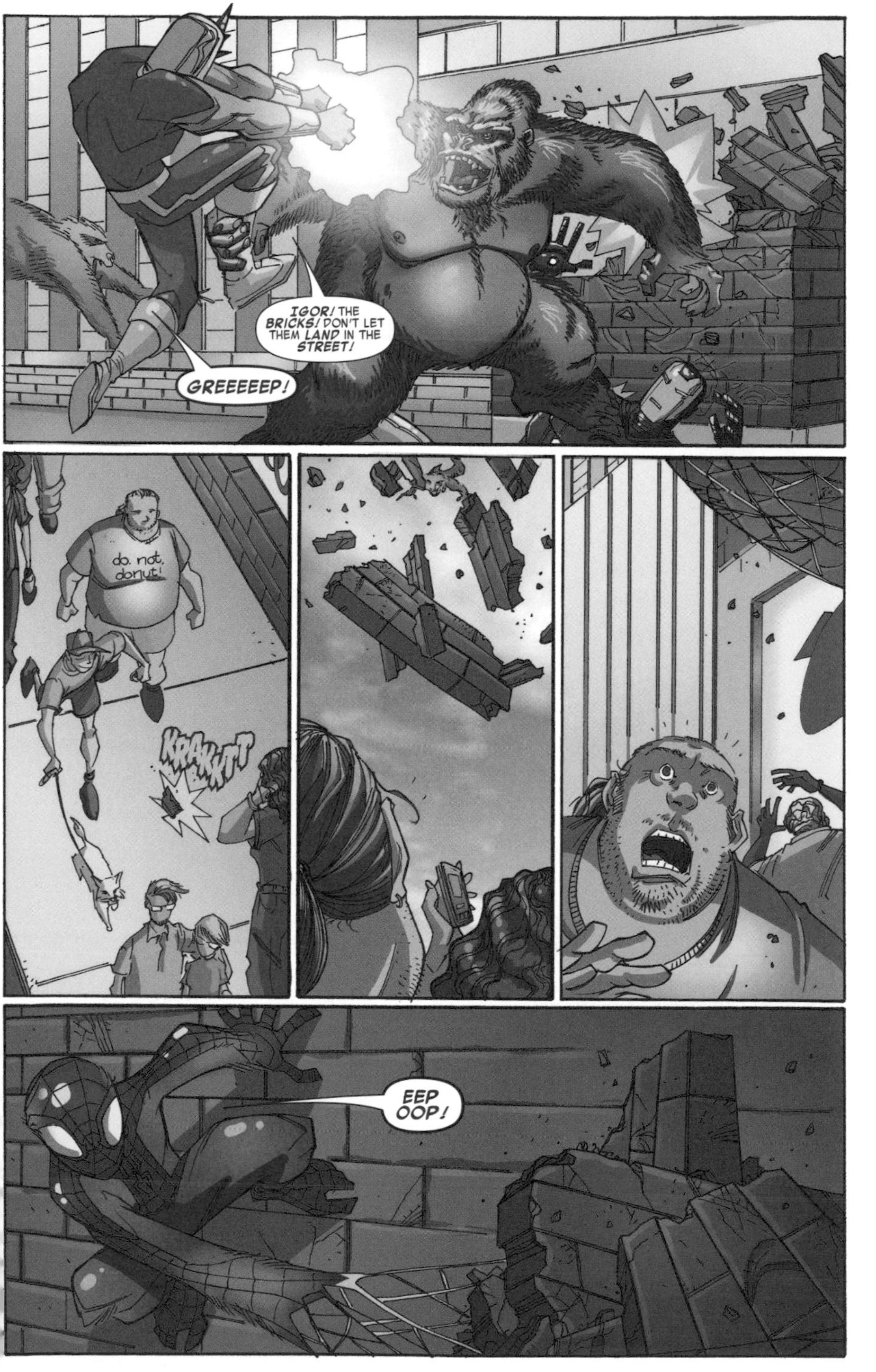
IGOR! THE BRICKS! DON'T LET THEM LAND IN THE STREET!
GREEEEEP!
do. not. donut!
KRAKKTT
EEP OOP!

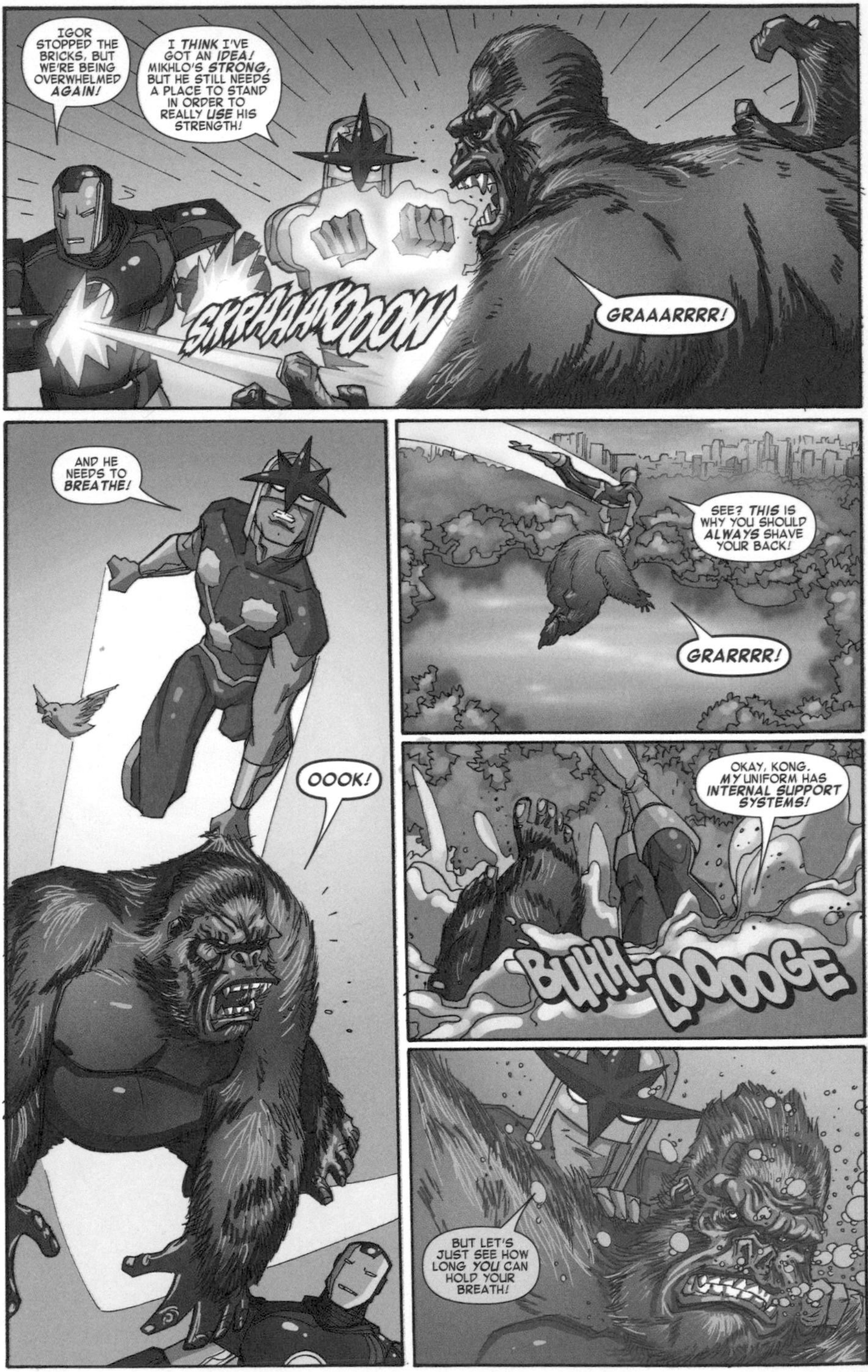
IGOR STOPPED THE BRICKS, BUT WE'RE BEING OVERWHELMED AGAIN!
I THINK I'VE GOT AN IDEA! MIKHLO'S STRONG, BUT HE STILL NEEDS A PLACE TO STAND IN ORDER TO REALLY USE HIS STRENGTH!
SKRAAAKOOOW
GRAAARRRR!
AND HE NEEDS TO BREATHE!
OOOK!
SEE? THIS IS WHY YOU SHOULD ALWAYS SHAVE YOUR BACK!
GRARRRR!
OKAY, KONG. MY UNIFORM HAS INTERNAL SUPPORT SYSTEMS!
BUHH-LOOOOGE
BUT LET'S JUST SEE HOW LONG YOU CAN HOLD YOUR BREATH!

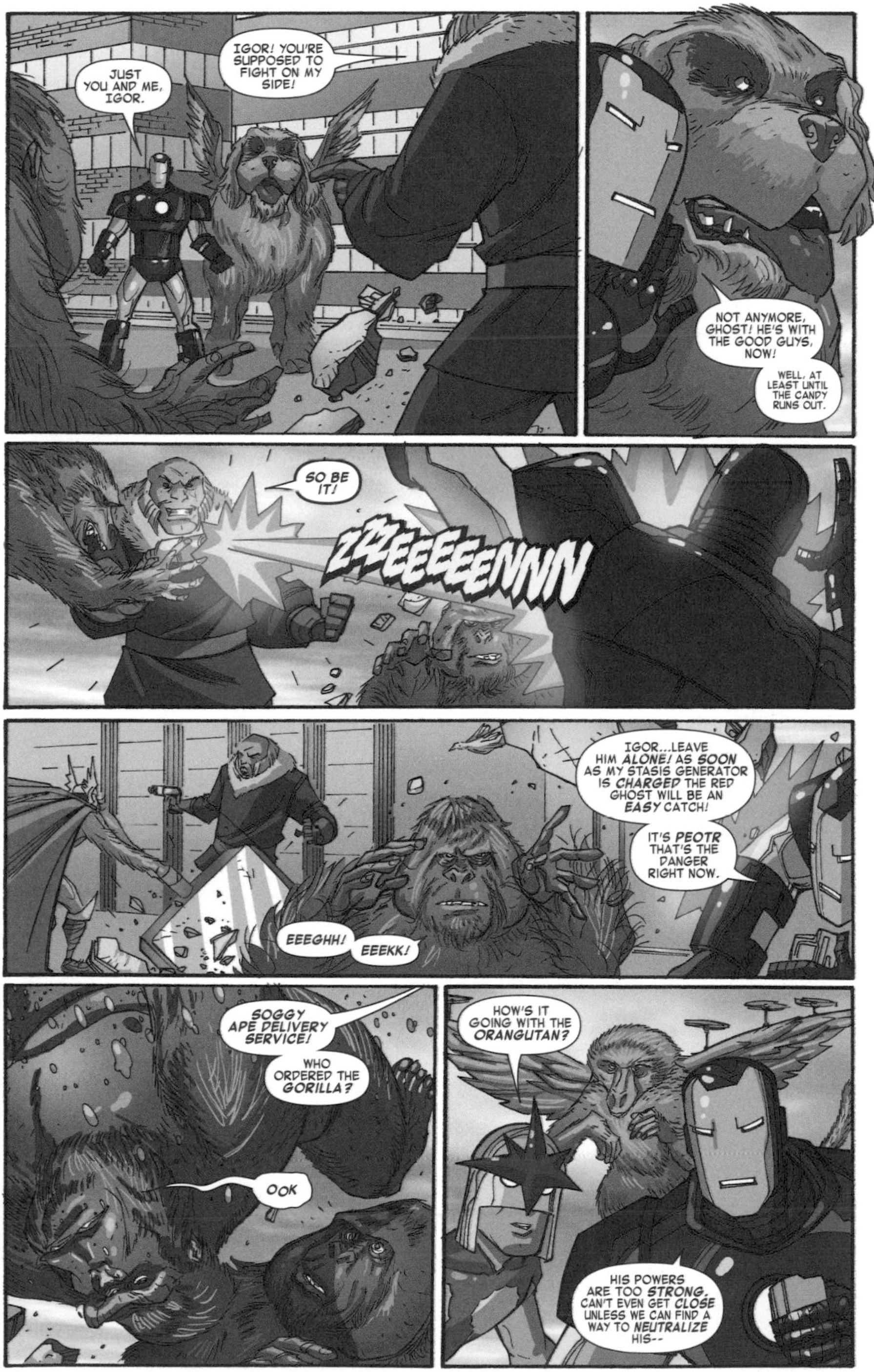

JUST YOU AND ME, IGOR.
IGOR! YOU'RE SUPPOSED TO FIGHT ON MY SIDE!
NOT ANYMORE, GHOST! HE'S WITH THE GOOD GUYS, NOW!
WELL, AT LEAST UNTIL THE CANDY RUNS OUT.
SO BE IT!
ZZZEEEEEENNNN
IGOR...LEAVE HIM ALONE! AS SOON AS MY STASIS GENERATOR IS CHARGED THE RED GHOST WILL BE AN EASY CATCH!
IT'S PEOTR THAT'S THE DANGER RIGHT NOW.
EEEGHH!
EEEKK!
SOGGY APE DELIVERY SERVICE!
WHO ORDERED THE GORILLA?
OOK
HOW'S IT GOING WITH THE ORANGUTAN?
HIS POWERS ARE TOO STRONG. CAN'T EVEN GET CLOSE UNLESS WE CAN FIND A WAY TO NEUTRALIZE HIS--

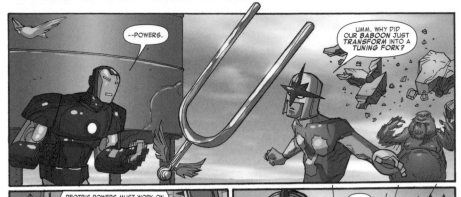

--POWERS.

UMM, WHY DID OUR *BABOON* JUST *TRANSFORM* INTO A *TUNING FORK?*

PEOTR'S POWERS MUST WORK ON A CERTAIN WAVELENGTH! IGOR'S EMITTING A FREQUENCY THAT'S MOMENTARILY *CANCELING* THE ORANGUTAN'S ABILITIES!

HE'S *VULNERABLE* NOW!

GOT HIM!

THWOKK

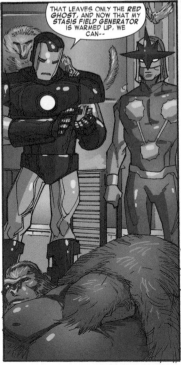

THAT LEAVES ONLY THE *RED GHOST*, AND NOW THAT MY *STASIS FIELD GENERATOR* IS WARMED UP, WE CAN--

SPAKT

TSSSSVVVT

HAH!

SO MUCH FOR *THAT*, IRON MAN. AND NOW THAT YOU CAN'T *STOP* ME, I'LL BE BACK FOR MY APES *ANOTHER* TIME.

IN FACT, SINCE I'M *COMPLETELY INTANGIBLE*, MAYBE I'LL JUST WAIT UNTIL THEY WAKE UP, AND--

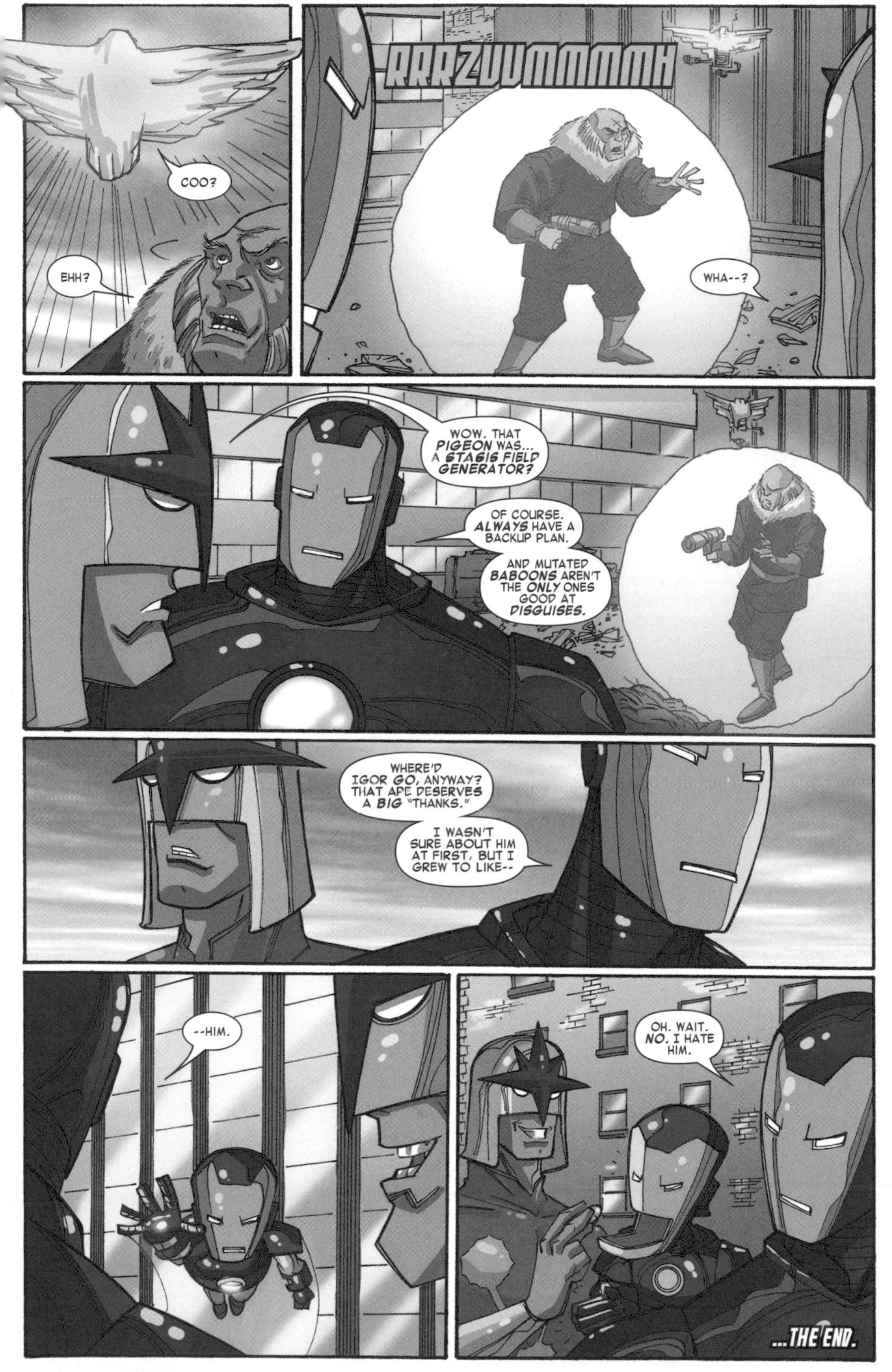
COO?
EHH?
RRRZUUMMMMMH
WHA--?
WOW. THAT PIGEON WAS... A STASIS FIELD GENERATOR?
OF COURSE. ALWAYS HAVE A BACKUP PLAN.
AND MUTATED BABOONS AREN'T THE ONLY ONES GOOD AT DISGUISES.
WHERE'D IGOR GO, ANYWAY? THAT APE DESERVES A BIG "THANKS."
I WASN'T SURE ABOUT HIM AT FIRST, BUT I GREW TO LIKE--
--HIM.
OH. WAIT. NO. I HATE HIM.
...THE END.

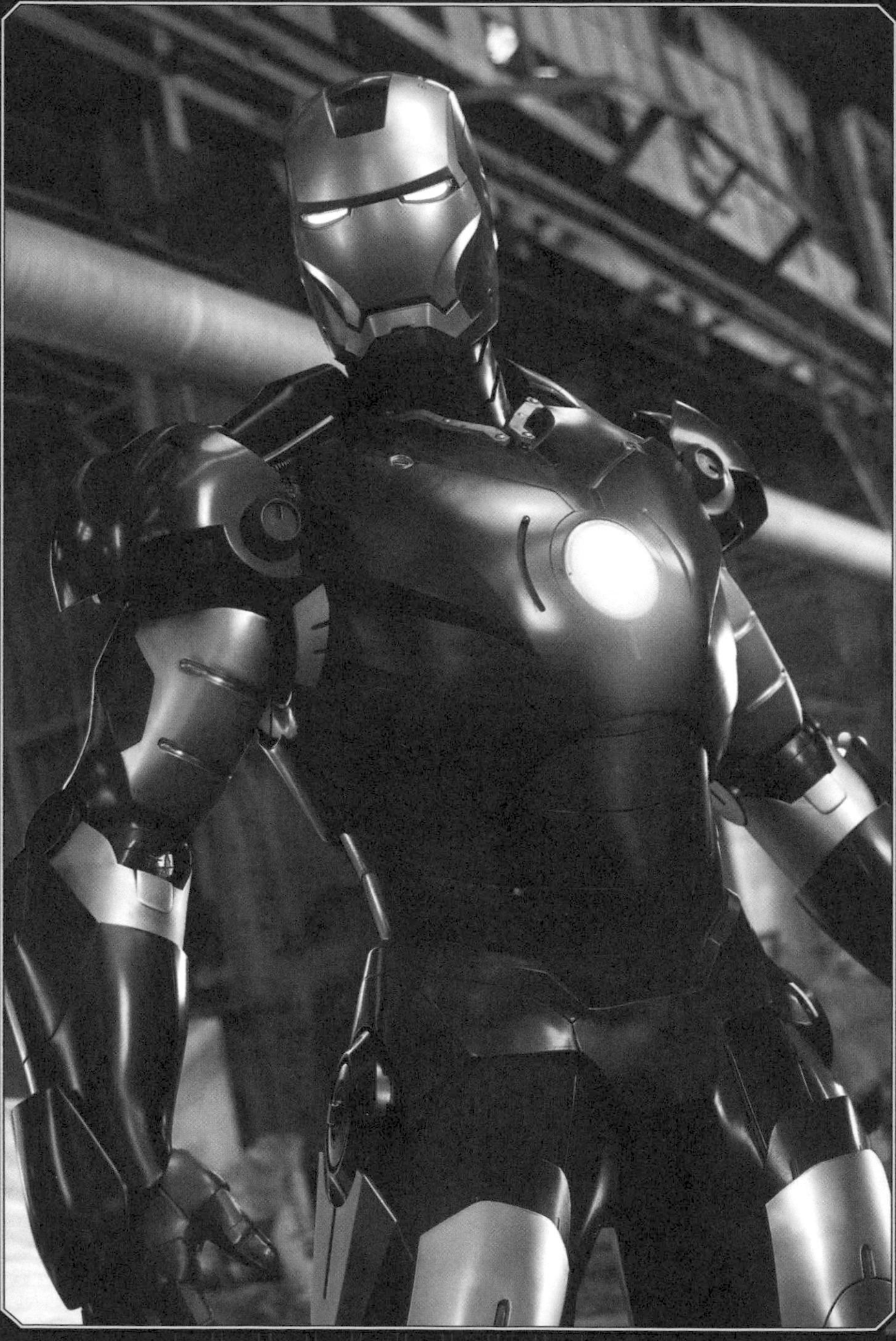

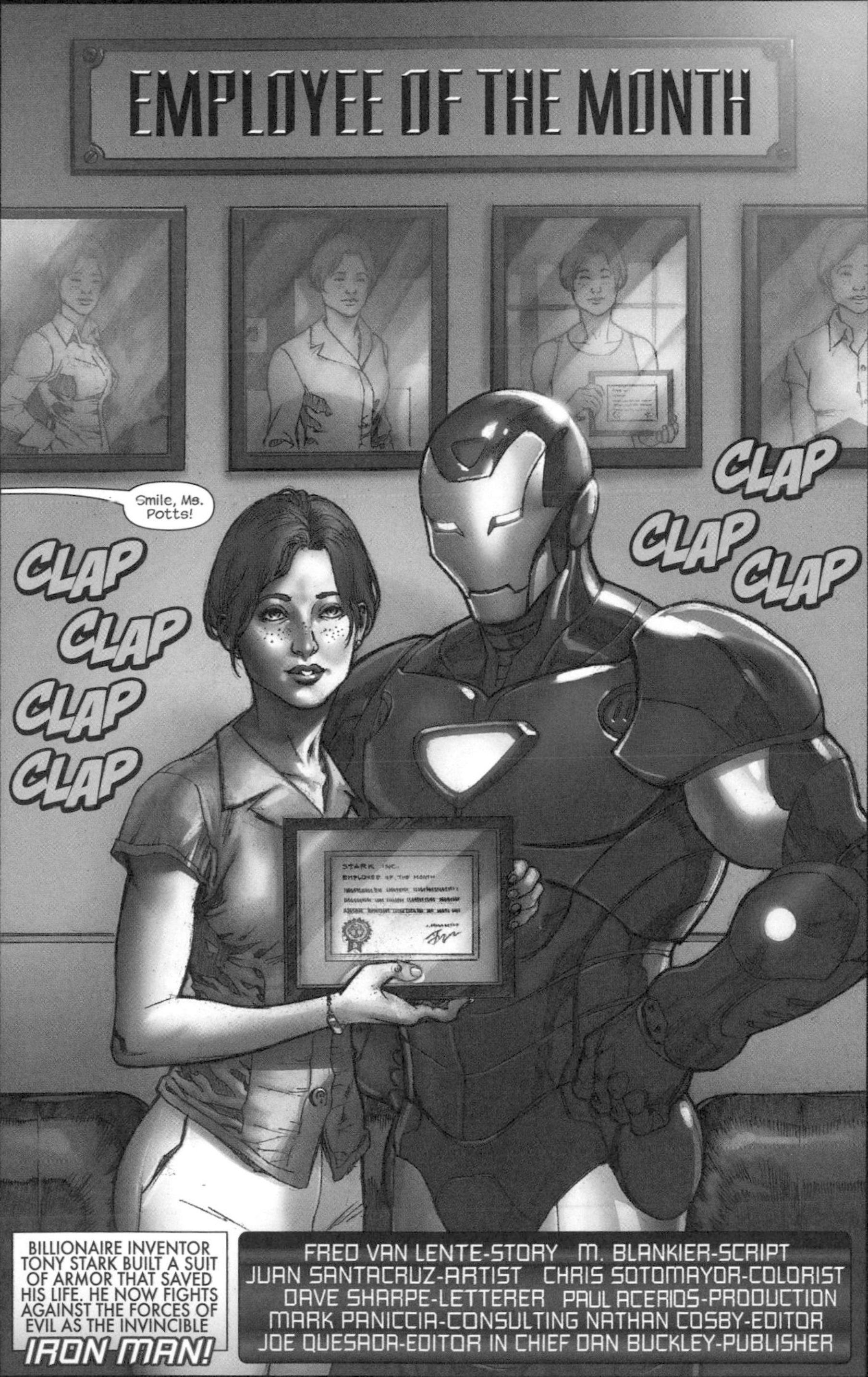
EMPLOYEE OF THE MONTH
Smile, Ms. Potts!
CLAP
CLAP
CLAP
CLAP
CLAP
CLAP
CLAP
BILLIONAIRE INVENTOR TONY STARK BUILT A SUIT OF ARMOR THAT SAVED HIS LIFE. HE NOW FIGHTS AGAINST THE FORCES OF EVIL AS THE INVINCIBLE IRON MAN!
FRED VAN LENTE-STORY M. BLANKIER-SCRIPT
JUAN SANTACRUZ-ARTIST CHRIS SOTOMAYOR-COLORIST
DAVE SHARPE-LETTERER PAUL ACERIOS-PRODUCTION
MARK PANICCIA-CONSULTING NATHAN COSBY-EDITOR
JOE QUESADA-EDITOR IN CHIEF DAN BUCKLEY-PUBLISHER

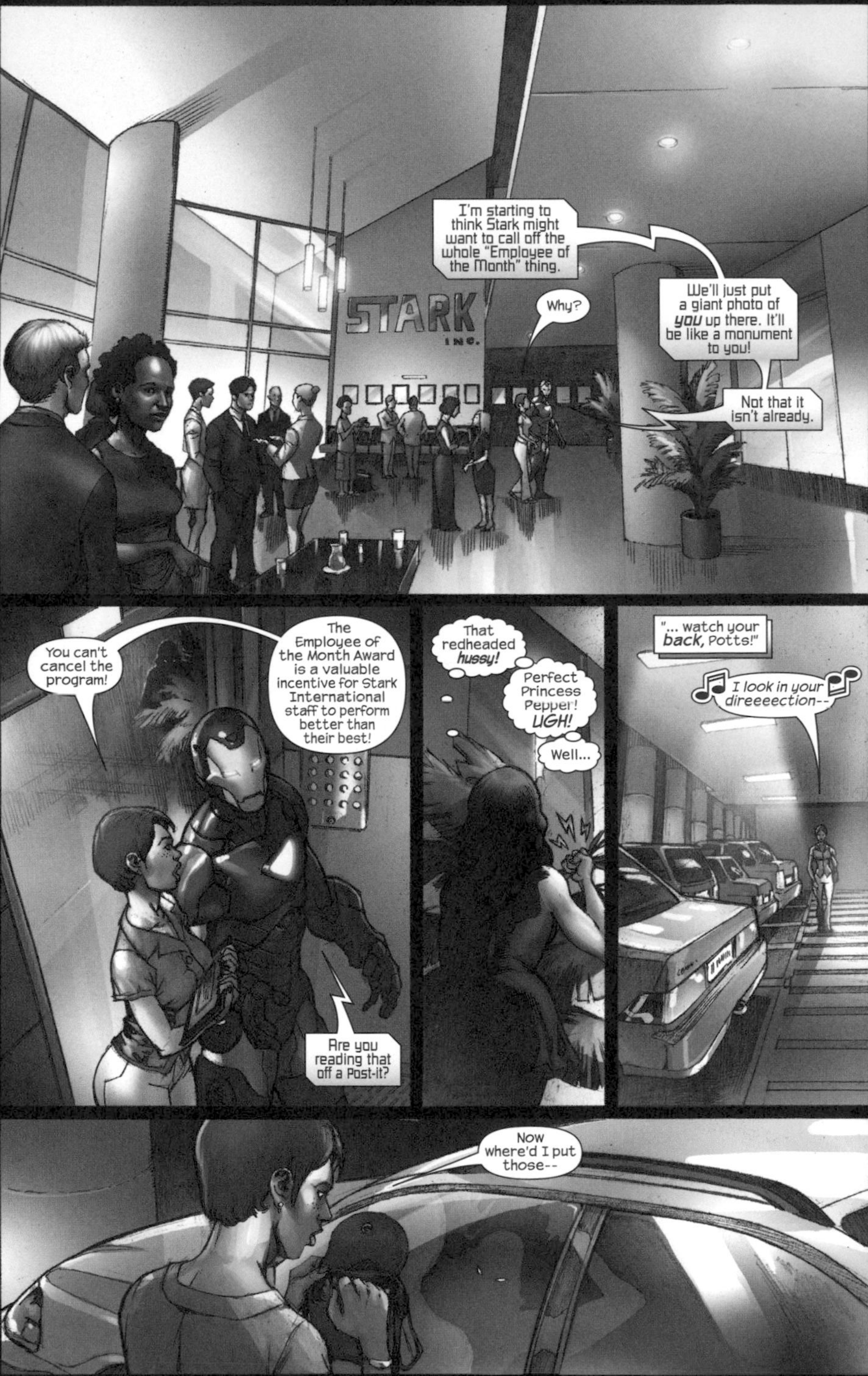
STARK INC.
I'm starting to think Stark might want to call off the whole "Employee of the Month" thing.
Why?
We'll just put a giant photo of *you* up there. It'll be like a monument to you!
Not that it isn't already.
You can't cancel the program!
The Employee of the Month Award is a valuable incentive for Stark International staff to perform better than their best!
Are you reading that off a Post-it?
That redheaded *hussy!*
Perfect Princess Pepper! *UGH!*
Well...
"... watch your *back,* Potts!"
I look in your direeeection--
Now where'd I put those--

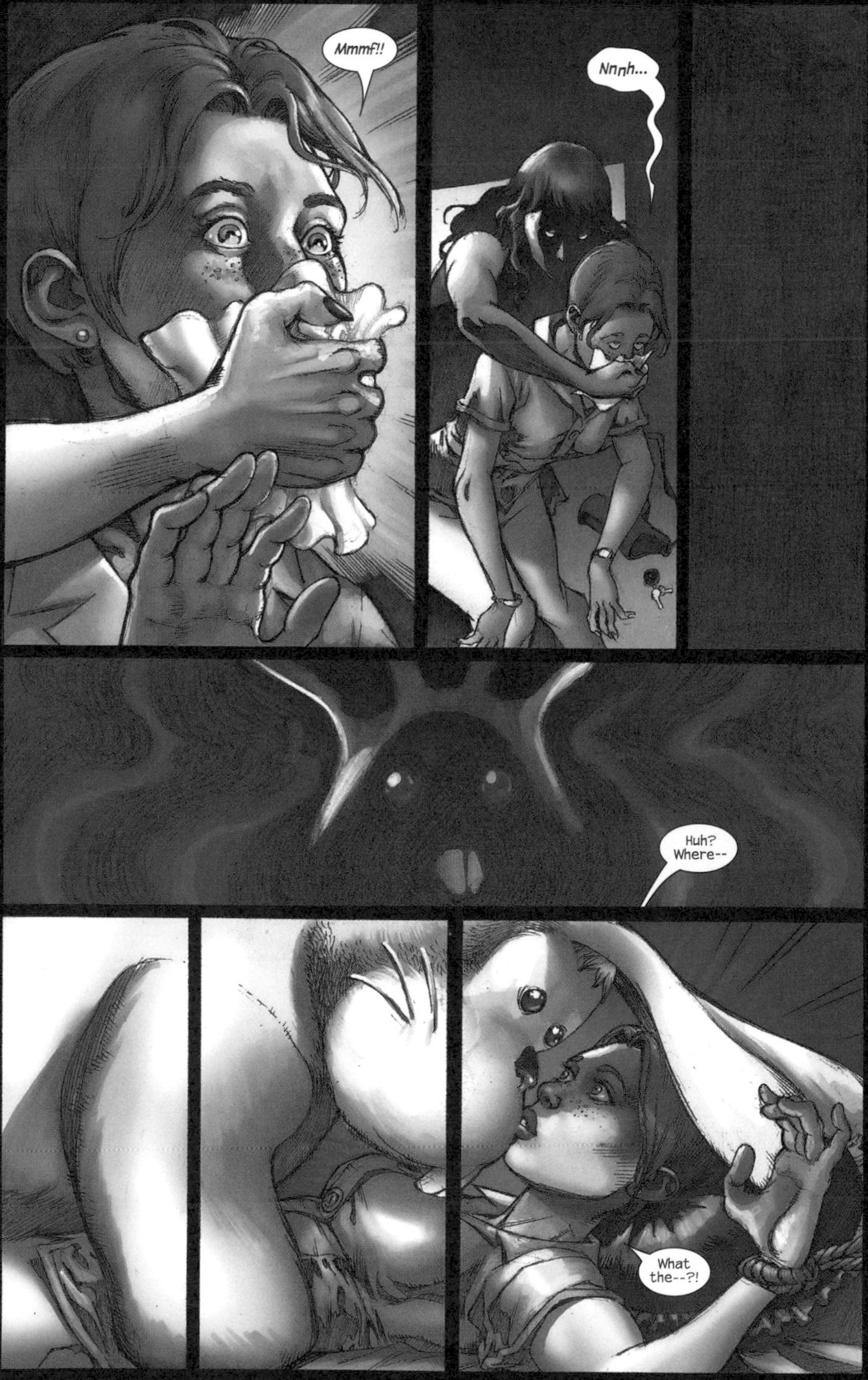
Mmmf!!
Nnnh...
Huh? Where--
What the--?!

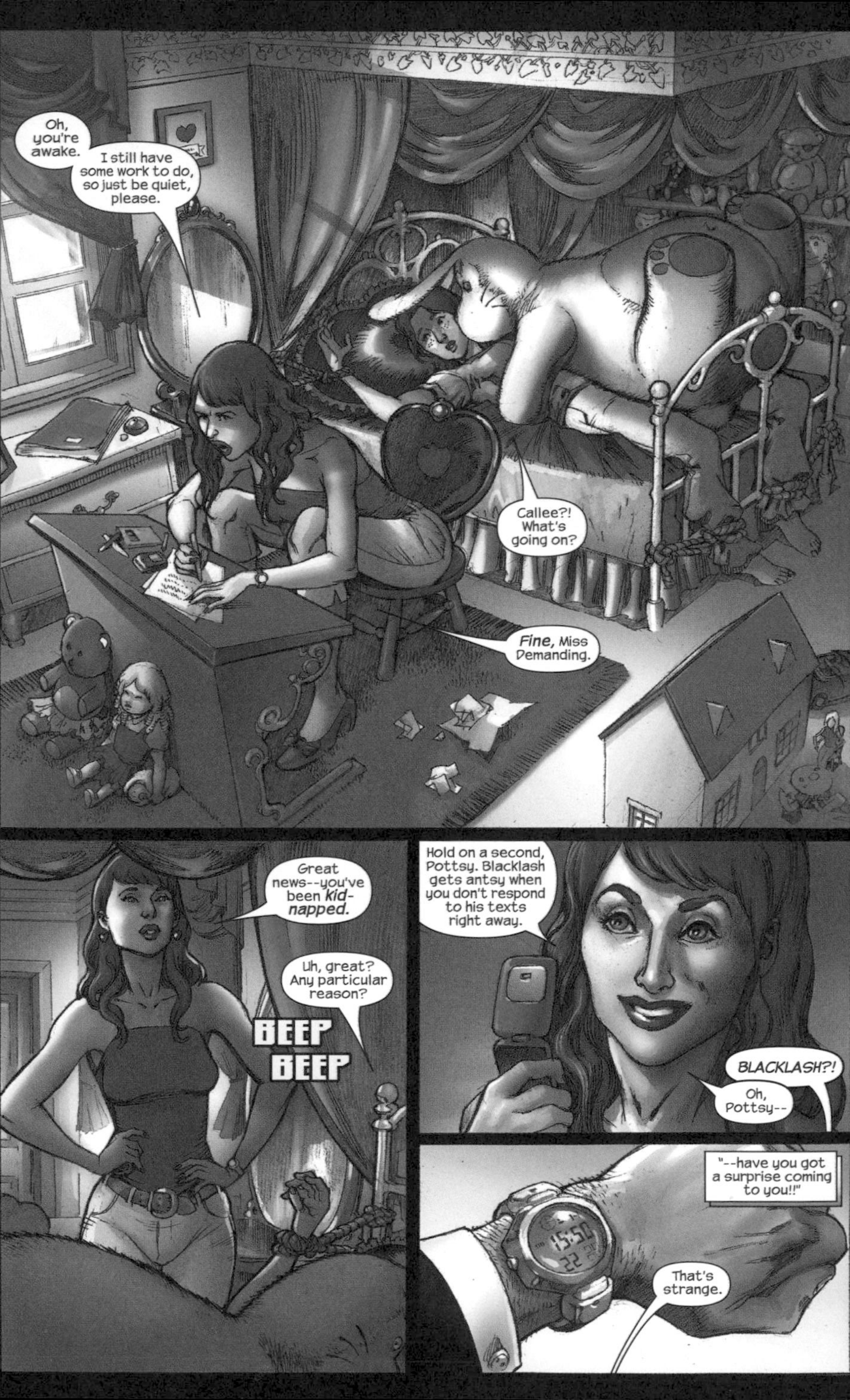

Oh, you're awake.
I still have some work to do, so just be quiet, please.
Callee?! What's going on?
Fine, Miss Demanding.
Great news--you've been kid-napped.
Uh, great? Any particular reason?
BEEP BEEP
Hold on a second, Pottsy. Blacklash gets antsy when you don't respond to his texts right away.
BLACKLASH?!
Oh, Pottsy--
"--have you got a surprise coming to you!!"
15:50
22
That's strange.

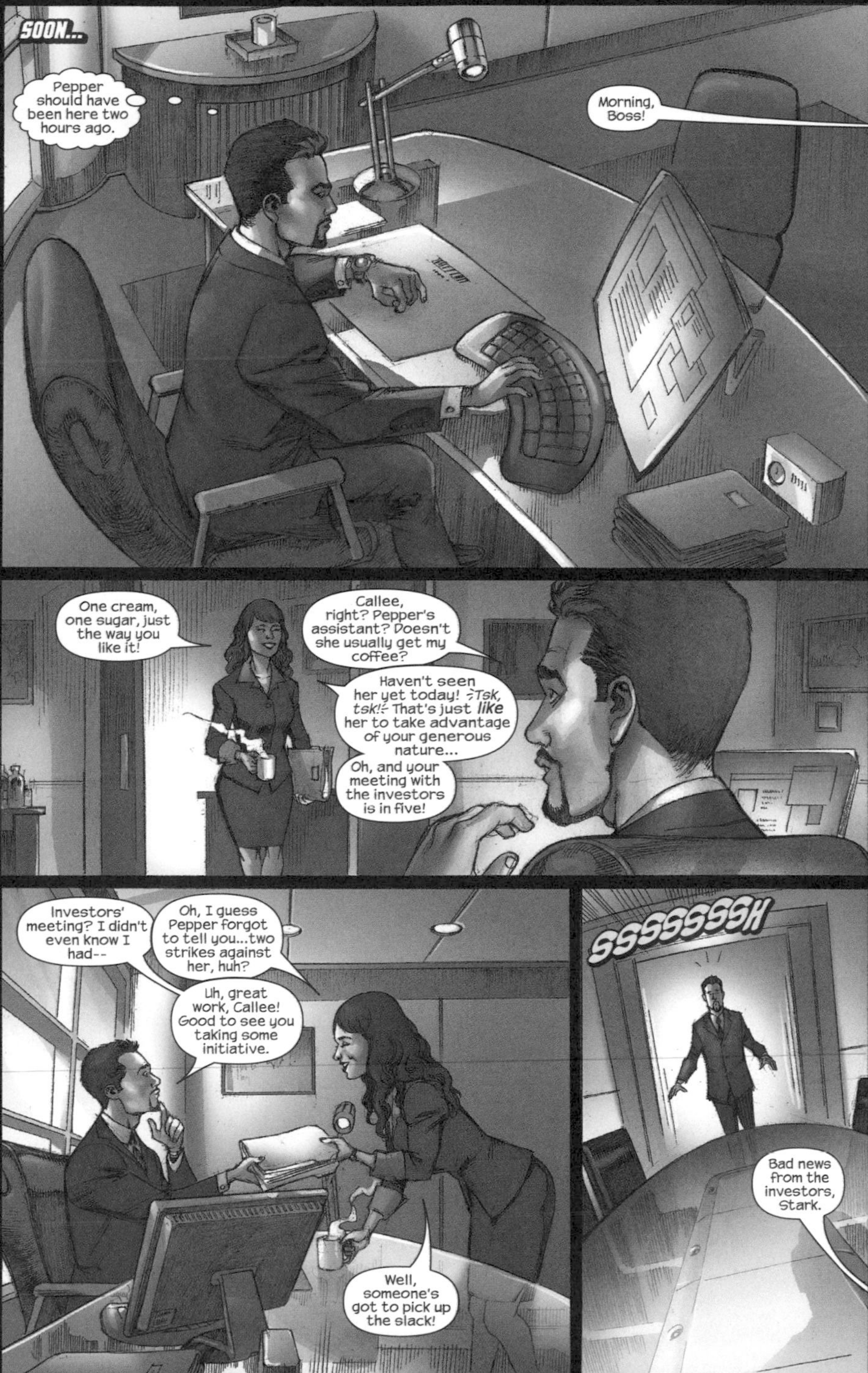
SOON...
Pepper should have been here two hours ago.
Morning, Boss!
One cream, one sugar, just the way you like it!
Callee, right? Pepper's assistant? Doesn't she usually get my coffee?
Haven't seen her yet today! -Tsk, tsk!- That's just like her to take advantage of your generous nature...
Oh, and your meeting with the investors is in five!
Investors' meeting? I didn't even know I had--
Oh, I guess Pepper forgot to tell you...two strikes against her, huh?
Uh, great work, Callee! Good to see you taking some initiative.
Well, someone's got to pick up the slack!
SSSSSSSH
Bad news from the investors, Stark.

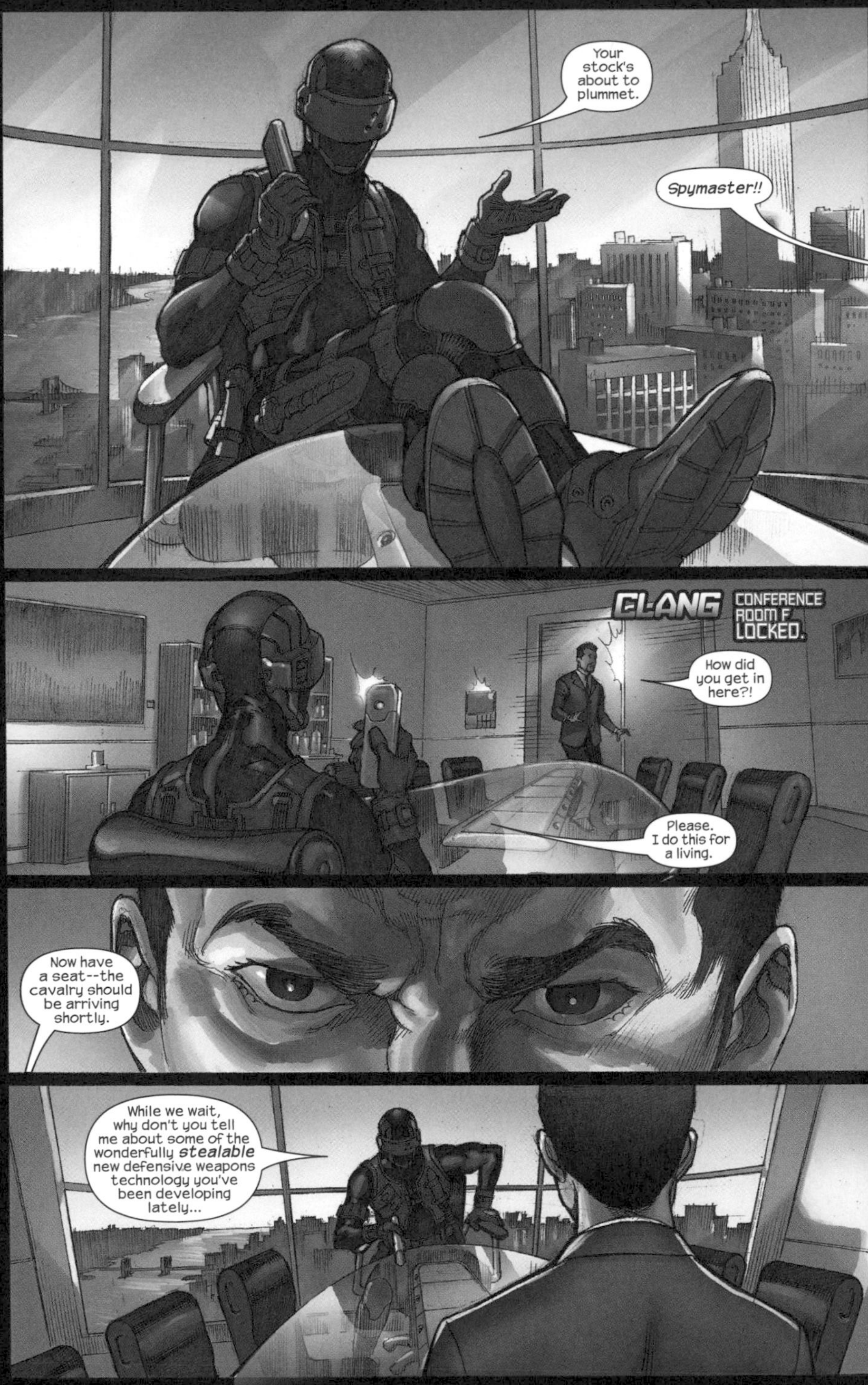
Your stock's about to plummet.
Spymaster!!
CLANG
CONFERENCE ROOM F LOCKED.
How did you get in here?!
Please. I do this for a living.
Now have a seat--the cavalry should be arriving shortly.
While we wait, why don't you tell me about some of the wonderfully *stealable* new defensive weapons technology you've been developing lately...

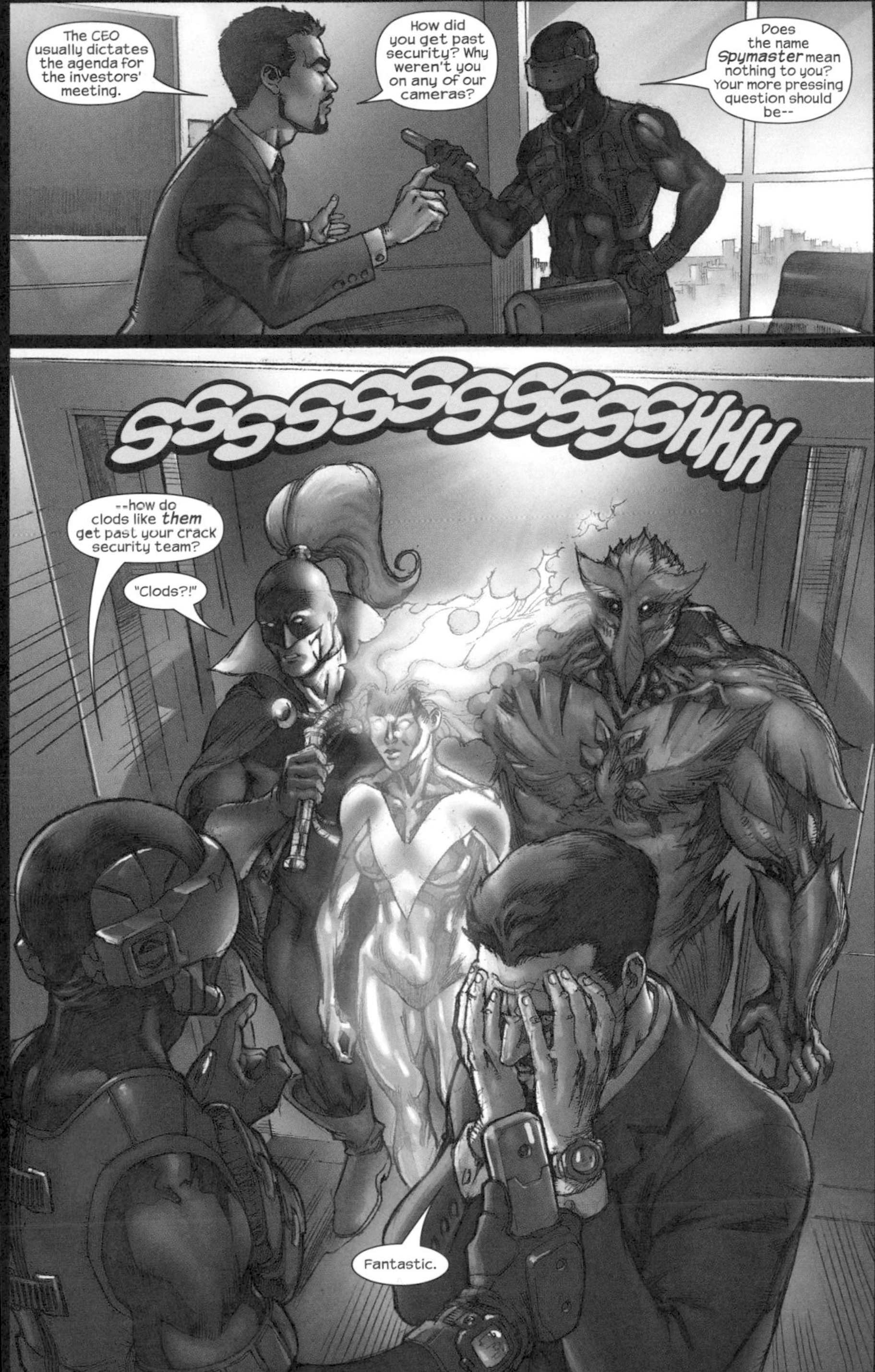
The CEO usually dictates the agenda for the investors' meeting.
How did you get past security? Why weren't you on any of our cameras?
Does the name Spymaster mean nothing to you? Your more pressing question should be--
SSSSSSSSSSSSSSSHHH
--how do clods like them get past your crack security team?
"Clods?!"
Fantastic.

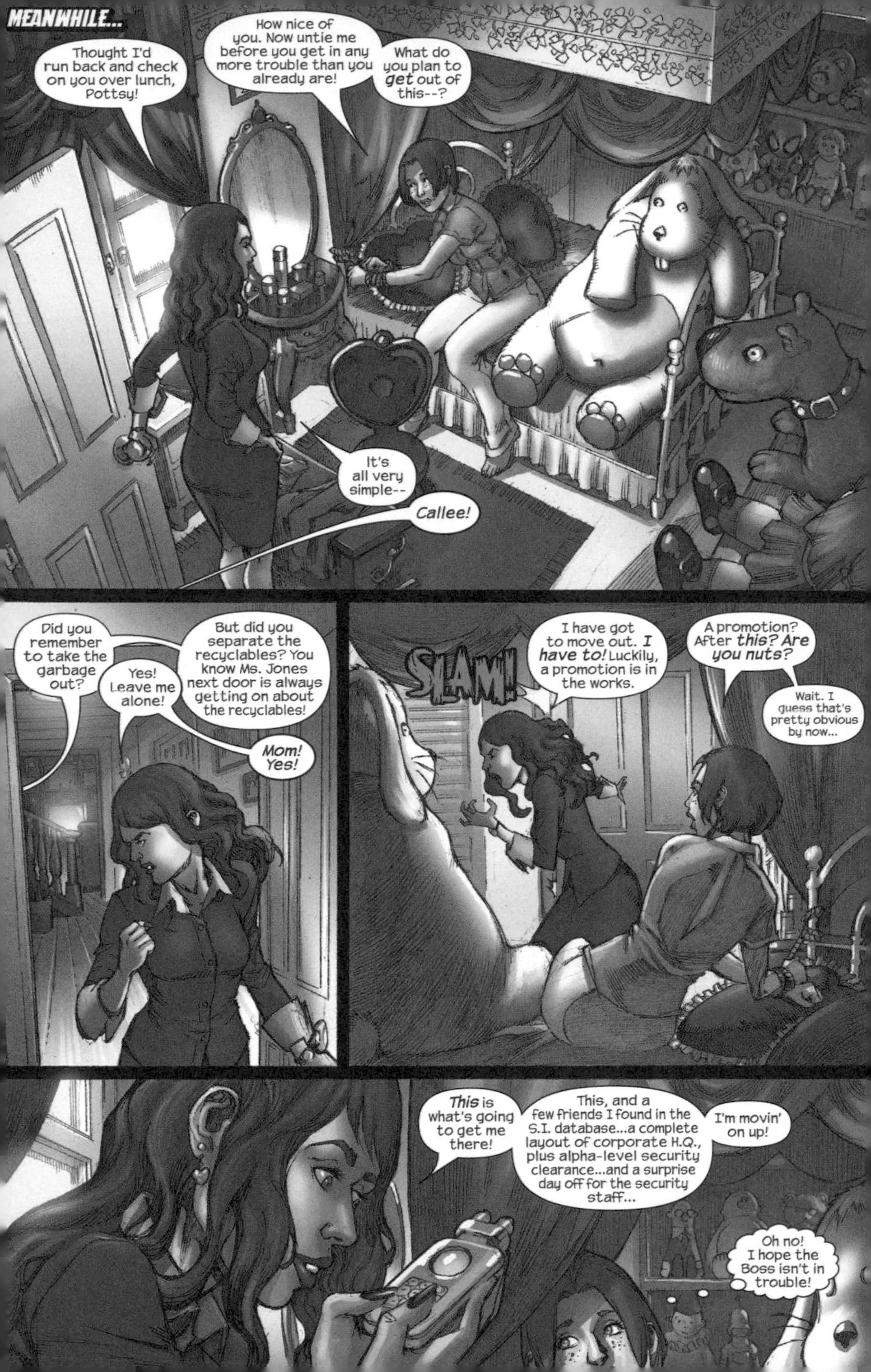
MEANWHILE...
Thought I'd run back and check on you over lunch, Pottsy!
How nice of you. Now untie me before you get in any more trouble than you already are!
What do you plan to get out of this--?
It's all very simple--
Callee!
Did you remember to take the garbage out?
Yes! Leave me alone!
But did you separate the recyclables? You know Ms. Jones next door is always getting on about the recyclables!
Mom! Yes!
SLAM!
I have got to move out. I have to! Luckily, a promotion is in the works.
A promotion? After this? Are you nuts?
Wait. I guess that's pretty obvious by now...
This is what's going to get me there!
This, and a few friends I found in the S.I. database...a complete layout of corporate H.Q., plus alpha-level security clearance...and a surprise day off for the security staff...
I'm movin' on up!
Oh no! I hope the Boss isn't in trouble!

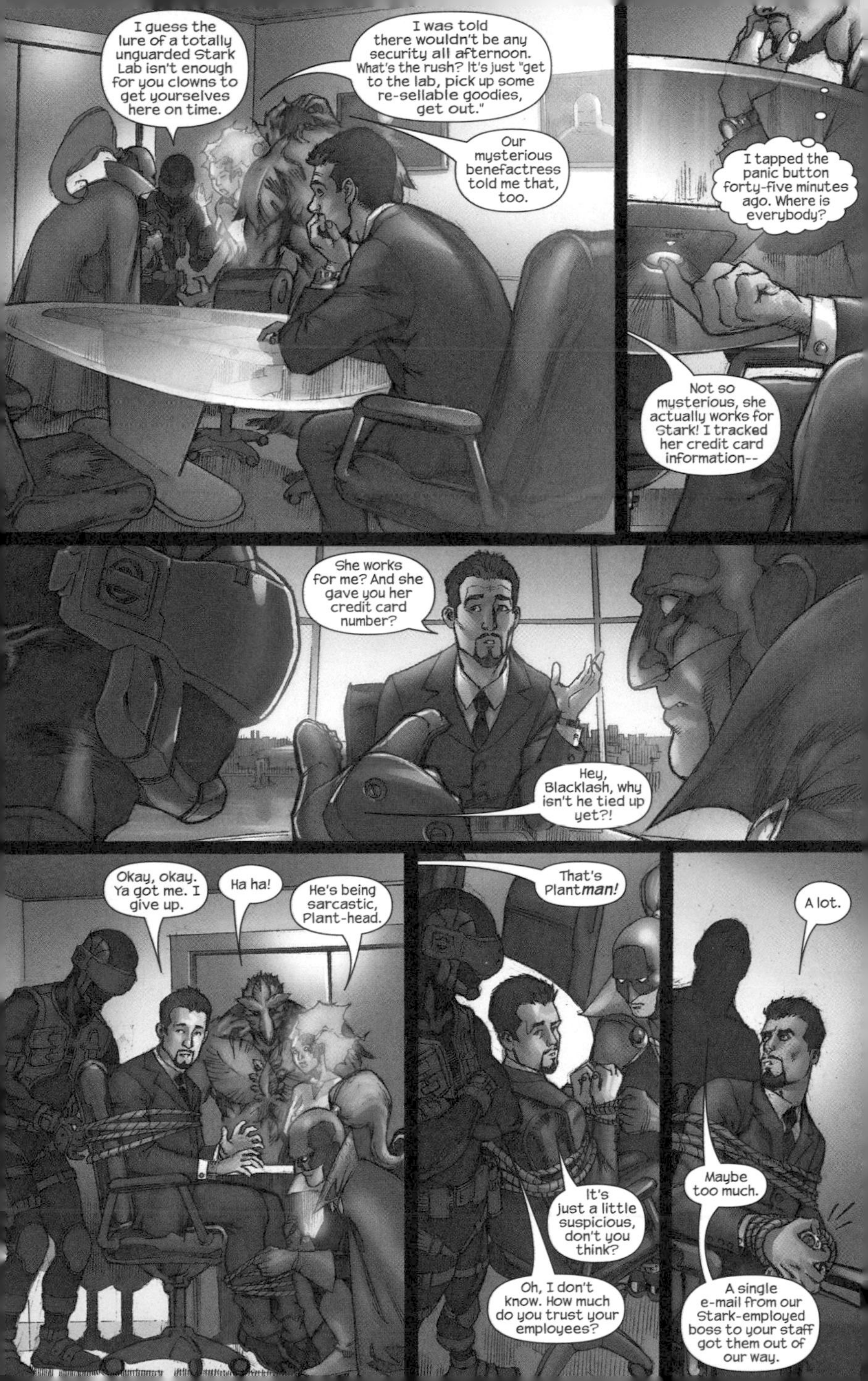

I guess the lure of a totally unguarded Stark Lab isn't enough for you clowns to get yourselves here on time.
I was told there wouldn't be any security all afternoon. What's the rush? It's just "get to the lab, pick up some re-sellable goodies, get out."
Our mysterious benefactress told me that, too.
I tapped the panic button forty-five minutes ago. Where is everybody?
Not so mysterious, she actually works for Stark! I tracked her credit card information--
She works for me? And she gave you her credit card number?
Hey, Blacklash, why isn't he tied up yet?!
Okay, okay. Ya got me. I give up.
Ha ha!
He's being sarcastic, Plant-head.
That's Plant*man!*
It's just a little suspicious, don't you think?
Oh, I don't know. How much do you trust your employees?
A lot.
Maybe too much.
A single e-mail from our Stark-employed boss to your staff got them out of our way.

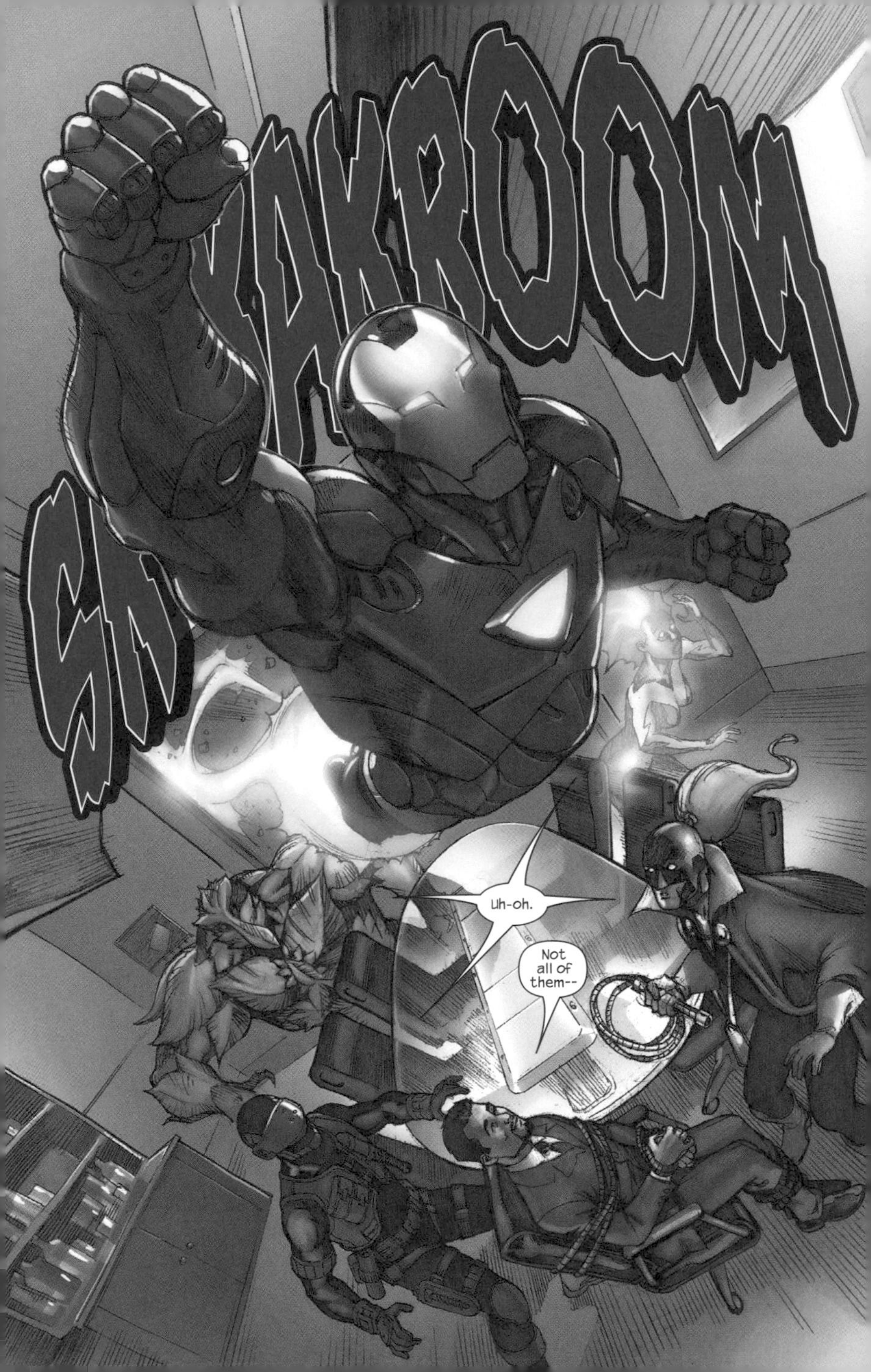
Uh-oh.
Not all of them--

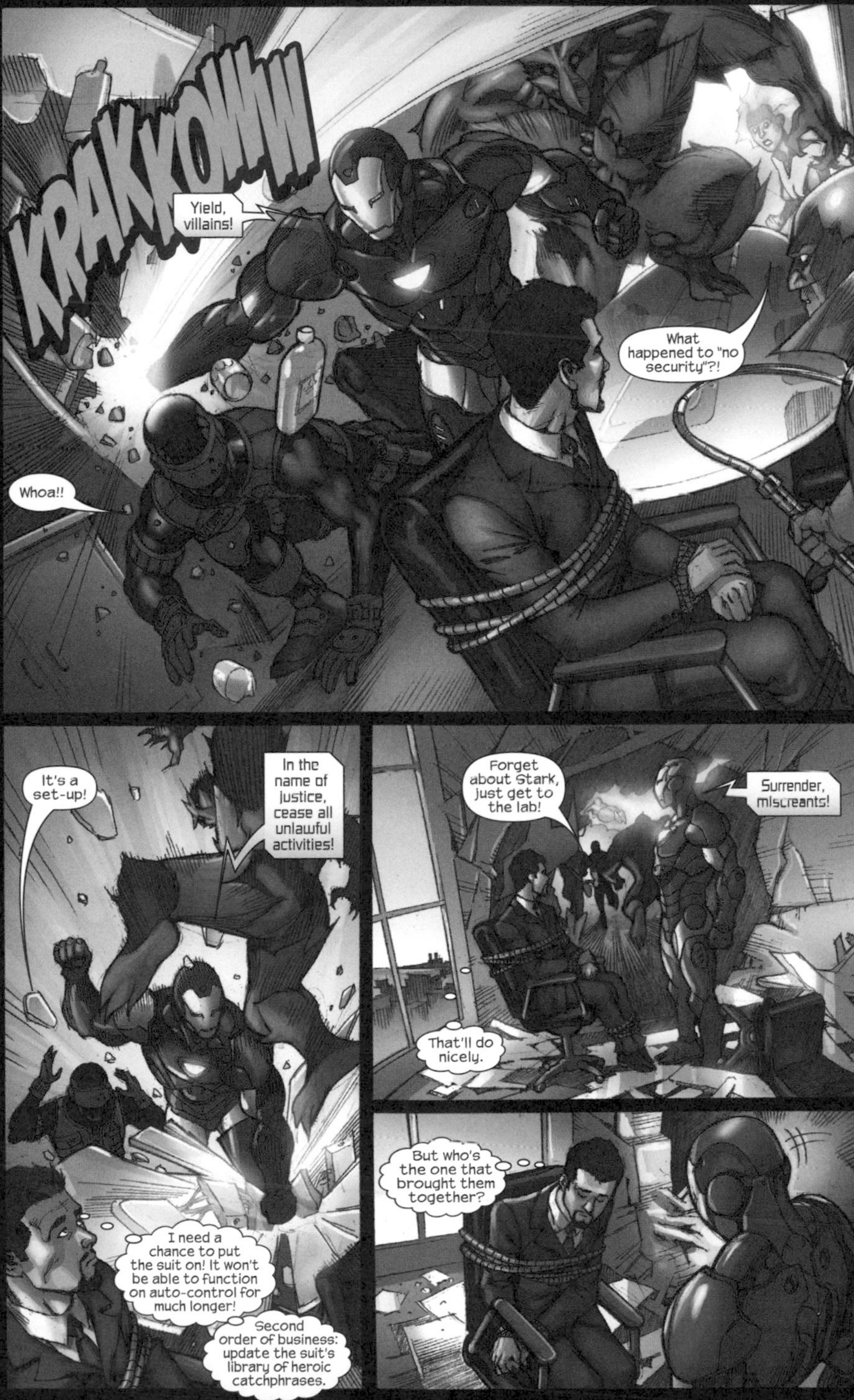
KRAKKOWW
Yield, villains!
What happened to "no security"?!
Whoa!!
It's a set-up!
In the name of justice, cease all unlawful activities!
I need a chance to put the suit on! It won't be able to function on auto-control for much longer!
Second order of business: update the suit's library of heroic catchphrases.
Forget about Stark, just get to the lab!
Surrender, miscreants!
That'll do nicely.
But who's the one that brought them together?

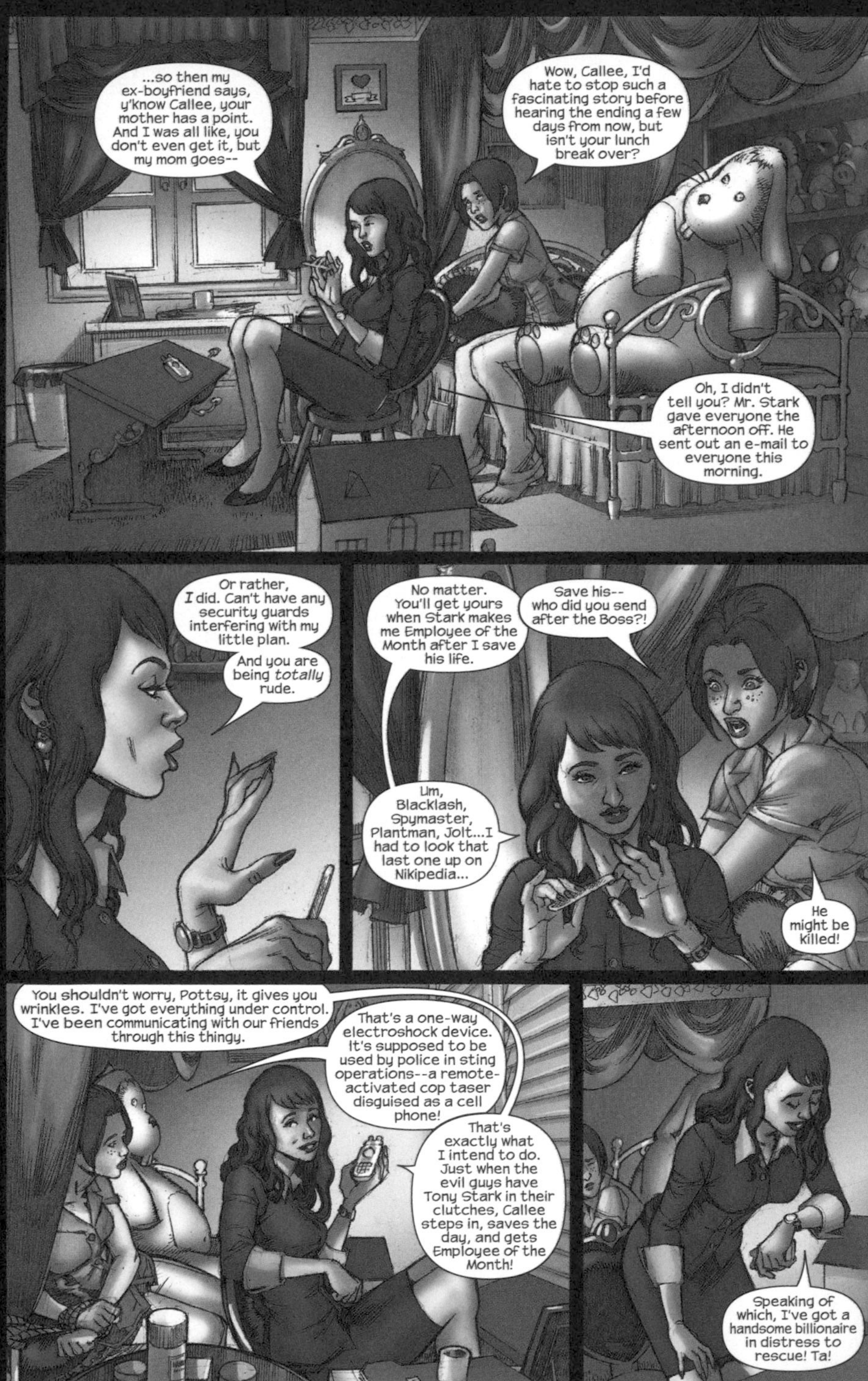
...so then my ex-boyfriend says, y'know Callee, your mother has a point. And I was all like, you don't even get it, but my mom goes--
Wow, Callee, I'd hate to stop such a fascinating story before hearing the ending a few days from now, but isn't your lunch break over?
Oh, I didn't tell you? Mr. Stark gave everyone the afternoon off. He sent out an e-mail to everyone this morning.
Or rather, I did. Can't have any security guards interfering with my little plan.
And you are being totally rude.
No matter. You'll get yours when Stark makes me Employee of the Month after I save his life.
Save his-- who did you send after the Boss?!
Um, Blacklash, Spymaster, Plantman, Jolt...I had to look that last one up on Nikipedia...
He might be killed!
You shouldn't worry, Pottsy, it gives you wrinkles. I've got everything under control. I've been communicating with our friends through this thingy.
That's a one-way electroshock device. It's supposed to be used by police in sting operations--a remote-activated cop taser disguised as a cell phone!
That's exactly what I intend to do. Just when the evil guys have Tony Stark in their clutches, Callee steps in, saves the day, and gets Employee of the Month!
Speaking of which, I've got a handsome billionaire in distress to rescue! Ta!

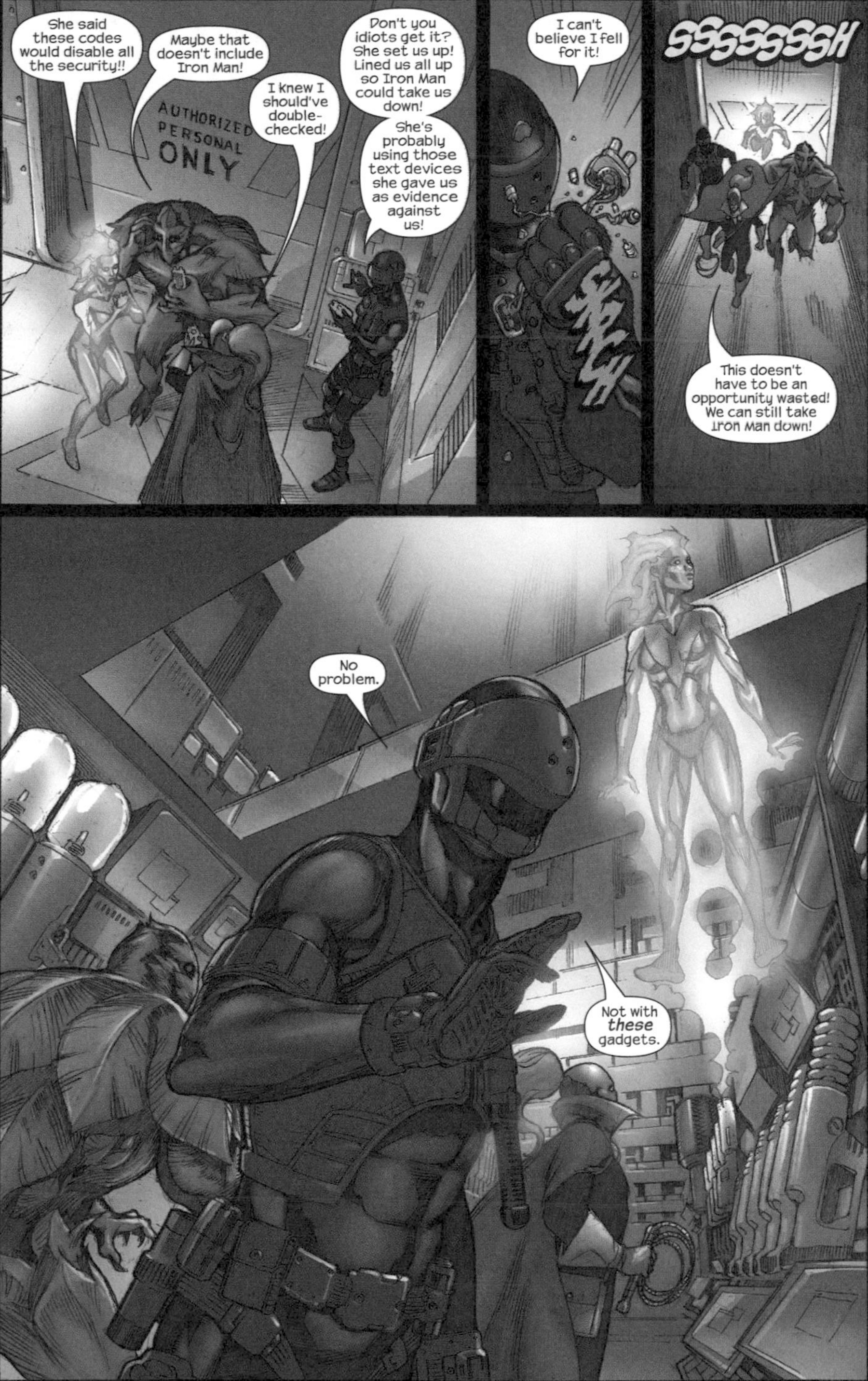
She said these codes would disable all the security!!
Maybe that doesn't include Iron Man!
AUTHORIZED PERSONAL ONLY
I knew I should've double-checked!
Don't you idiots get it? She set us up! Lined us all up so Iron Man could take us down!
She's probably using those text devices she gave us as evidence against us!
I can't believe I fell for it!
SSSSSSSH
This doesn't have to be an opportunity wasted! We can still take Iron Man down!
No problem.
Not with *these* gadgets.

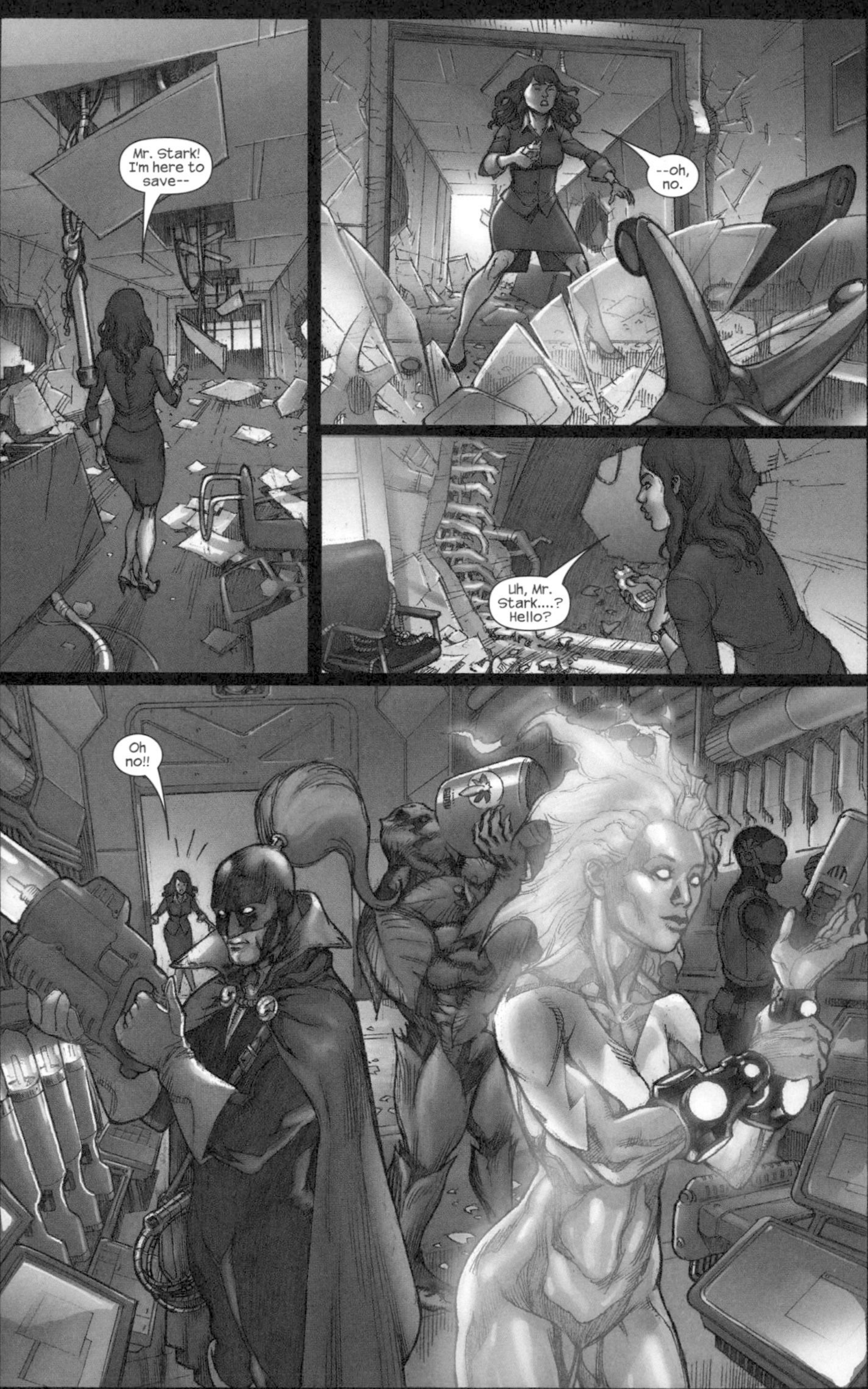
Mr. Stark! I'm here to save--
--oh, no.
Uh, Mr. Stark....? Hello?
Oh no!!

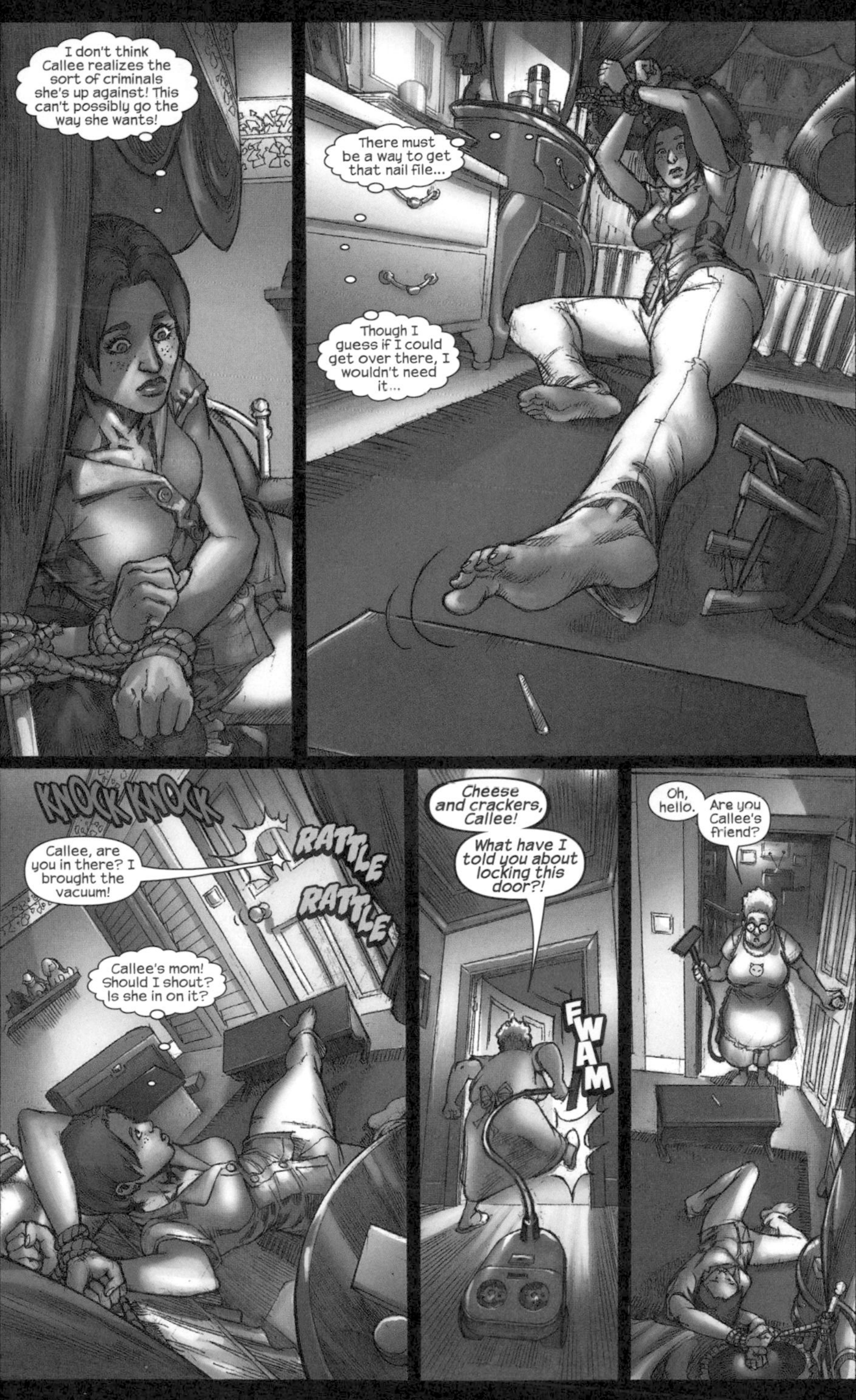

I don't think Callee realizes the sort of criminals she's up against! This can't possibly go the way she wants!
There must be a way to get that nail file...
Though I guess if I could get over there, I wouldn't need it...
KNOCK KNOCK
Callee, are you in there? I brought the vacuum!
RATTLE RATTLE
Callee's mom! Should I shout? Is she in on it?
Cheese and crackers, Callee!
What have I told you about locking this door?!
FWAM
Oh, hello.
Are you Callee's friend?

Speak of the devil. Just the gal we wanted to see.
Why isn't the electroshock code working?!
We cottoned on to your plan, missy. We destroyed the devices you gave us.
You told us those access codes would disable all of Stark security!
They do! Don't they?
Lucky for you, Callee...

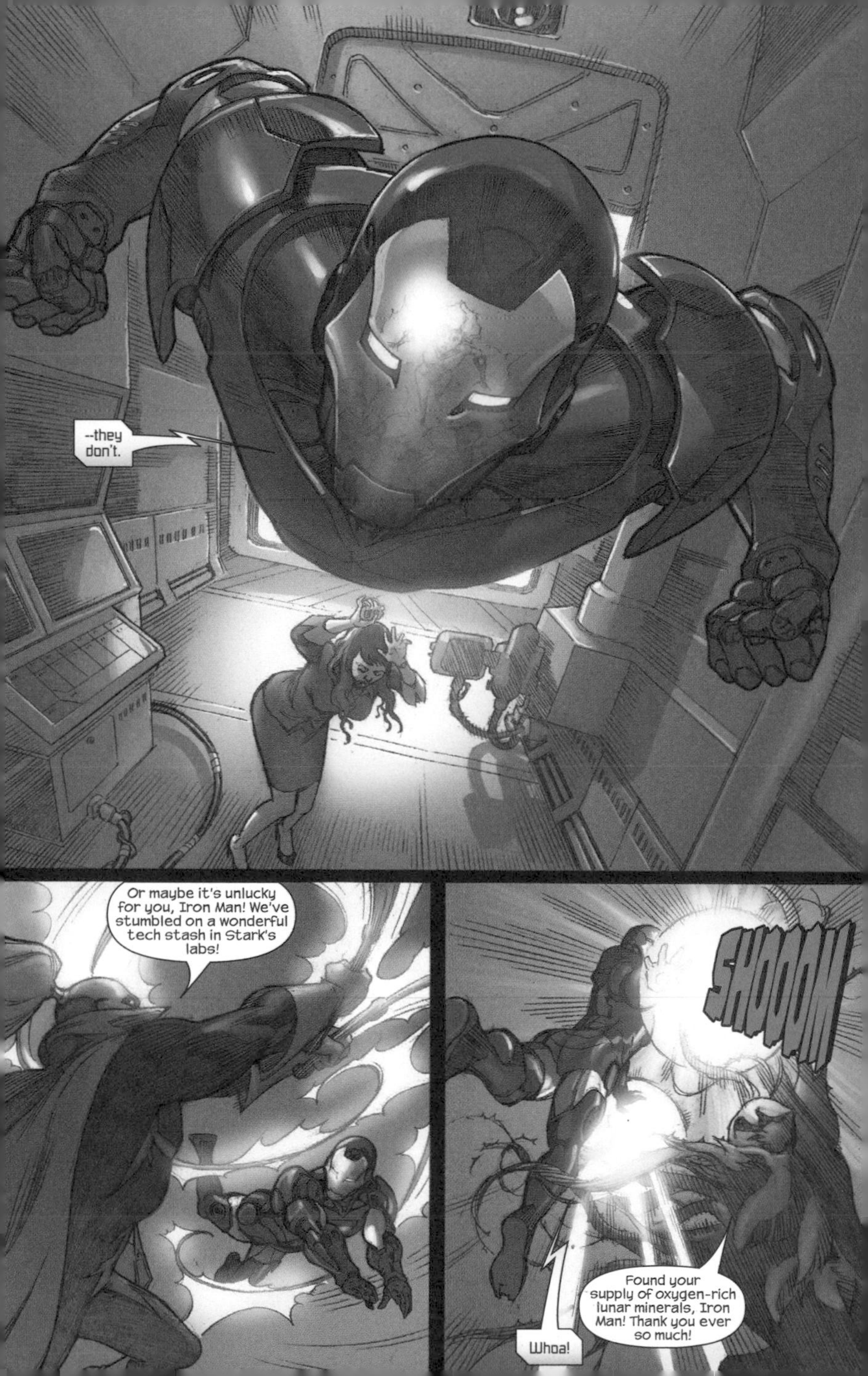
--they don't.
Or maybe it's unlucky for you, Iron Man! We've stumbled on a wonderful tech stash in Stark's labs!
SHOOOM
Whoa!
Found your supply of oxygen-rich lunar minerals, Iron Man! Thank you ever so much!

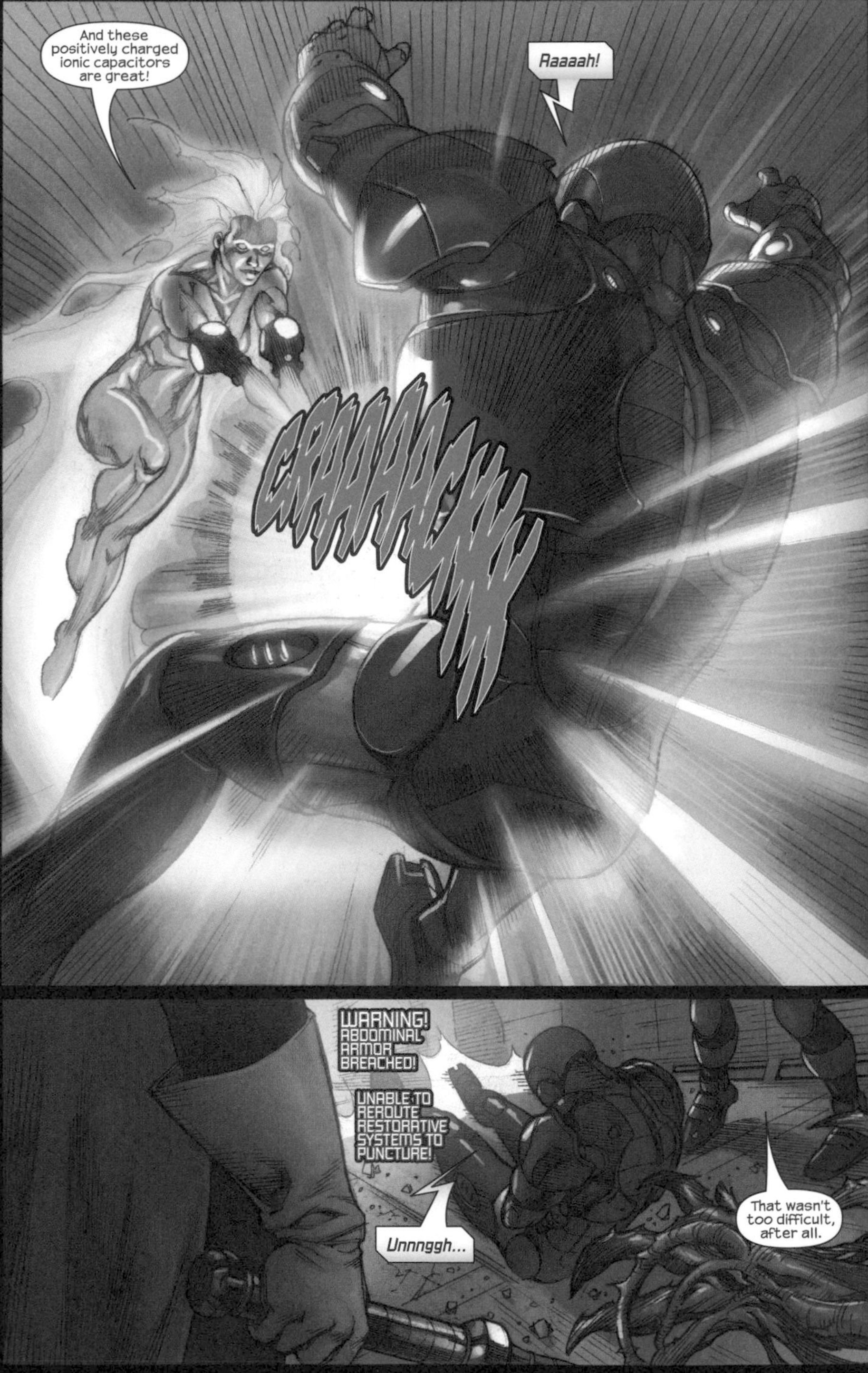

And these positively charged ionic capacitors are great!
Raaaah!
CRAAAACKK
WARNING! ABDOMINAL ARMOR BREACHED!
UNABLE TO REROUTE RESTORATIVE SYSTEMS TO PUNCTURE!
Unnnggh...
That wasn't too difficult, after all.

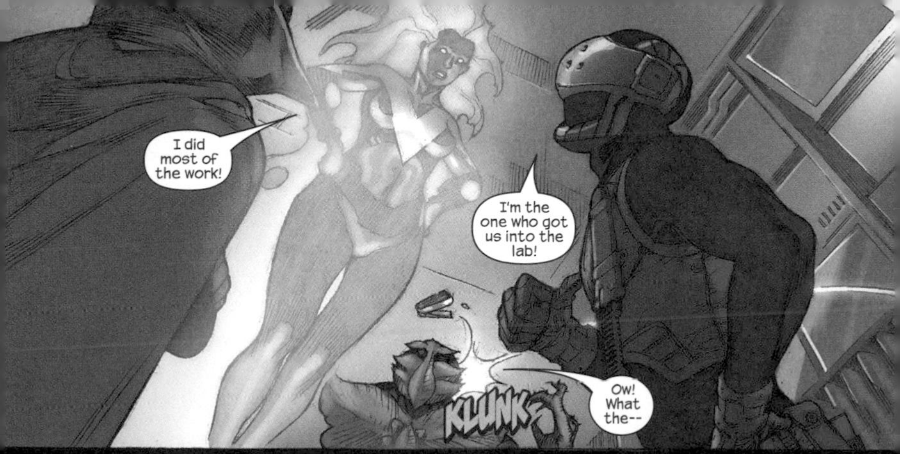
I did most of the work!
I'm the one who got us into the lab!
KLUNK
Ow! What the--

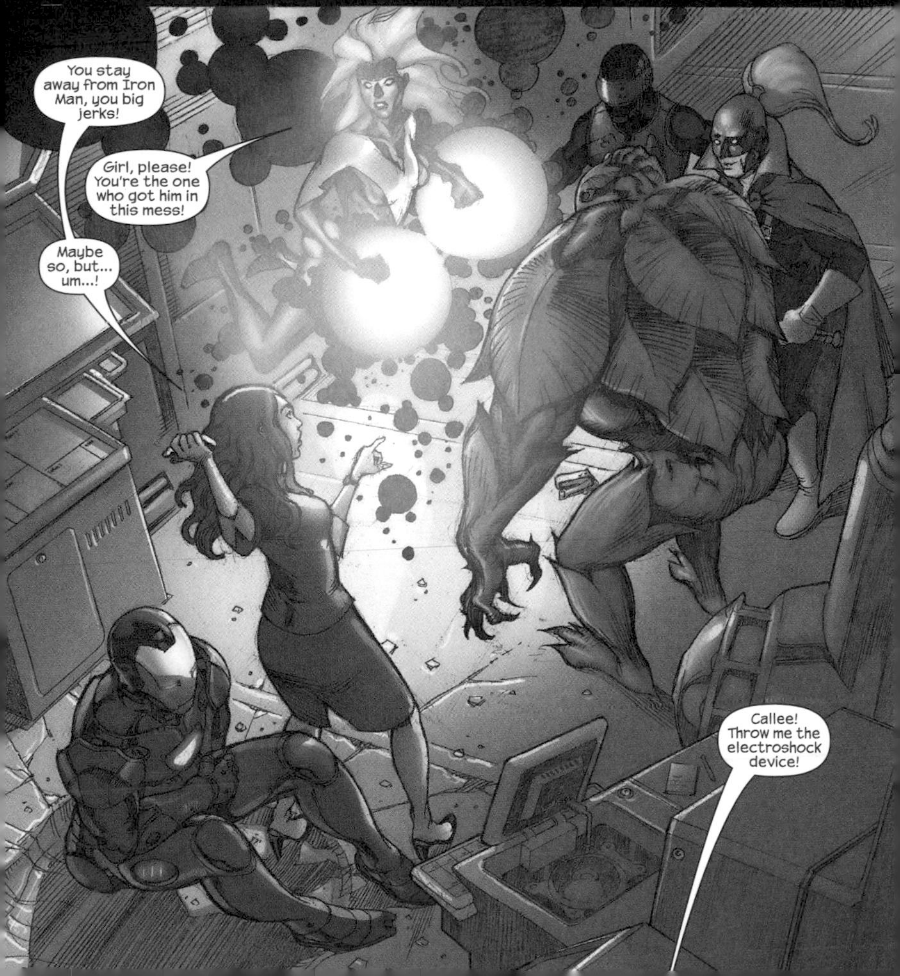
You stay away from Iron Man, you big jerks!
Girl, please! You're the one who got him in this mess!
Maybe so, but... um...!
Callee! Throw me the electroshock device!

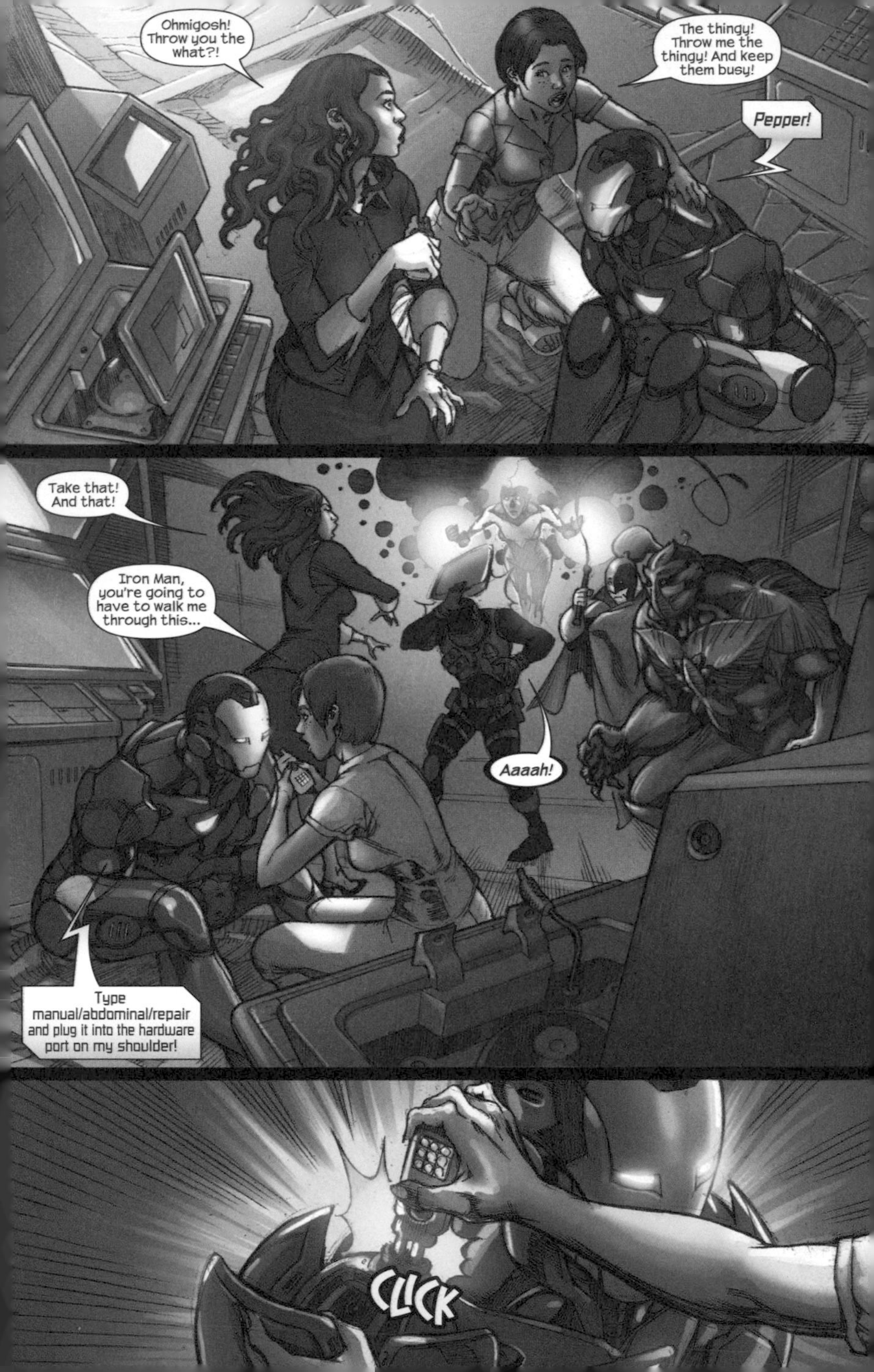
Ohmigosh! Throw you the what?!
The thingy! Throw me the thingy! And keep them busy!
Pepper!
Take that! And that!
Iron Man, you're going to have to walk me through this...
Aaaah!
Type manual/abdominal/repair and plug it into the hardware port on my shoulder!
CLICK

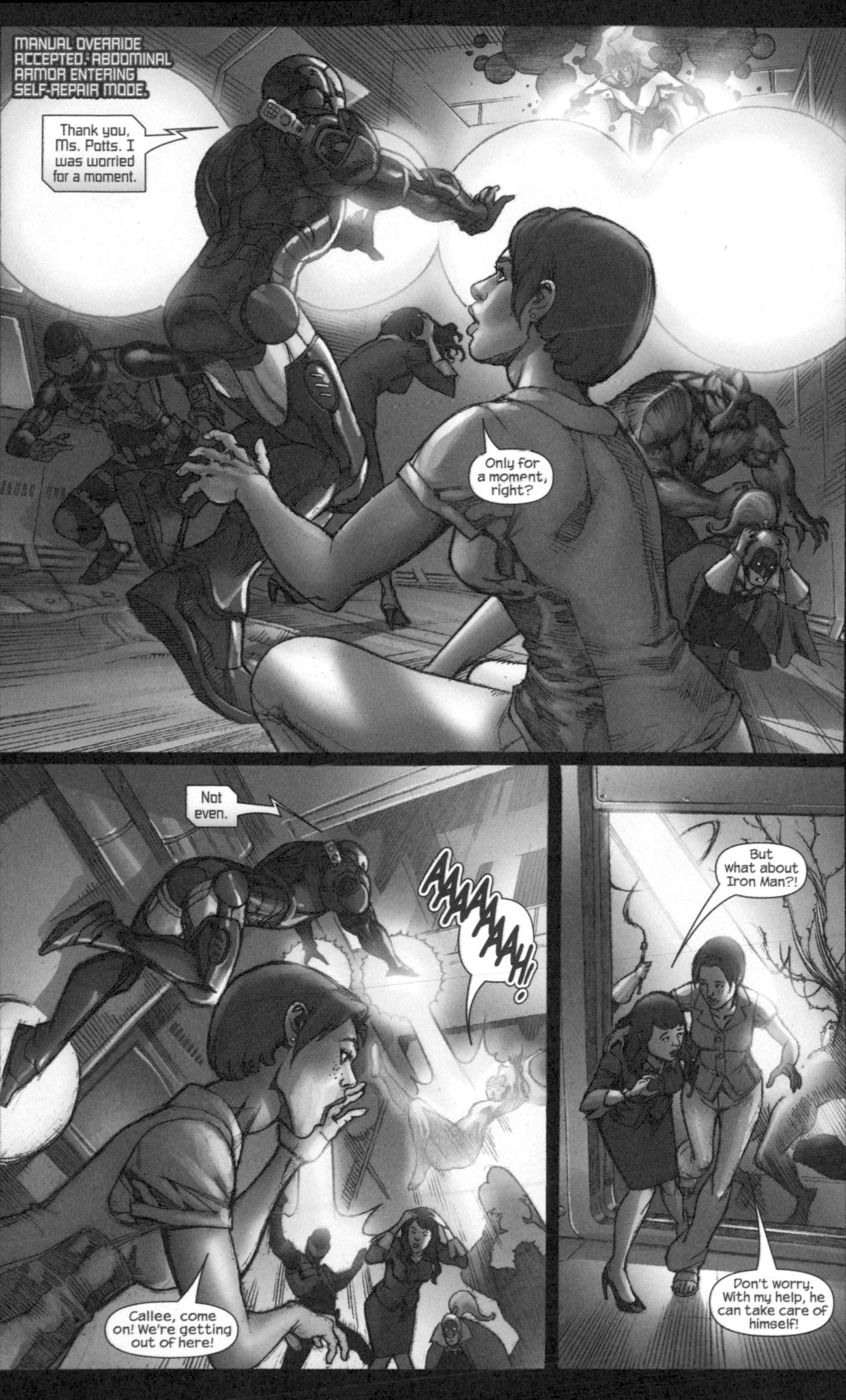
MANUAL OVERRIDE ACCEPTED. ABDOMINAL ARMOR ENTERING SELF-REPAIR MODE.
Thank you, Ms. Potts. I was worried for a moment.
Only for a moment, right?
Not even.
AAAAAAAAH!
Callee, come on! We're getting out of here!
But what about Iron Man?!
Don't worry. With my help, he can take care of himself!

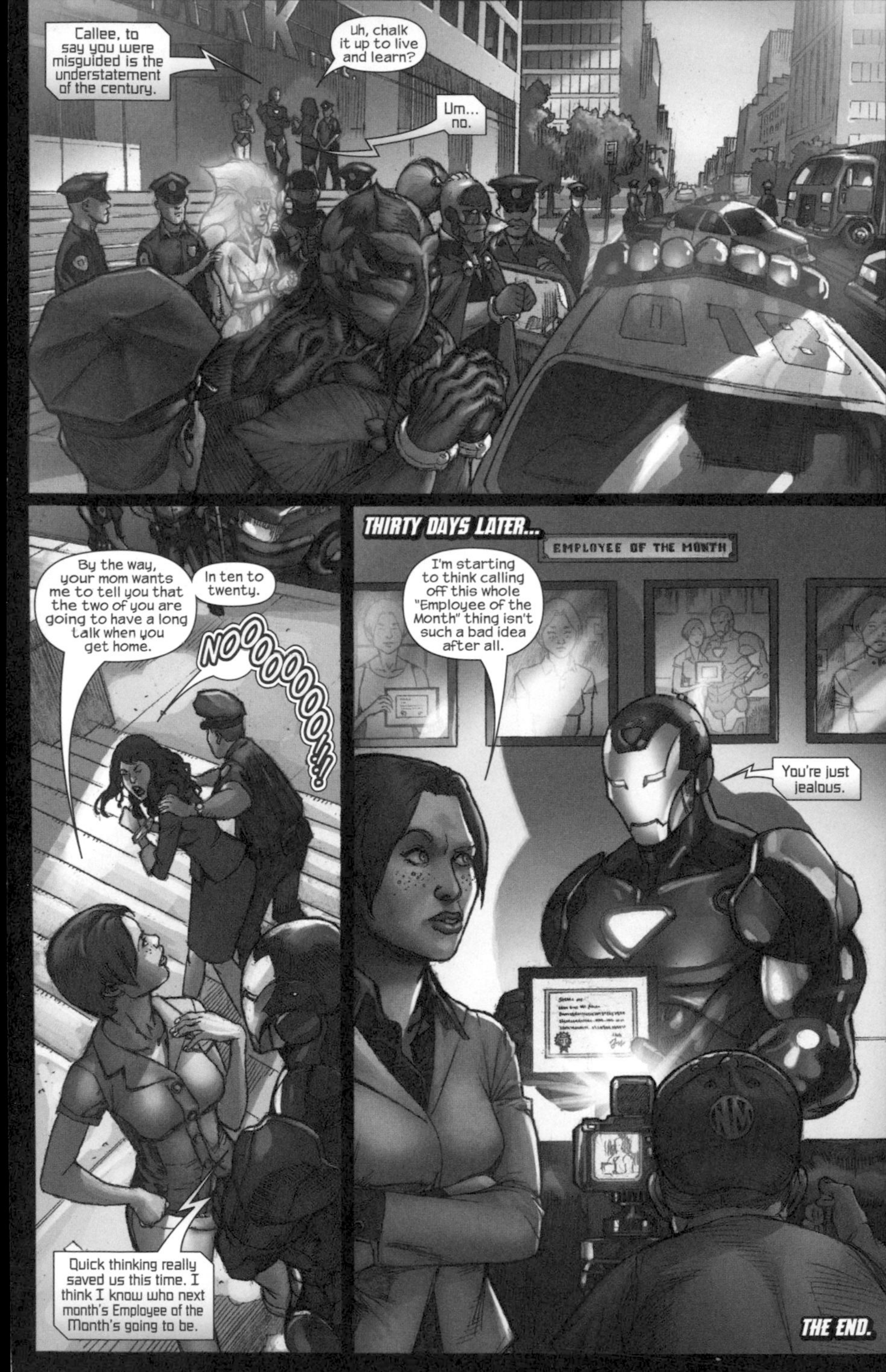

Callee, to say you were misguided is the understatement of the century.
Uh, chalk it up to live and learn?
Um... no.
By the way, your mom wants me to tell you that the two of you are going to have a long talk when you get home.
In ten to twenty.
NOOOOOOOOO!!
Quick thinking really saved us this time. I think I know who next month's Employee of the Month's going to be.
THIRTY DAYS LATER...
EMPLOYEE OF THE MONTH
I'm starting to think calling off this whole "Employee of the Month" thing isn't such a bad idea after all.
You're just jealous.
THE END.